THE MAKING OF A STRIKE

THE MAKING OF A Strike

Mexican
Silver Workers'
Struggles in
Real del Monte
1766–1775

Doris M. Ladd

University of Nebraska Press: Lincoln and London

Library of Congress Cataloging in Publication Data
Ladd, Doris M.
The making of a strike.
Bibliography: p.
Includes index.
1. Miner's Strike, Mineral del Monte, Mexico,
1766. 2. Compañía Real del Monte y Pachuca —
History — 18th century. 3. Silver miners — Mexico —
Pachuca Region — History — 18th century. I. Title.
HD5331.M72   1766.P325   1988
331.8'928223423'097246   87-5897
ISBN 0-8032-2876-7

For Tom, *con afición*

CONTENTS

!¡

Acknowledgments

Ed Beechert, more than anyone else, made it possible for me to write this study by reading it in its Protean forms, talking volumes about labor history, and pressing books on me every time I faltered. In Mexico City Enrique Florescano and Cuauhtémoc Velasco discussed their pioneer studies of workers in New Spain. To my gratification the staff of the Archivo General de la Nación greeted me companionably, like a long-lost employee. In the archives and in the cafes Dorothy Kerig, John Hart, Sue Cline, Linda Arnold, and Richard Boyer talked a lot and laughed a lot and for a moment created what I miss most, a community of scholars. In Pachuca José Vergara, José Arias, and the staff of the just-organizing Archivo Histórico del Poder Judicial welcomed me as their first foreign scholar. Padre Héctor Samperio of the Centro Hidalgüense de Investigaciones collected a number of valuable sources for me to read and talked about anti-labor biases in history and what it takes to be a good priest. At the University of Texas at Austin Jane Garner answered every question and more. In Seville doña Rosario Parras, director of the Archivo General de Indiás, and researcher Belém García López were as courteous and patient as they were competent. At Stanford University I found a fine collection of treatises on occupational diseases and hazards in historical perspective in the Green Library and the Lane Medical Library. At the Branner Geological Library I encountered many books on dust and ores and the surprising revelation that no eighteenth-century lodes or adits had ever been portrayed schematically before. The banks of Mexico City house useful collections of important colonial economic studies.

I am especially grateful to the people who helped me change this book for the better, people I know: Nettie Lee Benson, James Lockhart, Ed Beechert, Bruce Cruikshank, Dorothy Stein, and Jane Pultz; and people I never have met, my pen pals: E. P. Thompson, Peter Linebaugh, David Montgomery, Peter Stearns, and Alice Cook. July Green, cartographer at the University of Hawaii at Manoa, made the maps.

Funds for research in Mexico and in Spain were provided by the National Endowment for the Humanities and the people of Hawaii.

I have worked to write a book which would allow Mexicans, Mexican Americans, and Spaniards to become aware of the dignity of their heritage. An example of such a benison: Mexicans in the eighteenth century had a genius for social protest and for community action. In turn the Spanish crown had a genius for mediation. New Spain was no tabula rasa passively waiting for Europeans to write a script that would suddenly activate its economic life and assure its dependency. New Spain was a crucible of economic processes, processes that rewarded working people and nurtured ideals, convictions, and fortitude in those Mexicans determined to defend themselves. In an encounter between reform and constitution, modernization and tradition, you win, you lose. In this specific struggle Mexican miners won.

There is no one I would rather have take this book than Edward Thompson. So I have laid it on him.

!¡

CHAPTER 1

Introduction

In the summer of 1766 Mexican silver miners of Real del Monte, about a hundred kilometers north of Mexico City, developed a major industrial strike without a labor union or a political ideology to sustain them. It was the first strike in the history of Mexican labor and the first strike in North America. The word *huelga*, "strike", did not officially enter Spanish dictionaries until 1884, and the workers at Real del Monte never used it. Their efforts represented struggles that involved working, living, and being disappointed. They demanded rights that had been marked only in sweat and tears. They won those rights by organization and negotiations that were innovated spontaneously but confirmed officially. Their way was made possible by the counsel and actions of friendly people with status in the town.

The principal characteristic of a strike is not violence. To equate the two confuses symptom with cause. In Mexican colonial history peasant direct action, as recorded in criminal records, has been interpreted as violent and pathological. But William B. Taylor says there is a way to plumb such pathology: "My approach to criminal records is not limited to the pathological side of peasant history. I am equally interested in how violent incidents can reveal patterns of social behavior and their relations to cultural premises and external conditions—patterns and relations that can be translated from behavior recorded in criminal trials."[1]

Violence is a variable, not an attribute of popular collective action. Charles, Louise, and Richard Tilly counted twenty thousand strikes in France from 1890 to 1914. Most were orderly and nonviolent. Only three or four hundred were violent. Strikes tend to be controlled by local organizations that articulate clear, long-held grievances in a process that precludes their actions from being interpreted as "eruptions of violence."[2] George

Rudé, studying workers in eighteenth-century France and England, distinguishes between violence provoked by police or authorities and violence emerging from the actions of the crowd. In general, he says, strikers opt for property damage: they attack mine structures, machinery, workshops, or the houses of management. Assaults on people are rare. Violence is most common when the crowd is provoked, denied all means to legal redress, or punished after their peaceful assemblies are condemned as "hostile outbursts."[3] In the balance, Rudé found that "it was authority rather than the crowd that was conspicuous for its violence to life and limb."[4]

Self-interested perspectives result in double entendre judgments, and when meanings become distinct, class differences are revealed. George Rudé explains how this happens by analyzing the word "mob." Authorities view popular disturbances as the work of rabble, riffraff, criminals, canaille. The people in the "mob" are passive, with no ideas of their own, helpless in the hands of outside "agents." The participants involve themselves only for the base rewards of "loot, lucre, free drinks, bloodlust, or merely the need to satisfy some lurking criminal instinct."[5] This stereotype may occasionally fit a circumstance. Rudé concludes, however, that the term "mob" is usually employed against working people as "a frank symbol of prejudice."[6]

Rudé prefers to call the basic unit of collective action a "crowd." "Crowd" embraces a group of local working people with distinct and well-considered goals, people asking for "natural justice," insisting on their rights, and seeking remedies for very specific grievances. To answer the difficult question of how the values of a crowd originate, Rudé suggests that "traditional beliefs might, instead of becoming abandoned, be transformed and adapted to meet new needs."[7]

Another example of class differences in labeling is the usage of the word "riot," *tumulto* in Spanish. Authorities seem to use the dictionary description, where a riot is an "uproar," a "wild and violent disorder," a pathology. Rudé, applying the concept of crowd and using violence as a variable, gives the word riot a completely different meaning: "The riot, then, is the characteristic and ever-recurring form of popular protest which, on occasion, turns into rebellion or revolution."[8] The riot is important because it may be the only means of political action available to working men. The riot of redress is a principal form of popular dissent, but the crowd involved in it may or may not turn to violence.

To reveal crowd rather than mob behavior, Rudé instructs us to focus on what actually happened, on the event itself. Who participated? Who were the leaders? What was the target? What did the working men want? What forms of repression were used against them? What is the importance of this event in history? Causes, motives, and attitudes, Rudé cautions, will be the hardest to trace. The historian must use police and judicial records, must use all evidence warily because the primary sources are so biased.[9]

William Taylor examined 142 peasant tumultos or riots in Colonial Mexico from 1680 to 1811. Because they were spontaneous popular protests expressed by mass action, it was, Taylor said, "almost impossible" to pinpoint the causes. The riot was often over before the men with pen and ink arrived to describe it. For the incidents that could be identified, Taylor found that certain patterns of behavior emerged, in the one to three days of defiance, when new taxes, tributes, or monopoly excises were imposed or when priests or local authorities were suspected of abusing their power. All these peasant riots were apparently unplanned or at least short-lived.[10]

Like a peasant tumulto, the strike was a popular protest; strikers joined in a crowd, not a mob, and what ensued was or was not violent. However, it took a year and more to conspire and plot to organize the strike at Real del Monte in 1766. Because of workers' long cooperation in the work process, because they confronted the horrifying hazards and diseases as dangers that bound them together as brave men, because they witnessed with their own eyes the changing social relations of production every payday, they came first to experience, then to share resentment. Each worker had time to discover a clear definition of his own self-interest and his role in the cause. The extended time of discontent, the long organizing effort, the experience of solidarity forged by work and the awareness of danger, the stake of each individual worker in the outcome sets this strike, any strike, apart from other kinds of riots and protests.

When labor stops working, the collective action may or may not constitute a strike. When miners in eighteenth-century Guanajuato left their work to protest tribute, or taxes on tobacco, or the expulsion of the Jesuits, their actions were riots, not strikes. Workers, after all, are people with all the interlocking roles that serve to define human identity. Those incidents were work stoppages, it is true, but in them miners set aside their roles as workers and acted as freemen and parishioners concerned about their community.

The experience that makes Real del Monte unique is that miners there agitated about *work*. Their actions fulfill the criteria for a strike set up in John A. Fitch's definition: "a concerted suspension of work by a body of employees, usually for the purpose of adjusting an existing dispute over the terms of a labor contract."[11] But this Mexican strike occurred long before the incidents that Fitch describes. The definition must be modified a little.

There were stoppages, and one ended in joy because workers got what they wanted. It was a strike concerted by conspiracy, not by a labor union. The contract was unwritten, "traditional." What happened was disturbingly spontaneous from the point of view of the authorities; to the miners an action discussed and developed in pre-existing networks and communications systems that came to express the shared expectations of a community of workers.

Because their view of their rights developed from within their work and experience, because they themselves quoted no ideology, to express their story takes a special technique. I have tried to tell much of it in the miner's own words, from their perspective. E. P. Thompson was teaching us how to deal with historical facts: "The historian must work hard to enable them to find 'their own voices.' Not the historian's voice, please observe: *their own voices.*"[12] To heed the advice on facts and take one step further, to find the workers' own voices was, surprisingly, not difficult—because of the Spanish sources. The voices of working men can be heard, of course, in their grievances, and in this first Mexican strike the grievances were both articulated eloquently and written down. But there is much more. There was a royal notary present during almost every confrontation, every arbitration attempt, every investigation. The notary identified by name every worker who spoke and quoted him either directly or indirectly. In criminal cases every defendant was identified as to age, race, occupation, sex and marital status. Every accused worker and witness spoke his own piece; some had a second chance to talk when they were questioned on the contradictions of their testimony. In the Mexican historical experience, miners are not voiceless, are not inarticulate. In this history participants had opportunities to comment as they were making it. Uniquely, the protagonists, the workers, spoke for themselves.

A supplementary technique is to attempt to reconstruct the situation, how the context felt and looked. Workers themselves described their jobs and their problems. I have tested the idea that "as individuals express their lives, so they are."[13] But the environment they lived in, and often found too obvious to relate, is important, too. To deal with the contingencies revived is to deal with the question; why bother to read history at all? Carl Degler defends the reward of empathy: "an important justification of history is that it attempts to give a sense of what it felt like to live in another time, when different values and personal goals had to wrestle with the same timeless and insistent aspects of human existence . . . that engage the attention and energies of people today."[14]

I have also used historians' descriptions and primary sources to recreate the work and behavior of the men of Real del Monte. The novels of Mexican writer Rodolfo Benavides,[15] who was himself a miner in Pachuca, made up for the fact that I could never see a mine for myself. Some of the things I did see in the modern town of Mineral del Monte I have included. For analogy, books on the Comstock Lode in Nevada describe silver miners and mining in loving detail.[16] The reports of authorities in New Spain revealed the actions and pastimes of the miners as well as the justifications of law enforcement. The moans of Indians forced to work in a mine and the analyses of medical investigations, then and now, reveal the occupational diseases and hazards miners suffered, the dangers of the work. All these elements are pieced together into patterns which discover miners' social environment, the changing contingencies that shaped their behavior as strikers.

Since this is the first social history of labor dealing with Colonial Mexico in English, it might be useful to describe what labor history is. It is an analysis and story of workers' behavior in the past. Workers star; their work and working conditions, their protests, their growing awareness of solidarity. Industry, management, authorities, regionalism, violence all play supporting roles. The discipline analyzes an old experience, and new aspects are revealed and clarified. In the light are the motivations and intentions and the problem-solving devices of working men. The labor history perspective changes things: "It is as though light of a particular hue were cast upon everything, tingeing all other colours and modifying their specific features."[17]

Sources in labor history cannot be read by rote. Especially in criminal investigations, the evidence must be summed up in the light of another hue. The conclusions of authorities do not always add up according to conventional techniques of summation.

What little Mexican labor history there is has appropriately been written in Mexico. Today, colonial labor history is undergoing a renaissance nurtured by Enrique Florescano.[18] Fifty years ago, a Mexican historian dedicated his career to publishing collections of documents on working class history in the eighteenth century: wage labor, forced Indian labor,[19] and the strike of 1766, to be discussed here.[20] Luis Chávez Orozco was Mexican, he was dedicated, he was a painstaking researcher, and he never failed to remind us that past experience in Mexico is deeply felt.

For industry studies (where labor is often considered as a factor in production), mining is the best-developed topic in Mexican colonial economic history. In general scholars focus on an elite context of production of silver, the intricate relationships of industrialists with crown and capital as seen in laws, judicial proceedings, and the owners' protective association, the Mining Guild and Tribunal.[21] Three very different studies deal specifically with Real del Monte.[22]

Work-related values are intrinsic to the subject of a strike. Work-related incidents presuppose work-related contexts and yield work-related outcomes. Contingencies, incidents, and values come together in the historical experience known as "strike." It helps to read the best story of a strike ever written, Emile Zola's *Germinal* (1885), and the best analysis, Norman McCord's *Strikes* (1980).

One of the characteristics of the working life of miners up to the present day is that they, more than workers in other industries, have a high propensity to strike. This is partly because miners have their own communities and their own codes. Partly, they say, it is because mining is a physically demanding set of skilled tasks whose dangers and rewards draw "tough, combative, and virile workers"[23] to the job and fosters in them an independent spirit. Authorities at Real del Monte saw that spirit and despised it as "boldness," "insolence," "viciousness." John Leddy Phelan explained how to translate such hyperboles: they mean that the workers were "strong-willed, proud, and quarrelsome."[24] Alexander von Humboldt, in his visit to New Spain in 1804, saw the miners' pride and crowed about it.[25] Independence of spirit was a dominant theme in this, Mexico's first strike. The work, the perils, the luck, the rewards, the rebellion, the force, the slanders, the friendships, the community all touched the miners, shaped their lives, and helped them bring about their strike.

The process by which workers became strikers is the same kind of process found in all organizing labor, the same kind of process by which economic change conditions awareness and transforms worlds. This first strike in Mexico is especially important because it happened in the mid-eighteenth century in a predominantly rural society and because it developed within the context of the Spanish imperial experience in the New World. The attitudes of the Spanish government at the time were quite different from those of their European counterparts when they confronted militant industrial workers on strike. Spanish government sanctioned the grievances of labor and facilitated the workers' victory over the exigencies of expanding capital, creating an old and new accommodation that dignified the place of labor in economic development. This is not a story of defeated workers and starving families and lost causes. This is a story of Mexican workers, how they organized their strike—and how they won it.

!¡

CHAPTER 2

The Work of the Mines, the Matrix of the Strike

The work of the mine itself defined the behavior of workers as miners and shaped their awareness of their inalienable rights as strikers. Workers did not make a strike out of thin air, though assuredly there were no models or precedents to follow. They made the strike out of what it takes to wrest ore from a rock face and lug it to the surface, to talk back to implacable authority, and to share the experience with a community of workers who phrased disgust and resentment in the same vocabulary. The workplace was the community,[1] the work itself stimulated and supported their camaraderie. Miners' work is tempered by the goals of mining: to bring out silver ore, which will mean profits for the owner and bullion for the crown, a currency for international trade, a market for the farmer and craftsman, survival for dependents, wages for the miners and other workers employed to meet the goals and push up the threshold of danger so that all may survive. The intense specialization of tasks in the silver industry first individualized the worker in his skill, then forced him to cooperate in order to meet his quota and survive his shift.

Danger was a powerful catalyst in their association. None of the workers took survival for granted. Francisco de Gamboa (the greatest Mexican mining expert of the era) wrote that miners worked in terror of ladders giving way, rocks sliding, heavy loads breaking their backs, dripping icy waters, diseases, and the damp, hot, suffocating dark. Gamboa added that if the mine prospered, they worked so hard below that they disdained everything, even devils from the depths of hell.[2]

Silver in Real del Monte was a fully developed industry. To pry ore out from the vein below and load it on mules above required about thirty different specialized tasks. Experts said there were eighteen more functions in the refinery, where ore was transformed into silver, with two or three more taking place in the mint.[3]

All the characteristics of productive industry—great capital investment, division of labor, deployment of the large work force, and systematic work—were present in Real del Monte. The market for silver was primarily an international export market, for silver was a vital economic link that bound New Spain to its mother country. The crown sold the substances needed for refining and took a share of all ore produced. Owners were like tenants, claims were like leases, and the crown retained the subsoil as its own, though it only "evicted" when there was bankruptcy. Duties on silver production filled the king's coffers with ingots and pieces of eight, which meant that whatever happened in silver mines was closely attended by royal officials. In the Spanish heritage the mining enterprise was far from a lawless, rowdy "mining camp." It was, rather, a mining Real, a protectorate of the crown itself, a royal enclave where the working man had rights respected by a code of law endorsed by the king himself.

On the one hand the mining Reales of New Spain were separated, isolated in mountain fastnesses. Each was unique, each set of silver mines had its own ways, its own rules. On the other hand, because of the interest of royal officials, communications to the justices of head towns (like Pachuca) and even to Mexico City were swift. The soldiers could come with speed, but worker networks with grievances about the industry might find a ready audience in the viceroy himself.

Work and wage pitted the crew below against the managers and the boss above and bound the workers together in the struggle. Bosses and miners shared many commitments, but on the topic of profits their interests diverged, became explicitly antagonistic. Spanish has a sort of bifocal perception that focuses how class interests may divide our understandings of things. The word *barra* meant "share or stock" to the investor and "work gang" to the workers. The word *minero* meant "investor" to the capitalists and "mine foreman" to the workers. "Wages" meant living to the workers; to the owners, a factor in production that might be manipulated.

Ethnic rivalries did not seriously divide the free men of Real del Monte. Owners preferred the work of free labor and hired Creoles, mestizos, mulattoes, and bilingual Indians, who were all integrated by their efforts into the work community. The boss, a Spaniard, had the right to force village Indians to work for him as manual laborers in the dry diggings. Unique to Real del Monte were 133 Black slaves, brought into the Veta Vizcaína in the

1750s to work in the mines and in the drainage projects. Gamboa said there was one great advantage in hiring Black slaves: they could be punished. Antonio de Ulloa said they could be counted on not to steal. According to an inspection in 1771, there were 135 Blacks — 22 married couples, 58 bachelors, 3 single women, and 30 children — living inside the mine of La Palma. Stocks of beans (*habas* and *frijoles*) were stored in the kitchen. Each married couple had private lodgings in the south gallery. In the north gallery was a dormitory for the single men. There was a commons for laundry and several rooms set aside for child care and religious instruction for children and adults. On feast days masses were said for the slaves before a special altar in the mine. Blacks worked the ores of La Palma with Black work gang leaders. They were expected to keep to themselves, and they did.[4] The free workers hated the slaves and left them alone and treated the captive Indians as if they were not there.

In 1754 and 1755, eighty-four miners from Guanajuato were imported to relieve the chronic labor shortage. They were greeted with blows and fights and enough mayhem to drive them away and persuade the boss to give up the idea. The men of Real del Monte treated the Guanajuato miners like scabs.[5]

Workers in Real del Monte claimed the mother lode as their own. The Veta Vizcaína or Biscayan Lode traces its silver way east-west across the hills, and some sixteen mines historically had been worked there. By 1766 Pedro Romero de Terreros had rehabilitated about half, the "seven shafts of the Veta Vizcaína," and hired men to work the principal mines of La Palma, Dolores, San Cayetano, La Joya, Santa Teresa, Sabanilla, and Santa Agueda.[6] (See Appendix 3.)

Real del Monte, at the foot of the mountains, was and is a beautiful little town. Its streets were narrow and winding, with maguey plants and the women's vegetable gardens and bright flowers in pots near the houses, with deep green pine forests, brushwood, wildflowers, and pretty paths all around. In a thick mist all are shrouded into woods. Sunlight, moonlight, and clear skies "clotted with stars" restore their shapes. The town had two jails (civil and ecclesiastical), a handsome white stucco church with two bell towers (one roofed with tiles), a number of stores and taverns, a traveling market in the plaza, but no town hall, no printing press, no community center, no school. The cemetery served all those functions. There were no barracks and no tax offices, no convents or monasteries, no hospital. To the northeast was the workplace, below, in the dark, its labyrinths narrow and twisting to the stopes where the ore was mined, through the tunneling drifts to where the great shafts led to the surface. Drainage canals and adits redirected ground water to nearby streams and, as they used to say in Cornwall, purged the "houses of water."[7]

Church bells pealed the way to work or mass at eight in the morning, and the Angelus rang workers off the day shift or on to the night shift or reminded men it was time to leave the tavern and go home for supper. Rodolfo Benavides described what it was like to go to work and leave the bells and the creaking sound of the whims and to descend into a silver mine. Feet slapped on the notched logs and dislodged dirt that took all too long to find bottom. Smiths' hammers sharpened tools to a rhythm. There were no caged canaries to sing, no companionable noises of horses or mules. The sounds of the mine proclaimed a man's world. When workers arrived, the voices came, the thudding of picks, the wrenching of crowbars against solid rock, men's whistling, and occasionally, a muffled explosion.[8]

The basic unit of manpower below was the *barra* or work gang of five or six men—pikemen, a peon, the gang captain. Pikemen with miners' picks attacked the rock face, then with mallets struck in the point of a lever, or inserted wedges with a cutting edge of steel and pounded until the rock cracked. With the crowbar end of the lever they pried out, wrenched out ore and rubble. When the veinstone was impacted and the rock face too hard, an expert pikeman pounded a hole and inserted a *taco*, a paper cylinder wrapped around black powder, the packet tied securely with maguey fiber and sealed with a fine white clay. A shank protruded to affix the tallow fuse, which was lighted with a flint and steel or a candle flame, the work gang having retreated into a safe cavern. Rodolfo Benavides, who lived it, said that the explosion sounds dull and muffled, as rocks thud to the ground, the body feels a sudden touch of hot, humid air like the panting breath of a beast, the nose smells burnt-out powder, the throat feels choked and scratchy, and the eyes see a thick, blue smoke that stings.[9]

When the rocks stopped falling and the smoke dissipated, the *barra* would go back to work, the pikemen to their pounding, picking, and prying and the peons to their loading of the large cowhide sacks, some with ore, some with the white and yellow alkaline rubble called, in pidgin Nahuatl, *tepetates*. Humboldt said the work gang was composed of three peons to every pikeman and that may have been true for Guanajuato. However, the scarce work rolls at Real Del Monte show just the opposite: two or even three pikemen for each peon.[10]

The work of peons, they told Francisco de Gamboa, the royal arbitrator, was to support the pikemen in whatever they needed and to carry the sacks from the stopes to the dispatchers above. Gamboa considered the standard sack size at Real del Monte to vary from 146 to 196 pounds.[11]

The peons had to carry their heavy loads up logs hacked into hundreds or even thousands of shallow steps. The "ladders" were double tree trunks, eight or ten yards long, notched with a hatchet and joined by little lumber platforms. The notches barely fitted a footstep. Deep in the humid mine, cottony fungus festooned the ends of the logs and grew embedded in the knotty, splintering sides. The "ladders" were inclined at a forty-five degree angle. Rodolfo Benavides shuddered at the thought of them: "It was chilling to see how those men climbed up and went down those wet, slippery logs. No one bothered to consider that the only thing that stopped them from falling into an abyss four hundred meters deep was that ugly round little ladder, not two inches thick."[12]

It took tremendous endurance to carry more than a hundred pounds up 1800 notched steps. Alan Probert says that conventional ladders could not have been used because a barefoot man so heavily laden could not bear the pressure of rungs on his arches. Humboldt said the peons threw their bodies forward and counterbalanced their weight on a short staff. They walked zigzag to breathe easier in the strong drafts of air. For protection they placed a folded woolen shank over their shoulders, then stretched the load to their head with a tumpline. They measured their shift by the load (the sack) or by the trip (up and down). Peons maintained they worked harder and with more danger than anyone except the pikemen who set explosives. They said they feared accidents when they were tired and that climbing up and going down the ladders were the most arduous parts of their job.[13]

And the miners worked at all these tasks twelve hours a shift, night or day, without sanitary facilities, without any defense against the deadly quartz particles, the sight of stone, the sound of rocks, the stifle of dust, the water making slime ankle-deep in the stopes, and more icy water trickling, gushing from above. But Benavides remembered that there was beauty in it: "Water droplets running down the walls caught the candlelight and gleamed like little ornaments of crystal in a thousand strange and fantastic shapes."[14]

They stopped to eat in a cold, empty cavern. They sat down on a wet floor, put out their candles, unwrapped cold tacos from moist bandannas, and ate them in the dark. There was silence while they listened to water dripping down the rocks, there was talk, there were quarrels, there were fights.[15]

The men who worked the water directly had the most fatiguing job in the mine. Bailers were always scarce and in demand, and their function was essential. They worked to keep the tunnels free of water. They bailed by hand, then poured the water into large leather casks which were sent by crane and by pulley to the surface, where they were dumped into the river. Indians were forbidden by law to do this exhausting work, though Pedro Romero de Terreros set his forced labor to do it. While drainage operations were not considered skilled labor, bailers got preferential treatment: a full day's pay for a half day's shift. [16]

The scaffolding of timbermen made the rounded edges of rock look rectangular with crib lathing. Timbermen and their helpers sawed the wood below and fashioned the notched logs, the platforms, the planks, and the braces that shored up the arches of the mine. A maguey cable brought planks up from the sawmill and down from above, holes were drilled, and the scaffolding was fixed in place with bolts. They lifted the old wood away to the surface, where someone decided what could be used again and what would be dried in the sun to be burned "in the stoves and chimneys of the bosses." Timbermen told Gamboa that their job was the most difficult in the mine. While pikemen and peons might work at two or three locations in a shift, timbermen spent the whole time, without a break, in the same place. And when old wood was lifted away, that was a very dangerous place to be. Humboldt was not impressed. He said the woodwork in Mexican mines was carelessly constructed. Nonetheless, timbermen were paid more cash wages than anyone in the mine, a peso a shift. [17]

Manual laborers in the dry diggings (meaning where no ore was to be found) worked waist-deep in the waters of the adits and foot-deep in the tunnels. Their job was to clean dirt and tepetates out of the work places. Sometimes the alkaline rubble was used to fill old shafts or caverns; sometimes it had to be lugged to the surface. Men worked twelve hours a day on such projects. The free manual laborers told Gamboa that their work in the mine was just as taxing and risky as work in the adits, and the greatest risks they found in climbing up and down. Humboldt praised the muscle and endurance of Mexican laborers. He also admired the skill of masons who worked both on the surface and within the mine. He said they fashioned limestone walls and arches with great care. [18]

There were two contrivances in eighteenth-century Mexican mines that did not depend exclusively on manpower. Below, smiths set up small portable forges powered by charcoal fires and made tools and sharpened pikes and wedges dulled by pounding. They also took charge of doling out water for thirsty working men to drink. Smiths were in an awkward position: they stayed below like workers but because they sharpened the company's tools, they thought they were management. On the surface, whims, great spool-like capstans, were pushed round and round by mules and horses and saved peons trips by winding and unwinding the three-inch maguey fiber cables used to hoist and lower leather containers of water, ore, and rubble. Whims were not pumps. They were elaborate pulleys. Whimsites were described for the Veta Vizcaína in 1767. San Cayetano had six for water only; La Palma had five; the Dolores had one for ore and rubble and four for water; La Joya had three whims for water only; Santa Teresa had one for ore; and San Andrés had one for rubble. Whims required the services of horse prodders, and stable boys were also hired to look after the animals. Whim operators needed muscle as well as a way with horses, for they unloaded the sacks and buckets and turned the ore over to dispatchers. Humboldt thought whims were "poorly designed, carelessly constructed, and uneconomically operated."[19]

A shed roofed over with shakes protected the mine shaft, and in it, amid fodder for the horses, the ropemaker made maguey-fiber cables and ropes. Dispatchers received ore sacks above and below and broke up hunks of ore. On payday they mixed the ores and parcelled out the shares. Saturday was payday for cash wages, but quotas and *partidos* were distributed every day. The managerial staff sat around a table in the gallery: the timekeeper, the scale man, the mine foreman, and occasionally the mines' administrator and the owner himself. Close by, guards, watchmen, and dispatchers tried to keep the workers honest.[20]

After payday the quota sacks of ore were hauled outside and the rocks pounded and sorted, a task so easy, miners said, that even women and girls could — and did — do it. Humboldt listed the ores of Veta Vizcaína:

lacteous quartz
splintery hornstone
amethyst
calcium carbonate (limestone)
silver sulfides (argentite and haloids)
native pure silver occurring with sulfides
prismatic black silver
dull red silver (antimony sulfide)
galena (lead sulfide)
pyrites of copper and iron oxide
arsenic sulfide

Ore sorters separated the "rebellious ores," like antimony, galena, and lead for smelting; and they set apart the arsenics, the silver sulfides, and the "blacks" gathered from the lower part of the vein for amalgamation.[21] Teamsters took the sorted ore on mule trains to refineries.

In the territory outside, the boss hired roving gangs of stalwarts called *recogedores* to form a kind of "press gang." Their job was to round up "lazy, idle men" and force them to work the dry diggings. Recogedores were the most hated employees of the mines, a private police force hired by the company to solve the labor shortage with a whip.[22]

Management furnished the tools of a mining enterprise. At the beginning of each shift workers lined up around the table in the gallery. Pikemen picked up the twenty-pound mallets and the miners' picks and chose the eight- to twelve-pound iron pike with a gad point at one end and a crowbar at the other. Gamboa observed that the lengths varied according to the strength of the man. They also selected the iron wedges with a steel cutting edge, the one-pound size for hard rock, the two-pound for a soft face. Some picked up the papers, powder, and paraphernalia for explosives. Everyone who went below was issued three tallow candles, each one dipped to last four hours. Motten said miners who wore soft caps held their candle with a forked stick. According to Benavides, they made hoops of wood or metal, put them around the crown of their straw hat, and placed the candle in the hoop.[23]

The peons shouldered their burdens (Alan Probert has it on good authority that the rawhide ore sack looked and smelled like a dead mule),[24] and the shift was armed for work.

Two wage systems operated at the same time in the large mines of eighteenth-century New Spain, partidos and cash wages. Partidos or shares were the oldest and most widely used. In 1766 only Taxco and Zimapam did not distribute partidos. In the sixteenth, seventeenth, and eighteenth centuries in small enterprises, the employer would supply the tools, the worker his labor, and they would divide a day's haul of ore equally. As mines became bigger and work more specialized, a quota was set to be turned over to management. Then one or two additional bags would be designated for the partido, to be divided equally between worker and management.

In the mines of Real del Monte skilled workmen were twice-marked: by being assigned helpers and by participating in the ore-sharing plan called the partido. The partido was the skilled laborer's share of ore, and he claimed it as a traditional wage in addition to his industrial cash wages. Partidos were divided the day after they were collected, which meant that ore was shared every day. To determine the partido the day's sack quota was set by an experienced miner according to the difficulty posed by the rock face and the height of the waters and accommodated to the quality of the ore to be removed. Once the pikeman had met his quota, he could fill a designated number of sacks for himself. Pikemen, when they took a break, allowed their peon to use their tools to fill one bag of ore for every four bags he carried.

Timbermen were also allowed a partido when they had to dislodge a reef of ore in order to secure the scaffolding. When they finished, they might fill a sack for themselves. In the gallery they were required to give 25 percent of the ore they had collected to management.[25]

Every worker who went below received the same daily cash wage: four *reales* (fifty cents) for each twelve-hour shift. For one real he could buy a beef tongue, a pound of wool, twenty-eight ounces of mutton, or five pounds of beef or veal. For three reales he could purchase twenty-five pounds of candles, suet or charcoal. In 1761 a Black slave miner bought his freedom from Pedro Romero de Terreros for 936 reales. A modest house in Real del Monte cost two thousand. Miners fretted about their pay, confessing, perhaps, their custom of eating fast foods and drinking on the job:

"four *reales* can be spent in a day or a night inside the mine itself
in eating and fortifying oneself against the toil and dampness."[26]

What they did to increase their pay infuriated owners. José Alejandro de Bustamante, Romero de Terreros' predecessor and partner in Real del Monte, identified stealing as insidiously wormholing the formation of profits, capital, and the patience of the boss. He complained, "They rob tools, blasting powder, candles, sacks, rope, leather buckets" from the boss and from each other.[27] Workers hid their silver ore down in the rubble of the mine, even in the orifices of their bodies. In Guanajuato Humboldt was appalled by the ingenuity of the stealing, though it provoked in him an Aryan pride. While not suggesting that the men of Real del Monte were this clever in secreting silver ore, the "thousand tricks" of the men of Guanajuato are described so graphically as to make an analogy perhaps suggestive. Humboldt reported:

Honesty is by no means so common among the Mexican as among the German or Swedish miners; and they make use of a thousand tricks to steal very rich minerals. As they are almost naked, and are searched on leaving the mine in the most indecent manner, they conceal small morsels of native silver, or red sulfuretted and muriated silver in their hair, under their armpits, and in their mouths; and they even lodge in their anus cylinders of clay which contain the metal. These cylinders are called *longanas*, and they are sometimes found to the length of . . . five inches. It is a most shocking spectacle to see in the large mines of Mexico, hundreds of workmen, among whom there are a great number of very respectable men, all compelled to allow themselves to be searched on leaving the pit or the gallery.[28]

Peons had more opportunities than anyone to take ore because they often skimmed the top off of each sack they carried, thus stealing from the pike-men as well as the boss. Gamboa said they were hard to catch because each man hid it on his own, in his own secret place.[29]

What Bustamante found insufferable about worker-thieves in Real del Monte was their attitude: they were insolently self-righteous about it. If caught and punished, they might never return to work. They turned over to the owner his share as if it were "alms, and they consider what they steal to be a just wage for a day's work."[30]

The work-etched pattern, the underlying organizational potential of the work force, emerges from their network as workers. First, most important, is the *barra*, the cell of work below, a team of five or six men dependent on each other for their job, their comfort, and their safety. Next in this pattern is the *pueble*, the shift, which in the Veta Vizcaína at the time counted forty to fifty barras (311 pikemen and 150 peons) and 255 manual laborers. For the thirteen puebles of the work week (one night a week the mine was dark) there were 1555 pikemen, 750 peons, and 1275 manual laborers on duty. In the dry diggings were 160 pikemen and 45 peons.[31] The organizational structure used by the strikers, like the work of the mines, was pieced together by *barras* and *puebles*. Once patterned, it drew on the reservoirs of kith and kin networks in the community to fill out the numbers of strikers.

The intimacy that binds men to friends and family is extended in the Spanish heritage by the institutions of *compadrazgo*. The parents and godparents of a baptized child become co-parents and have a warm relationship that allows for borrowing and lending money, giving and receiving presents, exchanges of babysitting, mutual aid in household tasks, and in general sharing the burdens and celebrations of everyday life. Women used this network to develop a sisterhood among women and deep and lasting friendships with men. There are a few hints in these documents that miners visited their *comadres* on a regular basis, joked with them, talked with them seriously, and looked forward to their companionship. Men worked, went out, plotted, and hit the streets with their *compadres* as with their brothers. No role is insignificant because they, as workers and as people, created in New Spain a new form of resistance, the industrial strike.

Some miners were homebodies, they cleaved to their families. They left home only to go to work and left work only to go home. Some liked to sleep. All visited relatives and friends and celebrated baptisms, first communions, saints' days, and weddings and mourned at wakes.

Pastimes of the miners, on and off the job, served as a kind of cartilage of everyday life that held the strikers together and were interpreted as a cancer of conspiracy by authorities. The mines were worked twenty-four hours a day, seven days and six nights a week, and the men worked a twelve-hour shift by day or night, from eight to eight.[32] However, the partido made it possible for some workers to sign up for only three or four shifts a week and still make a decent living.

Men and women shared a few pastimes: dalliance, sex. Some workers lived in sin. Some of the more respectably wed tried to beat their legitimate wives. (Men went to jail when they tried that.) Men and women shopped at stores, fairs, and on Fridays and Sundays at the town markets. They sat outside their home and smoked and listened to a "scandal" of dogs barking at the black, cold night. They walked in the woods. Visits and promenades were popular. People gave *fandangos* to dance away a free night. Occasionally there was a night cockfight, the streets lined with torches, and music everywhere. Men and women went together to watch and listen "scandalously." Families went to church and often stayed after the service to watch the plays and puppet shows their priest staged for them in the cemetery. The strange thing about listening for "their own voices" is that one overhears surprising things. Parishioners in Real del Monte loved their passionate, kindly, eloquent, well-meaning priest.[33] "After all," wrote John Leddy Phelan, "the three major social activities were attending mass, making love, and playing cards."[34]

On their own men drank, gambled, participated in men's church groups (*cofradías* and choirs), discussed things, and brawled. Cards were played by day and by night: *albures, mus,* and threes-and-sevens. Many men loved to talk and spent hours in conversation at each other's houses, in taverns, in the cemetery. There were a few bullfights in the town plaza, but miners seemed to prefer fighting cocks, and they watched cockfights with enthusiasm in the cockpits and in the streets. Some men liked to drink. In those days the Mexican working man's drink was pulque, a whitish, sweetish fermentation of the sap of the maguey spiced with the spit of the maguey harvesters. Pulque, which is drunk by *medios* (half a pottery jar), was served in taverns and in *pulquerías*, both licensed and illicit. Such places also served turnovers and tamales. Most had live music, some even had dancing.[35]

Although a few men were called drunks, not a single man was accused of being drunk in any of the public demonstrations of this era at Real del Monte. Fornication, not drunkenness, was the workers' favorite crime, according to criminal records. Many men, when caught, married their partners with a smile. And, of course, there were fights: wrangles at home, skirmishes in the tavern, episodes where the men of one mine tried to win with rocks over workers from another. What happened to Luis Ramírez one night wasn't so unique. He went to a tavern in Real del Monte, drank a medio of pulque, played threes-and-sevens, quarrelled with someone, fought him with stones, and got a headache.[36]

A lively set of sounds sang the miners together in and out of work. It was a repertoire of whistles and catcalls that translated as passwords and counter-signs. In the working drifts, so far below the ground, sounds are muffled. The miners added to their minstrelsy an elaborate set of poundings, like the drumming of prisoners in jail. Their secret language worked in the mines, in the mountains, in the ravines, wherever miners wanted to communicate without being understood by any nonworker. Whistles, catcalls, and drumming formed in Real del Monte a language for work and a language for rebellion.[37]

!¡

CHAPTER 3

"Bitter Wages"

It is probably true that only workers can speak with full understanding about their "bitter wages,"[1] the diseases and injuries they contract on the job.[2] Only one freed miner, mestizo Felipe Estrada was specific about his condition. He complained of heart and lung trouble that crippled him. He could only go out on Sundays to Mass and for a walk around the plaza. He had not worked in one and a half years and sadly admitted that he would never work again. He was forty-one years old. In general, Real del Monte workers in the 1760s were laconic and vague about their working conditions: in their own voices they mentioned only their "excessive toil and fatigue."[3] Elaboration in the August 1 grievance were clearly literary and learned dramatizations phrased by the lawyer:

> It is frightening to read the phrases that authors use to express the terrors of this work: the continual risks of losing one's life, smothered in a landfall, plunged down an abyss, breathing noxious fumes, contracting pestilential diseases; all of which, added to the nature of the work itself, commends labor enough; four *reales* is little reward for it.[4]

One of the ancient authors referred to was Tertulian, who said that the hard tasks of mining served, as they had always, "as a punishment for slaves, a torment for martyrs, and as a means of revenge for tyrants."[5]

The miners of Real del Monte experienced their work as a torment. Exposure to the diseases and hazards of extracting ore produced the same effects on workers then that they do today, for the human body, not having lost any of its vulnerability, reacts the same. What is different now is that the miners have learned that working conditions can and ought to be changed (see Epilogue). However, in the eighteenth century there were no effective ways of lessening the hazards or preventing or curing the diseases. Rather than asking for protection, miners used the idea of continual danger to reinforce their conviction that they deserved just wages as a reward, as a medal for individual bravery and collective valor.

The work was dangerous. Grant Smith said that on the Comstock there was an accident every day and a man killed every week. Humboldt observed that Mexican miners of the eighteenth century seldom lived past the age of thirty-five.[6] A Pachuca miner in our time told of the hardships specifically in terms of death and disability, ironically in terms of "freedom" and the miners' native land of risk:

> Miners have their own country where they die of hunger and have the freedom to die hundreds of meters down in the bowels of the earth under tons of rock or down a shaft, leaving parts of their bodies smeared on the doorframes and posts; the liberty to move as far as the handle of a pick or the width of the drift allows; the liberty to die of silicosis and tuberculosis, yellowed and mummified, after their boyhood and youth have been disintegrated in sweat and blood on the handle of a pick.[7]

Fear of falling and being crushed was real for pikemen treading slippery logs with their heavy tools. It was an even greater risk for peons who had to work their way upward a thousand notches with a full one-hundred or two-hundred pound pack. Even children of seven or eight carried loads of a hundred pounds. One slip, one misstep, and the fall almost certainly would be fatal. Timbermen lowering and positioning scaffolding and ladders looked for rotten, splintering, broken, or swollen wood, which would indicate weakening from heat and water and use. The most dangerous moment for them occurred in the interval before the new wood was positioned. Then, carpenters, with no sure support, could fall into the abyss. The deepest point of the Veta Vizcaína was more than a thousand feet below the surface.[8]

When timbermen failed to support the shafts properly or when there were earth tremors, wooden structures collapsed, and masses of rock fell. Workers watched in fear for signs of a landslide. First, sand trickled into the stopes from above, then small rocks; massive pillars cracked, supports buckled, and at last tons of rocks pounded into the drifts. Miners could be crushed to death or buried alive. Zola captured the horror for the victim: "a land-slip, a complete slide, and the rock drank his blood and swallowed his bones."[9]

Millions of board feet of oak and pine yielded the logs and laths timbermen used to build the supporting structures of a mine. If this lumber ignited, it could spread devastating fires underground. Causes of fire were difficult to trace. Sometimes black powder exploded, and sparks flew. Some fires started when a worker set a candle too near the dry scaffolding. The first clue was the smell of smoke; the sight of flames came late. Tunnels blazed, ladders burned like red-hot coals. When the Quebradilla burned in Zacatecas, thirty-one workers died, and 250 escaped. In Real del Monte 80 to 172 miners were killed at the Encino. Heat prevents rescue, but smoke kills more than flame. Those who survived might suffer chest pains and depression, and at worst, persistent shaking of the limbs or even paralysis and loss of memory. The heavy smoke diffused into every part of the mine. Men coughed and choked, their eyes popping. Carbon monoxide, produced when fuel burns in an atmosphere low in oxygen, exercised its vampire effect, and men paled and died for lack of oxygen in the red blood cells.

Fires in silver mines could last for months or even years as flames continued to burn in faraway shafts. El Encino had to be abandoned in spite of its filaments of pure silver. On the Veta Vizcaína both La Palma and Santa Agueda burned, and both were still full of smoke in 1767. Eliot Lord explained why such mines were difficult to rehabilitate: "The stubborn hold which fire keeps in the exhumed chambers of ore, filled with masses of timber and waste rock, makes it formidable for months after it is apparently extinguished, for the unseen flames may burn fiercely at any moment; and unless constant watch is kept, the miners are never safe underground."[10] In any fire, Lord reminds us, watchers live the tragedy and keep the vigil; on the surface "the hearts of brave women break silently."[11]

Everyday conditions within the mines were deplorable. Rodolfo Benavides wrote that putrefying excrement infected the whole mine with a repugnant, unbreathable, asphyxiating atmosphere that nauseated people. Insects were a plague. Bernadini Ramazzini said that in Europe silver miners were subject to sudden drops of small stinging spiders and ticks, a plague supporting the miners' fear that small demons had worked their way up from hell to torment them.[12]

Propensities to contract diseases were even greater than chances of accidents. Some diseases of silver miners were debilitating, others were fatal, a few were both. Peons and pikemen might suffer "miners' elbow," which showed as a painful lump, red and swollen, and subsided as chronic rheumatism. Equally unpleasant were eyes chronically inflamed, so common to work below that it was called "miners' nystagmus." The irritation took a long time to develop and was progressively marked by headaches, dizziness, and the sensation of seeing all lights at night as spinning fireworks. Eyes cured themselves if the worker was transferred to the surface. In Europe, since minerals that caused disease were thought to cure disease, miners endured eyewashes of brass and saltpeter. When they complained of sore throats and inflamed gums, they gargled with milk, which was supposed to absorb the corrosive particles and restore their ease. Exposure to the salts of silver might cause a blue-brown mottling of the skin and "silver tattooing" in the throat, but silver itself was not otherwise harmful to human beings except in rare cases of kidney damage or arteriosclerosis. [13]

"Emanations," "vapors," and "noxious fumes" were—and are—considered perilous. There were danger signs when candles flickered faintly blue in air stinking from decayed plants, stagnant water, and human excrement. Rotting organic material gives off methane gas that turns candle flames blue and weighs down men's eyelids until they feel a "spider's-web veil which it left on the eyelashes." [14] Methane suffocates people, and if, in air, it moves into flame, it explodes. When fire is applied to hard rock containing arsenic and zinc compounds, as in blasting or when wooden wedges are set on fire to widen a crack, fumes may be released. Contact with such smoke causes the person to lose all feeling; the body swells up, and the worker is unable to move. [15]

Francisco de Gamboa, the leading expert on mining law in eighteenth-century Mexico, described "noxious vapors" in great detail. He wrote that miners had to flee from the galleries to avoid certain suffocation by "gaseous" substances that "put out candles, extinguish and annihilate men's spirits with the pestilential evil which emanates from arsenic, greasy and inflammable minerals, and sulphur compounds." [16] Both argentite (which used to be called "silver glance") and galena (lead sulfide) are silver ores associated with sulfur, and both are plentiful in Real del Monte. Native silver in the Veta Vizcaína occurs also with sulfur. Antimony and arsenic sulfides are common. Particles of sulfur are very irritating to the throat and lungs. When sulfur compounds exist in poorly ventilated work sites, workers may suffer shortness of breath and severe conjunctivitis. [17]

Men of the eighteenth century called the dust clouds of the mine face "fumes" and "vapors," too. Besides the sulfides, antimony and lead particles are hurtful. Exposure to antimony affects the lungs and entire upper respiratory tract and, when it occurs with sulfides, may cause cardiovascular problems. Lead poisoning is rare in silver miners, even though such men work with galena, a lead sulfide. Its effects tell more readily in smelters than in miners. [18]

Abrupt changes of temperature during the working day, from ninety degrees or more (Fahrenheit) in the stopes to the "raw cold" of twenty-three degrees in December at Real del Monte, had serious effects on the workers. Humboldt considered such sudden changes more harmful than the hard work of the mines. [19] The men had no place to shower and change into warmer clothes. An old miner remembered what it was like coming up hot and drenched with perspiration from the pits into the winter air: "The sweat freezes, and it sounds like firecrackers in the night." [20] Respiratory difficulties caused by the sudden change were treated with doses of quinine and stimulants. Heat prostration takes the form of high body temperatures (101–102°F), low blood pressure, and fast heartbeat, symptoms which slow work, especially when miners experience dizziness, impaired reaction time, and exhaustion. Freed from the heat, their nausea overcome, men craved ice, fruits, salt, acidic and highly seasoned food. [21] But whatever the cures and preventatives, abrupt changes in temperature weakened the body's defenses against bacteria and viruses, and in the mines tuberculosis and pneumonia were killers.

The mummifying death that comes when workers spit up their lungs and lie on their beds as exhausted skeletons racked with coughing is silicosis or, as it used to be called, "miners' phthisis." Miners of silver and gold, salt, alum, limestone, sulfur, lead, copper, tin, or mercury, and workers in quarries, foundries, and potteries contract, after a long time, silicosis. Related illnesses are the black lung of coal miners, the siderosis of iron miners, and the brown lung that affects spinners of flax, hemp, and cotton. These are all categorized under the general term pneumonocosis, which means a massive fibrosis of the lungs caused by different kinds of particles. None of the pneumonocoses is contagious; all are the "bitter wages" of the industrial laborer. [22]

The dust in the mines of Real del Monte was everywhere: the dust of the "country rock," feldspar and porphyry; the black dust of basalt, the blue dust of silver sulfide, the gray dust of clay slate, and the white dust of quartz. Those who worked the rock face head-on were the most exposed, the pikemen, the blasters, the peons who helped them, the manual laborers and forced Indian labor who sank the shafts and shoveled and transported rock all day. On the surface the women, children, and old men who pounded rock and sorted ore were also exposed to the dusts of the workplace. Anyone who poured out ore from the rawhide sacks and shoveled it back again knew dust as a constant on-the-job companion.

In an era which observed "noxious fumes" and "pestilential" diseases, Humboldt noticed the dust right away: "the health of the workmen suffer greatly in a place where a cloud of metallic dust is perpetually flying about."[23] A Saxon expert, Agricola, in 1556 maintained that the "wasting diseases" of miners were all caused by dust inhalation. He argued that dust itself had "corrosive qualities" that ate away the lungs and implanted consumption in the body. Agricola advised defenses against the dust in the workplace. The miners should wear loose veils over the face, gloves to the elbow, high boots. He lectured, "We should always devote more care to maintaining our health, that we may freely perform our bodily functions, than to making profits."[24]

Although learned men like Francisco de Gamboa read and quoted Agricola, it seems that profits, not precautions, were taken in eighteenth-century Mexican mines. Instead of protective gear, miners wore the traditional *cuera y gorra*, a leather or cotton tunic and a soft cap, and they went barefoot or wore sandals. Their shirtsleeves and trousers were rolled up, their arms and legs exposed, and they wore no gloves and no veils.[25]

It is not the large dust particles that damage the body, for they are trapped by the hairs of the nostrils and sneezed away, or they are coughed up, then spat out or swallowed within three or four hours after leaving work. It is the smaller particles that are so harmful. They settle in the alveoli of the lungs, and only some of them can be dislodged by coughing. An adult human body has three hundred or four hundred million alveoli, the tiny air pockets of the lungs, and to scar enough of them to impair transfers of oxygen and carbon dioxide in the blood takes many years. Experts in Real del Monte measured the structures of capital investment with care and counted the labor force, but they never calculated rates of dust inhalation. Today it is believed that five grams of dust adhering to the alveoli is fatal to the worker. In silver mines it may take from five to thirty years to accumulate that amount.[26] The process by which dust particles affects the lungs is not known, even in our time, but the results are clear. In the presence of the tiny particles, round nodules of scar tissue form in the affected alveoli, and their respiratory functions cease.[27]

Since silicosis is observably progressive, would-be healers have described three stages of symptoms for hundreds of years. In the first stage the worker has "cold" after "cold," each lasting a long time. He complains of shortness of breath, pains in the chest, and fatigue. The second stage is characterized by racking coughs in the morning, coughs that trigger vomiting and severe chest pains. His colds persist, he notices heart flutter. At this stage he may contract tuberculosis or pneumonia. The third stage, advanced silicosis, incapacitates the worker. Paroxysms of coughing are accompanied by severe weight loss. The heart pounds in the chest, and the pulse becomes more rapid. Weight loss is marked. The heart itself may dilate. The emaciated worker, for all these reasons, becomes an invalid.[28]

How many miners were affected by these diseases in Real del Monte and how many actually died of accidents and diseases cannot even be conjectured, for there are no "industrial hygiene" records available for eighteenth-century Mexico. One lethal sequence is common to mines everywhere: pneumonia, tuberculosis, and the influenzas kill many more workers than does silicosis itself. Those dying of silicosis are, then, the last survivors of the "bitter wages" for a lifetime of work.[29]

In colonial times all respiratory diseases, especially pneumonia, tuberculosis, and advanced silicosis, were considered medically incurable. Agricola recommended prayer and fasting to exorcise disease. Sixteenth- and seventeenth-century experts, always sanguine, recommended that patients sprinkle their meals with salts extracted from the mines where they worked, take a soothing balsam made of nettles, and drink a distillate of laudanum, oil of tartar, and rust. These medications were to be washed down with wine and greasy broth. Another treatment, used in the seventeenth-century mines at Annaberg, Germany, prescribed emetics, laxatives, sweats, and bleeding to purge the body of the poisons. However, as the symptoms worsened, most doctors conceded that the case was hopeless. Then, as now, the "bitter wages" ended with death.

Silicosis and poisoning by smoke were not just miners' problems in the silver industry; they were exacerbated by the conditions in refineries, in smelters, and in the great *haciendas de beneficio* controlled by Pedro Romero de Terreros.

Because workers could sell their share of partidos freely, small independent refiners bought ore and roasted it in little charcoal smelting furnaces.[30] The technical competence of such small, independent Mexican smelters was very highly regarded in Nevada a hundred years later. A silver miner from Virginia City was impressed: "The Mexicans here, with their little adobe smelting furnaces have contrived to extract from the same quality of ore more metal than the scientific gentlemen in San Francisco say there is in it."[31]

Very little is known about these small independent refiners in Mexico in the eighteenth century. However, one example from the judiciary records of Pachuca combines information on them with a surprising and unique environmental protection protest. Pablo Aparicio operated a smelter in his house near the old chapel of San Nicolás in Pachuca. His neighbors, men and women, complained in 1764: "D. Pablo Aparicio is injuring us with the smoke of pyrites and the dust of the ores that he burns. The fetid fumes are dangerous to our health, and we have lost chickens, birds, and domestic animals, which have died from them."[32] They also pointed out that waste materials from the smelting process were polluting the nearby stream. Since royal ordinance prohibited smelting in the neighborhoods, royal authorities turned down Aparicio's suggestion that the neighbors buy him out. Instead, he was directed to clean up the stream, remove his furnace, cease practicing his trade there by day or night, and refrain from bothering his neighbors.

Smoke irritated the neighbors, but it was liable to kill the smelter, whether he was an independent businessman like Aparicio or an employee of the great refineries of Pedro Romero de Terreros. The sulfur of the burning ores was more immediately irritating to the eyes, throat, and lungs of smelters than it was to miners. But the most hazardous element in the fumes of smelting came from the lead which was used as flux.[33] Harmful effects occur more rapidly when lead particles are inhaled as smoke or dust (because 25 to 50 percent is absorbed) than when they are eaten (and about ten percent is absorbed). Either way, the body cannot rid itself of lead. Lead poisoning is felt first as stomach cramps and pains that come and go in the muscles and joints. The anemia that follows is progressively debilitating. The disease inscribes a characteristic blue "lead line" on the gums, and jaundice yellows the eyes. Effects are especially marked on the liver, spleen, lungs, kidneys, and skeleton. The last stages of lead poisoning cause the worker to shake with palsy and to suffer coma, delirium, and convulsions.[34]

Most of the silver ores and all of the quota of the mines of Real del Monte were transported in mule trains to the great refineries of Pedro Romero de Terreros: Santa María "El Salto," San Miguel, and San Antonio. There were smelters at each, but the massive operations were geared to another kind of refining, the amalgamation of silver in the patio process, invented in Pachuca. Humboldt calculated that about 78 percent of the silver was amalgamated and only 22 percent smelted.[35] In the early stages of the patio process, dust was everywhere.

At the refineries women pounded ore to the size of small pebbles which would pass through a rawhide strainer. The pebbles were then crushed in an *arastradero* or stamp mill, where mules moved great slabs of rock to crush the ore to a fine sand. Because a refinery had more employees working and more ore to be ground, there was more dust than in a mine. Silicosis and its various respiratory complications were endemic in the great refining haciendas.[36]

Besides the pernicious effects of dust, sulfur and mercury fumes made refineries literally poisonous. The fumes, complicating the effects of exposure to fire and dampness, harmed many workers.[37]

Amalgamation in the patio process was likened to the making of a cake (*torta*), except that men's feet and legs, not spoons, stirred the mixture of ore mud, pyrites, and mercury. Workers trod the torta in the patio for days at a time. Humboldt was surprised at their robustness: "A great number of these individuals pass their lives in walking barefooted over heaps of brayed metal, moistened and mixed with muriate of soda, sulphate of iron, and oxide of mercury. All is done in sunlight and open air. It is a remarkable phenomenon to see these men enjoy the most perfect health.[38]

When the cake had "cooled," workers, often women, loaded the amalgam into sacks and squeezed out the mercury by hand. To recover what mercury might be left in the sacks, men and women heated pyramids of amalgam covered with a bronze bell over charcoal fires. The mercury vaporized, then condensed in a recovery trough.[39] The distillers' exposure to mercury fumes was prolonged and close, and distillation was dangerous, the most dangerous of all phases of silver production.

Mercury fumes or mists can cause poisoning if 0.4 mg. of mercury is absorbed a day. Effects may be lessened if the worker is removed from contact, but most people, once exposed, suffer some symptoms all their lives. Mercury can enter unblemished skin and produce symptoms. If it enters through a cut, it corrodes and ulcerates the flesh, producing intense itching, swelling, and deep pus pockets. Exposure to fumes or liquid produces the "mercurial tremor," which is felt first in the eyelids, mouth, tongue, and fingers. Gums are inflamed, lips swell, and the teeth loosen in their sockets. The person suffers from headaches and insomnia. Most frightening of all are the psychological disturbances, which begin with irritability, restlessness, speech impediments, and a fear of being with people. They continue with deep depression, failing memory, and loss of the will to live. The ultimate horror of the advanced phase of mercury poisoning is a classic psychosis. When English hatmakers used to soak furs in mercury and then chew them to softness, they went "mad as a hatter." Mercury poisons by inhibiting essential enzymes in the brain, and hallucination and delusion accompany its victims to their death by convulsions.[40]

Rodolfo Benavides described workers in Pachuca who died of mercury poisoning: "Mercury insinuated itself even into their bones and unbalanced their nervous systems, making them tremble constantly until they despaired and died in horrible paroxysms."[41]

That all these conditions existed to make miners' working life a torment could be interpreted as ignorance on the part of the mining industry. Or, in our time, it has been said that "Job casualties are a form of violence."[42]

In the eighteenth century men dealt with this kind of violence as best they could as individuals, and then they went right on doing what they had to do. The "voiceless victims" suffered with their families and died at home. The occupational hazards and diseases they knew so well seldom came up for discussion. They never became items for collective bargaining because they were problems coped with exclusively in the private sphere, far from the workplace. The lifetime of work in the mines might have been common knowledge, but suffering the "bitter wages" and dying from them were matters for the family, the doctor, and the priest. Those who still worked were watchful and fatalistic. Every day they went to face their tasks, and, to survive, they counted on their strength, their experience, their coolness, and their luck to last until quitting time. Every shift completed was evidence to them that they were daring and brave in the face of danger. Aside from themselves, they could only pray and learn to count on one another.

CHAPTER 4

Forced Labor

The pain and anguish of actually working in silver mines and refineries were also experienced and articulated by Indian villagers, compelled by authorities to leave rural areas and work in the mines. The plight of forced village laborers in the mines of eighteenth-century Mexico has been ignored.[1] Interestingly enough, it is contrary to the enthusiastic writings of New Spain's keenest foreign observer, Alexander von Humboldt. Humboldt insisted, memorably, during his visit to New Spain in 1804, that miners were all free men: "The labour of a miner is entirely free throughout the whole kingdom of New Spain; and no Indian or Meztizoe [sic] can be forced to dedicate themselves to the working of the mines."[2] Punishing people by forcing them to work in the mines had, he said, entirely disappeared from the Spanish world centuries before. Not only free, Mexicans were also the best-paid miners in the world.

The labor struggles at Real del Monte took place a whole generation before Humboldt's visit. He was mostly right: even in the 1750s and 1760s the majority of the work force of silver mines was free. But there was a minority, working men coerced from villages, not for crimes but in response to a labor draft, other men suspected of "idleness" or "vagrancy," all condemned to hard labor in the mines against their will.

In his original claim to the Veta Vizcaína, José Antonio de Bustamante won the right to compel communities from ten leagues around Real del Monte to send men to do forced labor in his mines, to force them to go "without pretext, excuse, or any reason for not complying," the work to include the drainage project and, when ores were found, whatever else might be necessary.[3] Since Indians were specifically forbidden by the Laws of the Indies to work in the drainage works of mines, this was a great concession in-

deed. In 1754 the viceroy confirmed Pedro Romero de Terreros in all Bustamante's rights and privileges. This included the same right to forced labor,
which village officials were directed to send to Real del Monte, by "the most
prompt and efficient means possible," under the threat of a hefty five-
hundred-peso fine. The law allowed four percent of the community's manpower to be commandeered.[4] If men refused to go, they could be condemned
to one year's hard labor at a factory if they were Indians, mestizos, Negroes,
mulattoes; or one year's hard labor at a fort if they were *españoles* (Creoles born
in Mexico).[5] Forced labor, though a minority of the total work force, surely
existed in the mines of Real del Monte, early and late in the eighteenth century.

Recruitment did not begin with Bustamante and Romero de Terreros. In
1726 Isidro Rodríguez de la Madrid tried to rehabilitate the mines of the
Veta Vizcaína by draining them and sent out the call for forced labor. The
response was a moan of horror from the pulque-producing pueblo of Zin-
guiluca in the province of Tulancingo. Local officials said that the village had
been tending maguey plants since "time immemorial," and all the men were
busily occupied with their trade. Armed thugs from the mines of Real del
Monte swooped down on the village, terrorizing everyone. When the Indians fled into their homes, the recogedores or press gang broke in after them
and threatened them with weapons. When the people sought refuge in the
church with their priest and hid under the altar, the men disdained the sanctuary and strode in, brandishing naked swords. In final desperation many of
the pulque workers ran away. The Indian officials were afraid that they
would never return and that the village would lose workers, tribute payers,
and family providers, leaving women and children destitute.[6] The mining
industry threatened villages with its insistence on force and forced labor, and
the villages felt it, but not consistently, nor were they always afraid.

Great pressure was applied again on the villages of the thirty-five-mile
hinterland of Real del Monte in 1756 and 1757. Their agonized reactions
displayed a wide range of behavior, but they were never "voiceless." Every
protest was grimly articulated into legal petitions by governors, village
councils, and parish priests. (Villages may be located on Map 1.)

When Pedro Romero de Terreros was confirmed as sole owner of the Veta
Vizcaína in 1754 (Bustamante died in 1750), his first endeavor was to set in
motion the paper work that would allow him to use force and threat in re-
cruiting labor. He apparently had four goals in mind: to open a new adit
(which was, in fact, completed in 1759); to renovate Mina La Joya; to "resur-
rect" the main shaft of the San Cayetano, which had been destroyed in a del-

uge (the job was completed by 1758); and to refine in his great haciendas de beneficio the increasing loads of silver ore worked from the newly exposed veins. He must have believed that it was past time to reap profits from his vast expenditures, for he made it clear that by 1758 he had invested 1,428,906 pesos. The King of Spain himself praised Romero de Terreros for proceeding with all these projects with "the most vigorous and bold constancy."[7]

The call went out to the neighboring villages, to Tulancingo, Cempoala, Actopan, Tetepango, and Ixmiquilpan. Romero de Terreros demanded a fifteen-day shift, at the end of which a relay crew with its own captain would relieve the first group. If there was no relief, the original crew would be compelled to keep on working. Like free labor, forced labor worked twelve hours. Or, they were supposed to. The protests were vigorous, constant, desperate. The legal briefs took years to process. Some villages complied, some were exempted, and one rebelled.

REAL DEL MONTE'S HINTERLAND OF FORCED LABOR

After Peter Gerhard, *A Guide to the Historical Geography of New Spain* (Cambridge 1972), pp. 44, 67, 209, 296, 336. This version by July Green, University of Hawaii at Manoa.

Village protests emphasized that workers were busy and occupied, not lazy and idle. When the call came in April of 1757, villagers of Actopan and Tetitlán were sowing the corn, beans, lentils, and chick-peas, which fed the people and provided the basis for their market trade. The men of Tulancingo were tending their maguey plants. In Huasca people were providing firewood, torch pine, and charcoal for Romero de Terreros' refinery at Santa María Regla, El Salto.[8]

Villagers also had many governmental obligations. They had to pay taxes and tribute to the crown and tithes to the church. The pueblo of San Bartolomé de Tetepango communicated its feeling of oppression. The villagers were "poor, miserable people. They paid the sales tax, tithe, and tribute, now comes this demand."[9] In addition, they had community obligations. In Cempoala they applied themselves to irrigation works to complete the Cempoala-Otumba project, which would bring water to the villages. In Tulancingo every four months people collected eggs and chickens for the viceregal palace in Mexico City. Every two weeks they took turns watching the flocks; every eight weeks they helped the priest with church affairs; and every three weeks they took a turn serving the village council and tribute collectors. Above and beyond all this, men did their own work. An Indian governor said there was not a single worker who was not in debt to his employer. When they came home, they tended their own animals, cared for their families, and went to church on Sundays and holy days of obligation.[10]

Strangely, since free miners almost never discussed their "bitter wages" in detail, Indians did complain explicitly. Work in the mines and refineries made them recoil and refuse to go because of the occupational diseases and hazards. Tulancingo declared that its people would rather run away and become fugitives than to work in Real del Monte:

> The hateful repugnance which they have for this work comes from
> the horror of the diseases some people from here have contracted.[11]

Diego Félix, an Indian of Tulancingo who had worked as a forced laborer in Romero de Terreros's refinery El Salto, hated it. He said he was forced to tread mercury into mineral mud, which was cold and oppressively damp, and they would not let him rest, not even when he was tired. The priest testified that many of his parishioners had died from the arduous work and from its detrimental effects on their bodies. The Indian governor concluded that the villagers of Tulancingo viewed their turn at El Salto like a criminal sentence to hard labor. What crime had they committed? Officials in Cempoala said that men came home gasping for breath, sickened by the dust of the stamp mills. Two villagers from Cempoala fell from the log ladders in the mines of the Veta Vizcaína. One was killed, and one was crippled for life. Bernardo Cervantes, legal counsel for the Indians of Cempoala and the only official to describe what appears to be mercury poisoning in agricultural Mexico, said that men staggered home from Romero de Terreros's refinery only to drum their fingers foolishly, their wits gone. [12]

The villages of Tierra Caliente, the "hot lands" to the east and west, all stated that their workers would die if they were forced to work in the frigid nights of Real del Monte. In fact, the Laws of the Indies specifically prohibited a forced change of climate if it impaired the workers' health. Santa Bárbara La Lagunilla fretted about going to the mines in the heavy rains of July and August. Tulancingo complained that no official was appointed to protect their interests, nor was medical help provided. At least if they stayed home they had counsel, healers, and a hospital. [13]

There was force, there was brutality. Peons were beaten, even beaten to death at El Salto in the stamp mills. Indian workers from Tulancingo, who had served time there, viewed the refinery with horror, as if it were a torture chamber. Isidro Pablo said he was cruelly abused because he could not finish the tasks he did not know how to do. All knew someone who could not work when he returned home because of beatings with sticks and whips at the refinery. A Mexican Creole, who had conducted work crews to Real del Monte, said that foremen took the Indians into the gallery and made them put on iron collars. [14]

The village of Santa María Tolopam defined mistreatment in detail. There was a continual shortage of food. Indians had to work day and night without proper rest. Not knowing the work, they were given many lashes, and some were whipped until they fainted and awoke close to death. The village insisted that there was no real labor shortage at Real del Monte:

> The truth was that don Pedro needs more workers
> because he treats the ones he has so badly. [15]

Workers sickened, they were injured, they were badly treated, and they didn't make any money. The customary pay was two and a half reales a day. But forced laborers all too often went home without any money at all, and all too often worked twenty-four hours for one shift's wages because their relief crew had not arrived. It was possible to spend too much money in the company store because workers had to buy their own food, firewood, and aguardiente. Four bran rolls, which Indians did not consider nutritious because they were not tortillas, cost half a real. Every payday money was taken from their wages for a kind of funeral insurance in case they died on the job, one-half real for the Mass and one-half for the coffin. Although the Laws of the Indies and the viceroy's directives commanded that the goings and comings be reimbursed, none of these villagers ever collected portal-to-portal pay. Tulancingo said:

> Pedro Romero de Terreros does not lack workers because of a shortage of labor; he lacks workers because the pay is so bad. [16]

The victims of forced labor arrived home tired, sick, and without funds. It was as if they had been punished by hard labor, flogging, *and* a fine. "All this," the Indian villages concluded, "was veritable tyranny." [17]

Tulancingo tarried. In January 1756 the district magistrate of Tulancingo was suspended and fined five hundred pesos because no laborers had been sent to Real del Monte. In February the viceroy chided the new officials for failing to form work crews. In March twelve men were sent to the mines and eight to the refinery of El Salto. Tulancingo's officials composed the most eloquent and persuasive of all the protests. They stressed the repugnance the population of Tulancingo and its subject villages felt about the diseases and bad treatment in store for them in the enterprises of Pedro Romero de Terreros. They took a survey of men who had worked in them and were not afraid to accuse the bosses of vicious brutality, overwork, exposure which resulted in horrifying symptoms, and unfair underpayment. Philosophically, they pointed out that in a chronic shortage of labor, no one could gain. Romero de Terreros promised to pay more duties if, after labor were coerced to produce it, there were more silver. But torn away from their agricultural pursuits, the men of Tulancingo would pay fewer *alcabalas*, less tribute, and less tithes and produce less of the provisions the mines themselves needed. Maguey plants would die without their care, pulque producers would lose profits, and the government would lose revenues from pulque. Forced labor, Tulancingo pointed out, hurts the miserable Indians, hurts the village, hurts agriculture, hurts the district, hurts the royal treasury, and even ends up with a negative impact on the mines themselves. "What the royal treasury gains in an increase of mining duties, it will lose in everything else." [18]

Tulancingo affirmed the valuable activities of villagers in their everyday life. Indians took turns at tasks that served the communal welfare. Their work, on the land and with animals, was work they knew well. They were well treated and well cared for. They paid taxes and tithes to contribute to the general welfare of the kingdom, the royal treasury, and the Church. At home they lived in harmony with their families and at peace with their neighbors. They made time to exercise their Christian duties. They were, in short, free, responsible people—workers, villagers, and family men—and they were needed at home. This petition got results. On September 7, 1757, Tulancingo and its subject villages were officially exempted from the labor levy of Pedro Romero de Terreros.[19]

Actopan first complied, then rebelled. Tulancingo was reprieved, but Actopan was punished and, after a brief respite, compelled to return to work in the mines. At first, in February 1756, work crews obeyed the directive of the viceroy. But in April 1757 a gang of Actopan workers escaped and returned home to proclaim to their villages that they had been sold into slavery and condemned to a death sentence. They had had to work in deep-mine drainage projects twenty-four hours without rest because only two crews had been sent from Actopan instead of four. Soaking wet, they went off the shift only to be locked up in a dark, subterranean gallery with none of their customary food to eat, but only expensive cheese, bran rolls, and aguardiente they were forced to buy from the company store.[20]

Overworked, undernourished, and fatigued, the Indians said they came home only to sicken and die. A Mexican merchant resident of Actopan corroborated their story: "I myself have seen them come back, thin and pale to transparency. I asked them, in their language, if they were ill, and they said it would take them fifteen or twenty days to recover."[21] They also said, stubbornly, that if they had to die, they would die at home. An Actopan farmer sympathized, "Indians are really sold and compelled to undertake hard and dangerous work. Because of their country ways and ignorance, they do not know how to do it."[22] Indians said they would not refuse to work for other miners or even go to the refinery at Atotonilco El Chico, but the mines of Romero de Terreros were notorious for their mistreatment of Indians. Even recogedores from Real del Monte, sent to round up the Actopan Indians, told their host that they had heard the Indians were overworked and locked up in the mines of the Veta Vizcaína.[23]

The situation at Actopan was uniquely and incredibly complicated by the fact that an Indian governor, the district magistrate, and his wife had embezzled the funds allocated to pay the village forced laborers. At the mines, the Indians were paid, not the legal daily wage, but only enough to settle their account at the company store. Each worker was given a chit for the balance, to be redeemed when he got home. But the money did not reach the Indians. The embezzling officials applied the funds to a debt owed the royal government for tribute. The Indians said they were condemned to death because of the ladders, the water, the diseases, and the fatiguing work. But they said

they had been sold into slavery because they were not paid. The commissioner for tributes suggested that the Indians' version was correct. Once the Indian governor had given him a writ issued by Romero de Terreros. The governor said it was a loan. When the draft was cashed in Mexico City, it was
apparently applied to service the debt of tribute owed by the district of
Actopan.[24]

In 1757 there were 4,945 tribute-owing workers in Actopan and its villages. Experiencing hard times, Actopan had not paid its tributes since the
harvest of 1756. Notwithstanding, in November of 1756 their tribute was
increased, just as the first crews went to Real del Monte. Almost two
thousand of the tributaries owed back payments to their *encomendera*, Mocte-
zuma's heiress, the Duquesa de Atrisco, who had mortgaged her share in
advance to a Spanish nobleman. The Indians of the Actopan region owed
7,237 pesos to state, church, and the lady. The few free blacks and mulattoes
in the area (eighteen) owed two pesos each. When the call to Real del Monte
came, more men ran away than joined the work crews. Royal tribute accountants and the village priest calculated that eighty workers, fleeing their
obligations and abandoning their families, were fugitives.[25]

In April 1757 Pedro Romero de Terreros insisted that Actopan send him
more working men in the hour of his "gravest necessity." The villages of the
Actopan district requested Otomí interpreters to explain that it was the sea-
son of spring planting and that they could not comply until their crops were
sown. They agreed to send some men, but they could not furnish the full
173-man crew. Royal authorities did not listen. Each village was directed to
form labor gangs for Real del Monte forthwith.[26]

The problems provoked the largest rural crowds ever to protest industrial
relations in colonial Mexico. The people of the Actopan district were mobilized by members of the escaped work gang, who came home, as the authorities saw it, "to sow sedition." The first rising was in a tiny village, on Monday or Tuesday. Then on Tuesday, market day in Tetitlán, an Indian cacique
ran to the plaza to find it full of "flags and a drum and the people going to
war." Charmingly, his first reaction was to go home to dinner. Then he took
his family and hid in the church. When he came out, the crowd had
dispersed.[27]

Wednesday, April 27, 1757, was market day in Actopan. Between three
and four in the afternoon three hundred or four hundred people, angry and
excited, entered the plaza of Actopan. Townspeople said there was no recog-
nizable leader. A band of Indian women carried a red flag, and one woman
waved a dust cloth. Men carried flags, white and striped. Their target was

the church, where some of the embezzlers and the recogedores from Real del Monte were hiding. A young curate came out to calm the crowd. An Indian picked up a rock, and a townsman shot him twice. The Indian, who died with the rock in his hand, was the only fatality. None of the Actopan townspeople were killed, though a few were injured. Indian injuries occurred when they were arrested. No property damage was reported. There were no "excesses."[28]

After the gun went off, the Indians retreated and encircled the town, just out of range. Their numbers swelled to about a thousand. They beat the drum and sang hymns and danced until the moon went down. By dawn they had retired to the mountains. The deputy district magistrate organized the townspeople (Mexican Creoles and a mulatto) into a posse. Fear, the need for community defense, and a fine of twelve pesos for those who would not serve mobilized a guard that stood all night against a threat of "continual alarms." The deputy called for militias from Ixmiquilpan, Tetepango, and Pachuca. By May 1, there were 195 militiamen and twenty-five martial horses (the viceroy had sent a mounted detachment of the Palace Guard) in Actopan, all quartered by townspeople.[29]

In colonial Mexico soldiers seldom, if ever, forced peace with weapons of war. Priests made the peace. The curate of Actopan had tried and failed twice to woo the Indians into repentance: once at the church door and once outside the town, when he and his fellow-curates were sent flying back to their church. On Saturday, April 30, after three days in the open air, the Indians asked the priest for the love of God to forgive them and explain their plight to His Majesty: "We do not wish war or trouble or anything except to be in accord with the district magistrate, the governor, and the holy church, and we want no more to do with this business of the mines."[30] The priest responded by going out with his fellows and preaching to the Indians "with words of love." Afterwards, they disbanded and went home. About two thousand Indians came to church at Actopan on Monday. A curate exhorted them to peace and tranquility — and absolved them. They seemed sorry, and their way home was blessed with relief.[31]

The priest and two Indian governors begged the deputy to pardon the Indians from the forced labor levy of Pedro Romero de Terreros. The Indian magistrates said they could not keep the peace if their sons were forced to go to the mines where their lives were in mortal danger. The deputy said he had no power to pardon them because the viceroy himself had commanded it. The priest apparently used his good offices to persuade the Indians who had risen to go again to Real del Monte.[32]

The posse rounded up suspects in Actopan with a heavy hand. Of twenty-five captured, ten men and two women said they were clubbed or struck on the face or shot while being apprehended. The Indians' defense attorney chided, "The posse rounded them up for no other reason than they were Indians."[33] Most were fleeing or working or leaving the church where they had hidden. One woman was taking a drink of water from the well. All but one of the Indian suspects were eventually freed.[34]

An Indian and a mestizo were judged guilty and punished. The Otomí cordage and sweet pulque seller said he was drunk and didn't know what he was doing when someone gave him a flag. He was sentenced to fifty lashes and six months' hard labor in a factory, but because he had been held unlawfully in jail too long, he was spared the flogging. The mestizo, who turned himself in, was accused of signaling the crowd to enter Actopan. He was condemned to perpetual exile ten leagues roundabout the district.[35]

A new hard line from Mexico City doubled and tripled the penalties for failing to form work crews. If local officials failed to procure labor, they were to be fined a *thousand* pesos. If workers refused to go into the mines, they would be exiled to four years' hard labor in the Mariana Islands (for Creoles); Indians, mestizos, or mulattoes, would receive two hundred lashes or four years' hard labor in factories in New Spain. The embezzlers, too, were reprimanded. The Indian governor and the district magistrate and his wife were to pay the Indians who had worked for nothing in Real del Monte out of their own pockets. An official believed that the mines were draining the district of much-needed labor, and that more workers had gone than Actopan could afford. He concluded wearily, "there is no Indian left here who is capable of going to the mines who has not already gone."[36] Royal authorities could reform and threaten, but they never questioned the principle that entrepreneurs had the right to impose their will on villages—or that villages had a sacred duty to obey crown, church, and capitalists.

Royal authority in the Spanish heritage was wont to temper punishment with understanding at the highest level of government. Even in the case of forced labor, it sought a proportion between the necessities of large enterprises and the needs of small villages. Even in cases of rebellion, Indians were to be pacified and attracted back to the straight and narrow of the Pax Hispanica with suavity and promises of peace and privilege. According to the Laws of the Indies, Indians could, of course, be compelled to labor against their will. But while they were doing what they did not want to do, their welfare could never be ignored. Mexico City insisted that forced laborers deserved good food and equitable pay, the comforts of the church, the support of an advocate inspector to look out for their interests, the solace of healers and a hospital, and sick pay from their employer if they were injured on the job or had an accident.[37]

The opinion of Domingo Trespalacios y Escandón, issued from Actopan in May 1757, reflected the authorities' struggle to achieve a sense of checks and balances. Indians, he stressed, must be dealt with charitably, in a Christian manner. They must be protected in their work and succored in their distress, with a spirit of protectiveness, helping, and warmth. They must be looked on favorably as faithful vassals of His Majesty while they were learning and becoming accustomed each day to their new duties. They might not work overtime. They might not be locked in, anywhere, any time. Rather, they must be lodged in accord with their full and natural liberty, as free people who came and went voluntarily to the mines. They might not, under any circumstances, be forced to work in the unhealthful and fatiguing conditions found in drainage projects. In mines or in refineries they might be used only as manual laborers. If anyone mistreated them, the man who gave the orders would be fined two thousand pesos, and the one who administered the abuse would receive two hundred lashes. If mistreatment were charged a second time, the owner would lose his enterprise and be exiled from the Indies. Workers must be paid on Saturday afternoons, *en tabla y mano propia*, from the pay table into their own hands. Owners had an obligation to pay for care for the sick. Laborers must be given corn to eat and paid portal to portal. Mexico City's rule was that Indians in transit should travel no more than six leagues a day. Indians deserved their full pay, and no one could garnishee their wages for any reason. And finally, if Indians needed to tend their own crops, they might send substitutes to take their shifts in the mines.[38]

The viceroy congratulated Trespalacios on his dealings with rebellious Actopan: those who "led" the resistance to the labor draft were punished, and the followers were pardoned but threatened with the full power of the law if they rebelled again. He seemed to have concluded that previous decrees in defense of Indian laborers were not enough. On July 9, 1757, he issued a new decree, and the language was blunt. Forced laborers were not, under any circumstances, to be mistreated. If they were, he who abused them would be fined a thousand pesos, and he who ordered it or permitted his employees to abuse them would be fined two thousand pesos. Every complaint from the villages except the labor draft itself was touched upon. Good treatment was imperative. Indians were to do no hard or excessive or dangerous tasks, nothing that would sap their strength or endanger their health or induce them to take great risks. They were not to be irritated or enraged.

Their goings and comings had to be paid, their wages had to be paid directly to them. Employers were forbidden to withhold any portion of their wages for any reason. The viceroy, the highest authority in the land, proved himself, at least in general, sympathetic to working men and their grievances and implacably opposed to lawbreakers, be they labor or management.[39]

It would be interesting to know how many villagers ended up working in Real del Monte in the forced labor levy and to what races and ethnic groups they and other workers belonged. To their great consternation, royal authorities found out that they did not know, either. No mine or refinery had the faintest idea what sort of men it employed. Employers counted heads and they counted reales on the pay tables, but they knew nothing about their workers as individuals. No one kept records, not the mines, not the refineries, not the royal treasury offices, not the Indian governors. Hoping to rectify what must have seemed like a great sin of omission to the paper pushers, Trespalacios directed in May 1757 that records be kept by the enterprise, recording payroll and daybooks, and reporting the information to the district office of record. The Veta Vizcaína sent a list, but it ignored ethnicity. It bunched the villagers: there were eleven manual laborers from Actopan and forty-one peons from Actopan, Cempoala, and Pachuca. Three forced laborers were working the drainage projects, but they forgot to say from where. It is, then, impossible to describe the miners of Real del Monte, either forced or free, in terms of any birthright categories except sex and, sometimes, the name of their village.[40]

On October 22, 1764, Pedro Romero de Terreros cracked the whip again. In all the past, he complained, he had not received even *one-twentieth* of the labor he required and deserved. He had hired more recogedores, to no avail. Since the opening of the adit, he had undertaken many new, costly, difficult, and onerous works, like canals to dump the groundwaters into the adit and the new tunnel to connect the Dolores Mine to the San Cayetano. There had been a payoff—the growing quantity of ores to refine—but there weren't enough workers to produce the silver. The people, he said, had a natural resistance to work because they were inclined to laziness, especially if they were Indians, or to joblessness and vice if they were Blacks. So he begged royal officials not to accept the "frivolous pretexts" of villages but to force men to work the mines as if they had been drafted into the royal service. He himself had worked hard, spending two and a half million pesos to rehabilitate his mines, but his hard work was for naught if there were not enough workers to produce and make profits.[41] In October the royal officials of Pachuca asked the viceroy for action. They explained that the walls of

Romero de Terreros's principal refinery, El Salto, had been broken down by torrential flooding in 1762. They predicted that, if there were more labor, the output of the mines would be a bonanza, and the refineries would produce 200,000 *marcos* of silver a year. They warned the viceroy that cunning villagers never lacked for an excuse to evade their duty. And so the call went out again, to Actopan, Tulancingo, Cempoala, Tetepango, Mesitlán de la Sierra, San Juan Teotihuacán, and San Mateo Texcoco.[42]

In February 1765, Mexico City issued the predictable enabling order to speed up the formation of work crews. There was punishment for anyone who would not go, punishment for anyone who tried to impede anyone else from going. But there were strong protection clauses this time. Indians were enjoined to denounce any bad treatment to the viceroy himself, and village authorities were counseled to question Indians to see if the rules had been infringed. *"The need for labor,"* directed the *fiscal, "is matched by the need of labor for good treatment."*[43]

Tizayuca and Pachuquilla were exempted because they had been relieved of tribute until the villages recovered from an epidemic. Suits were filed against Tluipustla, Cempoala, and Tulancingo, villages which had not complied.[44]

In April 1765 Pedro Romero de Terreros was apparently provoked enough to write a defense of his labor practices. He stressed the evil consequences of the lack of labor that caused vast quantities of ore not to be refined. He believed that at least five hundred more pikemen and peons were needed for the operations of the Veta Vizcaína. He had hired four recogedores, but they had only captured forty pikemen. Obviously smarting from the criticisms of Indians, he insisted that he treated his workers well. The trouble was that the villagers, naturally lazy, were influenced by hacendados who did not want them to leave their fields, by district magistrates who did not want to lose tributes, and by parish priests who invented ways of backing them up. It was not true that restraints had been used on Indians; no chains, fetters, or iron collars had ever been used in any of his enterprises. It was not true that the work was unhealthy. Men came from all over to work at the refineries of El Salto, San Miguel, and San Antonio without any harm to their health. Great quantities of mercury were never used. Treading powdered ore and mercury was such an easy task that anyone could learn it at a glance. Even the most ignorant peon could master it the first time he tried. The owner did not punish mistakes. In refineries the shifts and pay were equal for all, forced or free. But work in the refinery could be completed in four hours, and workers had long intervals to rest, chat, or even sleep. Rest was never a problem. Indians from Tulancingo were given a chance to rest after their journey and were lodged in a comfortable workshop. As for the company store, it was stocked with foodstuffs sold at current prices for the workers' convenience; those who did not like it could shop elsewhere.[45]

When conditions do not change, the song remains the same. The same villages continued to protest against Romero de Terreros in the same ways well into the next century.[46]

On the eve of the strike by free men at Real del Monte in 1766, there abides the fact of a critical and continual shortage of labor in the mines. Painful as a raw nerve throbbed the old horror of depopulation, and it recurs. If labor were not compelled to work, the entrepreneur would quit, and the mining camps would be *depopulated*. If villagers were forced to labor in the mines and chose instead to run away, villages would be *depopulated*. When the strikers of 1766 threatened management, they swore they would walk out and leave the mines *depopulated*.

Finally, there was such overwhelming evidence in so many of the villagers' briefs that a viceroy could come to wonder if Pedro Romero de Terreros might indeed need watching because his labor practices were "irregular."

In Real del Monte itself were other groups of working men who, like the Indian villagers, were compelled to work against their will for Romero de Terreros. Miners and workers hated the stalwarts who acted out the overt brutality of management's coercion. Recogedores, on the boss's orders, rounded up "lazy," "unoccupied" workers for manual labor in the mines. On horseback, armed with whips, riding crops, lassos, and machetes, the recogedores searched out the haunts of miners for working men who were not on the job. Like press gangs they terrorized the cemetery, the taverns, the pulquerías where men stopped to listen to music, eat tamales, and drink a medio. They scoured the streets of the town, the trails of the hills, and the paths of the barrancas where families lived in huts they had made themselves. Breaking and entering was a specialty. Beatings were standard operating procedure. They bragged that a team of recogedores, on the best day of their lives, might bring in a hundred laborers. Recogedores, in spite of their monopoly of force, were sometimes resisted because they were so brutal and because their victims were assigned to the dry diggings, without hope of profit sharing.[47]

Miners dreaded the specter of sitting down to a drink after a full twelve-hour shift only to be roughed up and lined up for the next one. They lacked a way to prove they had worked all day or all night. Typically, they tried to fight their way out or run away. Often a skirmish resulted, and the encounters sooner or later attracted the attention of bystanders who became participants. Women did not hesitate to enter the fray to protect their men. Hatred of recogedores spread from working men to their families and friends. An encounter could provoke a commotion, and in such a confrontation, some were wounded, some went to jail, some went to work, and some escaped.

Mariano Flores was in the tavern one afternoon about two. The recogedores burst in, he tried to hide in a trunk, but he did not fit. They spied him, he resisted, and they captured him. On the road to the mine his brother found them. Together, they began to stone the recogedores, then ran for home. Neighbors covered their escape with stones. The brother broke the reins of a recogedor's horse, leaving him "defenseless." Mariano ran inside the house and hid. The women of the house, his wife, his mother, and his sister, blocked the door and pleaded with the recogedor to leave him alone. "Shut up, you great bitch," the recogedor yelled at the sixty-year-old mother and, to defend himself, laid about with his machete until he had cut off her finger. He flogged the wife and sister until they were sore. The brother, appalled, came out with a saber and, defending the women, wounded the recogedor. The recogedores said they were both wounded, the work crew they had rounded up had run off, and their horses had been driven away. All this time the crowd gathered and yelled, "Finish off these *carajos.*" It took, the recogedores modestly told the authorities, a "superhuman effort" to apprehend the fugitives and drag the whole resisting family off to jail by their hair.[48]

These recogedores were brothers, from a family that had done the same work for generations. They said they were sick of the miners' "natural insolence." The men they had rounded up were demons, the most perverse, blustering, arrogant, provocative troublemakers in the Real. They reminded authorities that many recogedores had been wounded, even murdered, in Real del Monte by miners who were insolent, lazy, rebellious, and full of vice. They were supposed to use force, their work was dangerous, and so they did use force.

To the miners and their families, the recogedores were cruel, tyrannical, despotic, barbarous, and inhumane. All pleaded self-defense. There was, they said without enough exaggeration, much bad feeling in Real del Monte against the recogedores.

The community was even more appalled when recogedores rounded up innocent bystanders. They would not listen when men told them they had other jobs. They simply made fun of them, grabbed them by the hair, lashed them with a quirt, even ran them down with their horses. In this manner they assaulted a postal guard, a shoemaker, a smelter. When they found men talking in the cemetery, they beat their heads against the wall. They even jumped the mayor of Acayuca, who had complained to Mexico City about their mistreatment of village Indians, and abused him and beat him up. They captured a "truant" royal bureaucrat on his way to breakfast at the treasury office, boys on their way out of Sunday school, and traveling salesmen on their way home from Mass. They even trapped messengers and house servants. Once they seized an Indian employee of the royal saltpeter works, beat him when he tried to identify himself, and forced him down a mine when he had never seen one before. The provisioning of Real del Monte with meat, vegetables, charcoal, and firewood slacked off because sellers feared capture. A poor Indian peddlar was forced to leave his burro with its load of eggs unattended all day while he labored down the mine. Townspeople agreed with miners: recogedores could be insolent, degrading, and brutal.

But legal. The presence of recogedores was sanctified "constitutional" to the welfare of the mining industry by a specific clause in the mining ordinances. If there were no partidos, the hard fact was that no workers would volunteer. And so, when there was no silver ore to act as incentive, only recogedores and force could supply manual labor to the dry diggings.[49] Public sentiment, then, tended to run directly against the letter and intent of the law. In fact, the presence of recogedores in Real del Monte was an ever-renewable incitement to riot, a past and future bond of resistance between miners, their families, and their friends. The clashes between man and press gang would always produce sparks. The tinder depended on how many onlookers there were. Most days there were few, and the clash took place outside. In the strike summer of 1766 there were three recogedores, thousands of furious people outside, and a few authorities trapped inside the galleries, with no way out.

!¡

CHAPTER 5

The Strike

From June to October, 1766, workers in Real del Monte reacted to injustice and taught themselves how to discipline the growing momentum of discontent into discussions, demonstrations, petitions, and an organized strike. There were two official statements of grievances by workers. A work stoppage involved enough miners to shut the industry down. There was violence, extraneous to the strike but a crucial stimulus for arbitration. The most esteemed Mexican authority on the theory and practice of mining in New Spain, Francisco de Gamboa, came from Mexico City to decide the dispute. Assemblies of workers and the spokesmen they selected participated directly in the negotiations. It was, in short, a major industrial strike, and it was recognized by the highest authorities.

The incidents that provoked the miners of Real del Monte to strike began as modernizing efforts to cut costs and increase profits after the enormous expenditures made to drain the waters and rehibilitate the mines of the Veta Vizcaína. Pedro Romero de Terreros, the boss, was a Spanish immigrant who became one of the wealthiest men in New Spain. Taking advantage of his interests in his uncle's Querétaro business, he converted the profits into a merchant fortune. Seeking ways to invest his money, he came upon a Mexican miner, José Alejandro de Bustamante, and his grand scheme to rescue the mines of the Veta Vizcaína from the floods of groundwater by digging deep adits to drain them. Bustamante's great venture, the double-bore adit of Azoyatla, was begun in 1739 and finally petered out at a loss of 100,000 pesos. Bustamante died of gangrene after a fall from his horse in 1750, leaving Pedro Romero de Terreros his claim, his strategy, and his dreams. In 1755 Romero de Terreros commissioned a new adit, Nuestra Señora de Aranzazú, which was successfully completed in the summer of 1759. (See

Table 1, p. 143.) In the official inspection of 1762, a team of experts walked the adits and praised the new paths and the costly, good supporting structures. They dwelt on the thick oak beams and the transformation of San Cayetano from a flooded disaster into a safe, exemplary mine. A sympathetic bureaucrat in Mexico City estimated the total expense at five million pesos. The official inventory of 1762 lists Pedro Romero de Terreros's costs at 1,410,502 pesos for the adits, the refineries, and the mines.[1] (See Appendix 3.)

It was not that Romero de Terreros had no return at all on his investments. From 1738 to 1762, mostly before the completion of the drainage system, seven million pesos were taken out of the Veta Vizcaína; and from 1762 to 1781 (the date of his death), twelve and a half million. His mines accounted for more than half of all the silver produced in the Real del Monte–Pachuca area.[2] (See Table 3, p. 149.) He had, then, made a profit. It was, rather, that having invested money and sweat and care, he wanted to exploit the new opportunities fully. After years of coping with dirt and water, he wanted silver.

Pedro Romero de Terreros was more than a speculator and consolidator of capital. He was obsessed with his commitment to economic development. Once great shafts had been deepened, waters controlled, and many new veins of ore exposed, he expected his reward. He insisted that his free workers take pay cuts to minimize costs and, along with plentiful forced labor provided by the crown, that they work harder, more efficiently, more honestly to produce greater quantities of rich ore.

Presented with physical obstacles, he was patient and indefatigable. Underpinning his strengths and weaknesses was a persevering piety, at times arrogant and insensitive, at times devout and sincere. In the summer of 1766 tragedy delved deep into his character to transform his empathy for people. His lovely, clinging noble wife, frantic with terror of childbirth from the beginning, succumbed to her eighth pregnancy in ten years and died giving birth. Romero de Terreros determined grimly to raise his newborn son and the other six surviving children by himself at his hacienda refinery of San Miguel Regla.[3]

He had paid his dues, in business and in grief. And in sweat and personal risk. He was no absentee profiteer. José Antonio de Bustamante once said that mine owners who made their own inspections in the pits were "as rare as the phoenix."[4] Romero de Terreros was that kind of rare entrepreneur. He had congratulated himself on his public-spirited effort to create jobs in Real del Monte so that decent wages could bring the poor out of their misery. He believed he deserved rewards for all he had done, for all he had suffered. Presented with human obstacles, he was increasingly impatient and self-righteous. But he did not become tyrannical and vengeful until his workers tried to kill him.

Some of the changes in the work fell upon the laborers swiftly, like a knife in the dark. Peons, paid four reales a shift since the time of Bustamante, were cut to the slave's wages of three in June 1765. This sudden pay cut was the first overt cutback in production costs.[5]

Other changes had come more slowly, apparently even covertly introduced as isolated experiments. Two large groups of miners complained officially that the size of the quota sack had been doubled. Peons complained, but pikemen were bitter. They swore that the increased size of the sacks had made the quota so large that they could not meet it in one twelve-hour shift. Joseph Zavala and Juan Antonio Velazco said that it had taken them five, six shifts to gather ore into the too-large bags. The mine administrator (Marcelo González) and the timekeeper (Francisco Lira) proved that they were as hateful as the miners had thought by saying that there had been no change, that the sacks were the same as before, and that "if they worked more than twelve hours, it was to fill the partido." The workers, surprised, agreed: *Of course no one ever turns in the quota without the partido.* The confrontation merits emphasis. It explains why workers said they were not issued enough candles and blasting powder. They meant, not enough to complete what they considered to be a day's work: quota *and* partido. It explains the opposite view: suddenly hoping the partido was not necessary, management would naturally think, when workers insisted it was, that they were lying.[6]

As if doubling the work load weren't enough, workers complained that the partido was being unfairly manipulated by the scale man on payday. "Little by little," they said in their August 1 petition, "Don Pedro Romero has been changing the custom." Expressing an anguish, not a chronicle, they did not relate an exact sequence of events, but apparently the changes in partido had been tolerated for six months to a year. The miners singled out timekeeper Francisco Lira of Santa Teresa, scale man Cayetano Celis of La Joya, and José Serrano Velasco of San Cayetano as troublemakers who mistreated miners with sticks and harsh words as they cheated them.[7]

The miner dreamed of what the August 1 grievance defined as the "deep-rooted, firmly established custom" of dividing the partido "one rock for the boss, another for himself." He asked for an experienced man, the captain-taskmaster, to set the quota, judging it by lode difficulty, water level, and ore quality. This detail was never officially investigated, but it was stated again later in complaints against inept and inexperienced captains who could not find quality ore. More than anything, the miner asked for a predictable, profitable payday, without haggling.

The payday partido might amount to three or four reales on a bad day, and three or four pesos on a good day. But "little by little," management had begun to change everything, and the changes hurt. It is important to consider how deeply devoted the workers were to their traditional partido wage: they considered it "the only protection a pikeman has in a mine." They were committed to the proposition that it was the "only thing that permits miners to live in decency."[8]

The first change came, the miners said, when management sought to solve the problem of unequal ores. Both miners and management agreed that the partido sacks contained higher quality ore than did the quota bags. The miners justified the inequality by reminding authorities that the boss took half anyway, the custom being that the partido of pikemen and peons was shared by miner and boss fifty-fifty. Management, however, always interpreted it as stealing. And so, the first innovation: when inequality was proclaimed in the gallery, one-half of each partido was exchanged for one-half of the quota, and the mixed result was then divided. Miners did not like the change, but they suffered it when it was done fairly. Then the mixing was stopped, and a new quota of three bags to one bag of partidos was imposed. Again, the miners acquiesced. Then, in July 1766, a new quota of four to one was levied, and the partido sack was rented to the miners, not loaned. At the same time mixing was reimposed. This time the miners protested, saying the technique was unfair. Dispatchers poured the quota out, then poured the partido on top of it. The worker, forced to leave the gallery, was "in the dark" when the mixing was done. When he returned, he swore in a long growl that the best ore had been taken away for the boss.[9]

Another grievance reveals economic bonds that linked pikemen and peons with workers above and with the community of the town. Before the division was made in the gallery, ore from every quota sack and every partido sack was set aside for the convents of San Francisco and San Juan de Dios, Pachuca. This was charity plus a vague sort of burial and hospital provision. After the miner received his share of the partido, he meted out a shovelful (four pounds) for his designated healers (doctor, surgeon, druggist); a capful for the dispatcher and whim operator for hoisting out the ore and carrying it to the gallery; and a fistful (one pound) for the smith.[10]

The miners, disapproving, said the compulsory custom was being abused and demanded that it revert to being voluntary. "Every day," they charged in their August 1 grievance, "we are paying the company. In a word, we are contributing to a fund that enables don Pedro Romero to finance the equipment his mines require." At Santa Teresa the smith confessed that it was true, the miners were paying him. He had received no wage for eight years. He lived solely from what the miners gave him, a portion which he had to divide equally with the boss. Two peons complained that the smith did not sharpen their tools but preferred to punch them. All said he was wont to grab a double share.[11]

Workers added up the charges and the abuses, and how did they feel? The July 28 petition answers directly: "We have found ourselves wiped out, consumed, beaten . . . weary and vexed because we cannot stand so much tyranny."

And what did these Mexican workers do when confronted with such tyranny? They talked and vented their anger. They organized their strike. They sought justice from the law. They might have been, were, a little rowdy about their petitioning, but their network, which had been elaborated from work and their efforts to adapt, continued to seek justice by specifically nonviolent, legal redress from the constituted authorities.

Workers began organizing in June or July of 1766. The conspirators were a barra of pikemen who met so secretly at Nicolás de Zavala's house that almost no one knew what they were doing until the first workers started to walk out.[12] But Nicolás de Zavala, Domingo González, and José and Vicente Oviedo have more to their credit than a work stoppage. They began to articulate the miners' complaints in a serious way, and they made sure those grievances would be heard.

One old man, Real del Monte's deputy district magistrate, had worked in the mines for thirty years. Antonio Valdemoros Pintos studied the problem and concluded that workers might end the strike and be enticed back to work with a two-to-one ratio of quota to partido. He huddled with the administrator and asked a senior treasury official to draw up a proclamation. It promised miners a work week divided half for quota and half for partidos. Partidos and pay were guaranteed according to custom. Recogedores were instructed to force men to work in the mines. Conservative as it was, the proclamation was torn up by the administrator at the last minute because he feared it would incite, not pacify, the workers. Royal authorities had seized the initiative, had unilaterally found a way to change the practices that so disturbed the miners. But management let it go.[13]

The organizers intensified their efforts. Apparently the priest of Real del Monte, Dr. José Rodríguez Díaz, encouraged them to present a written petition of grievances to the royal authorities. Perhaps he even gave the miners a peso to buy a fold of stamped paper and have a bite to eat when they went to Pachuca to present it. [14] Nicolás de Zavala went alone to the house of a lowly treasury scribe. Antonio Núñez de Lovera was terrified. He refused to write anything down because he said the royal officials would never take a petition from working men seriously. Zavala left and returned. The scribe refused again. He said a better tactic would be to go to Mexico City, where there were lawyers and a chance to present the writ to the viceroy himself. Zavala went away and came back again. This time he said that the senior treasurer in Pachuca had assured him that they would get justice because he himself was still upset that administrator González had not allowed the publication of the decree guaranteeing a two-to-one partido. (The treasurer later denied that he had ever talked to Zavala.) Lovera was persuaded. He wrote a draft of the July 28 grievance. [15]

Nicolás de Zavala and Juan Diego de León circulated the petition and got seventy signatures and affirmations for it. Zavala, León, Diego Xarillo, Miguel Sánchez, Tomás Juárez, and seventeen other workers took the writ to Pachuca, but royal authorities said it was not in order. They went to the house of a schoolmaster and signed it properly. Then, without incident, they presented it to the royal treasury officials in Pachuca. [16]

In the July 28 grievance fifteen pikemen signed and fifty-one affirmed the first statement of complaints "in their own voices." It was a defense of the partido and a complaint against management for their sudden, unfair manipulations of mixing, tools, and divisions. The workers accused administrator Marcelo González and timekeeper Francisco Lira of treating them badly. A priest later testified that it was common knowledge that the administrator, timekeeper Lira, and Cayetano Celis of La Joya and José Serrano Velasco of San Cayetano had been provoking trouble and causing discontent among miners for a year. The July 28 grievance shows that the workers were sick of it: "today all is done to profit the boss and make the workers perish." Nicolás de Zavala signed first. [17]

When the workers returned to Real del Monte, Administrator Marcelo González set the recogedores on them. Juan Diego de León, Diego Xarillo, Miguel Sánchez, and Tomás Juárez were caught and forced to work all night in the dry diggings of La Joya. After the shift, timekeeper Marcos Jaramillo detained León, accusing him of being one of a group of shameless rascals bent on putting the Veta Vizcaína in a bad light. Since he had not eaten for hours, León asked the dispatcher for something. "I asked for bread, but he gave me blows." Someone advised him to run away to Guanajuato, but after being detained in the gallery all day, León ran away to hide in Atotonilco el Grande.[18]

On July 29 about noon, some 250 workers entered the treasury office in Pachuca with, the royal notary wrote disapprovingly, "the greatest scandal and brazen licentiousness," to demand the results of their petition. Outside, the streets were full of men, women, and children, cramped together in the narrow lane in front of the fortress-like treasury, seated in the adjacent churchyard, in the plaza, around the fountain, in the cemetery. The royal officials said they spoke to the miners "sweetly, softly, and convincingly," promising that they would investigate their claims the next day, urging them to return to work while the treasury employees finished their top priority mission, preparing a shipment of silver for the mint. Since that was not labor's priority, most of the crowd did not disperse, and the next day they accompanied the authorities up the steep mountain road, past the yellow and white flowers growing on the slopes, to Real del Monte.[19]

The work stoppage that the crowd had acted out in front of the royal officials in Pachuca was confirmed by mine foremen in Real del Monte. On July 30 timekeeper Lira of Santa Teresa checked in only ten barras, and five the night before. There were no work crews at all in San Cayetano and Dolores. Only La Joya had sixteen barras at work. Old deputy Antonio Pintos lectured the workers on equalizing the value of quota and partido. At Santa Teresa the royal officials observed a division. They emptied nine quota sacks on the floor and on them dumped the pikeman's two and a half sacks. They were mixed "to everyone's satisfaction." Then sacks were filled and weighed again. The pikeman received his two and a half sacks and spread out the ore for the division. Timekeeper Francisco Lira maintained that was how it was always done. The workers denied it. When the royal officials asked how the miners were treated, Lira said, "Not all are alike. Some are good, some are impudent and pernicious. It is the audacity that must be controlled."[20] Administrator Marcelo González promised to end mixing, but the miners would not accept the quota he set. And in the mines, arbitration, if it had begun at all, broke down in two hours.[21]

On Thursday, August 1, Domingo González and Pedro José Pintos led a crowd of three hundred back to Pachuca to demand, since thay had not received justice, that their petition be returned so that it could be submitted to a higher tribunal. Afraid that the working men would commit "the most appalling incidents" in their arrogant disorderliness, the royal officials promised to comply.

But González and Pintos made a bold decision. They would send their case to the viceroy himself, and this time they would engage a lawyer to write their petition. With José Vicente de Villanueva, José Manuel, José Hesabino, and José Antón Osorio, they hired a lawyer to draw up a second grievance in the name of twelve hundred workers. The lawyer, Manuel Cordero, was sympathetic and eloquent, and the August 1 petition is one of the great documents in Mexican labor history.[22]

Its predecessor, the original July 28 grievance, is a special interest, pikeman's complaint. Like it, the August 1 grievance tells the beads of quotas, tools, oresacks, and mixing in the dark. However, the August 1 workers felt "more afflicted and oppressed." Uniquely, adamantly, they stood behind the four-real daily wage for peons or manual laborers. They defined violence forthrightly as the arbitrary acts committed by management to victimize labor. They threatened, not with a strike, but with the desertion of the mines by workers if their just complaints were not redressed. The August 1 grievance is a class grievance, loud for labor, broader in philosophical scope. It expressed resentment against the "scabs," the Black slaves, the workers brought in from Guanajuato. It blamed the boss, not the foremen, for the troubles and called his actions "tyranny." Claiming the justice of God as their touchstone, labor demanded a fair share of the profits:

> If mines are profitable, God intends all who participate to benefit. . . . We workers who are the instruments have come to benefit the least, for drained in so many ways of what is rightfully ours, we profit nothing.

This injury, sir, is the injury of an entire people, more than 1200 men.[23]

The organizing barra—Domingo González, Juan Barrón, and the brothers Oviedo, José and Vicente—went to Mexico City and presented the August 1 grievance to the viceroy himself. They got results. Though the viceroy directed them to go back to work, he sent instructions to the royal officials to pay them with the two-to-one partido. Mixing, an old custom at Real del Monte, would continue whenever quota and partido ores were unequal. Royal officials and the district magistrate proclaimed the viceroy's will to management and labor on August 6, 1766, in the gallery of Santa Teresa. Workers were directed to go back to work. But the envoys felt betrayed. Juan Barrón shouted discourteous and skeptical questions about the two pages he claimed the royal officials had suppressed. Apparently one of the items not read was the viceroy's promise to investigate the specific grievances of the miners. It was taken as unseemly when Barrón shouted, "You'll be responsible for what happens if you don't do what we ask!"[24]

On August 8 authorities seized the envoys and arrested them. They proclaimed that González, Barrón, and the Oviedos would be held until the strike was over, until four full shifts had been completed. Workers believed that their spokesmen and messengers had been taken hostage in an act of terror. A protest group went peacefully to the district magistrate, Miguel Ramón de Coca. He said the hostages would be released, and took off their chains but kept them prisoner. The workers pleaded with him to release them, for they had committed no crime. "Release them, for the sake of the king's crown." He answered, "not even for the crown of the Virgin." The phrase would return to haunt him. He fought them off from horseback and left the people upset, moving up and down the mountain, angry.[25]

What *was* the crime of the hostages? Romero de Terreros knew. He was in Mexico City, tending to his children and the estate of his wife, grieving, held there by torrential rains. In a letter dated August 1, he begged the royal officials to imprison the men who had not only failed to return to work but who had actively prevented others from doing so. He maintained that the workers' depositions were "all malice." He assured the royal officials he would ask the viceroy to put pressure on the men to go back to work.[26] The four miners, then, appear to have been arrested for fomenting a conspiracy to strike and inciting to "riot," their crimes complicated by carrying the petition to Mexico City and raising their voices to the royal officials.[27]

A desire for peace held the workers strong through the following days of aggravation. Pedro Romero de Terreros, feeling ill, returned to Pachuca on August 9. He rode up the mountain in the rain to the mines, arriving at eight in the morning of August 13 to find no workers at either San Cayetano or Santa Teresa. He felt aggrieved: "I have never sought to be unjust to any of the workers . . . the payroll is never less than three thousand pesos a week."[28] He was uncomfortable and felt sorry for himself, and not every man would face an angry crowd of workers with just a token bodyguard, but he had his duty. On Thursday, August 14, he grimly set forth to try a second arbitration attempt.

Outside, some two thousand workers selected eleven of their most intelligent and experienced pikemen to speak for them. Inside, Pedro Romero de Terreros held court in the galleries of the Dolores, San Cayetano, and Santa Teresa. His efforts changed dangerous mutterings to cheers—for a moment.[29]

Romero de Terreros did a lot of breast beating. Have *I* failed? Do you not always receive your wages? Haven't I allowed the partido even though the law does not require it? "Have I not provided for you, tolerated and with-

stood all your mischief, . . . robbing tools, candles, powders, ores? Have I
not pardoned thieves and freed them because their wives were pregnant or
laden down with children?"[30]

The workers tapped their feet while he proved that sacks of quota held
baser metal than the partido sacks, a fact which no miner ever disputed. He
told them he was not to blame for the mixing rule. *They* were, when they
chose the best for partidos and then instead of giving their best to the quota,
fooled around "in idleness, grumbling, suspicion, and other illicit talk
which . . . I have heard personally, with my own ears."[31]

Diego Xarillo and Miguel Santos, both seasoned pikemen, trusted by
their companions and still smarting from their encounter with the recogedores and their forced shift of labor, patiently detailed the difficulty of
equalizing task and partido ores. Inexperienced captain-taskmasters were always at fault when inferior ores were brought up. This had in fact happened
recently at Santa Teresa. But all conceded that it was true: the miner tried
harder when he filled the partido.

The most fascinating exchange "in their own voices" took place in the
Santa Teresa between the boss and veteran pikeman Miguel Santos.[32] Santos
said that about wages there was no complaint (a clue that no peons or manual
laborers were present); of the robbery of tools, candles, and powder, they
knew nothing. He and his companions had not stolen any ores and were not
guilty, "but if you think we were, why have you not punished us?"

Romero de Terreros retorted, "I could have had you punished with the
stocks and twenty-five lashes, but I did not do so because I am a Christian."

He mocked their desire for an experienced captain. Then he waved about a
cloth-wrapped parcel, which turned out to be his mining claims. "Who is
the owner of the Veta Vizcaína?" he demanded.

Miguel Santos got that one right, "Señor don Pedro Romero de Terreros."

"I thought you had forgotten. Now, what division do you want?"

Santos did not hesitate. "Four bags of quota and two of partido, as the
Viceroy directed."

"You're lying."

Santos replied, "I lied about nothing."

Romero de Terreros explained that the convents' alms, not his share or the
workers', were meted out in the first division.

Santos looked at the richest man he had ever laid eyes on and was puzzled.
"What are a few alms to you?"

This reply made his employer angry. "What hurts me is to offend God,
not to give what is owing to God."

They observed a division of ores. Romero de Terreros took time out to explain that if they did not want to pay the smith, they could take their own water below in canteens or skins, he wasn't forcing them. He rambled on about the order of work. If one day they had to work the dry diggings, the next shift they should be assigned a rich face, on his word; though, he confessed, he was aware that such a division of labor did not, in reality, exist because the timekeeper was more concerned in placing his friends and compadres in the most lucrative tasks.

Santos said, "You speak the creed. But what about the partidos?"

Romero de Terreros was angry, again. He turned to a Santa Teresa pikeman, Juan José Orizaba, who also signed the July 28 grievance. "You talk, he's getting hot in the head."

The pikeman repeated, "Sir, my comrades want the partido in the form he explained."

Terreros gave in. "To demonstrate to you that I care about you more than you care about me, and because I hope that in the hour of my death God will pardon me as I pardon you, tell me, will you do your duty?" No more robberies, a full twelve-hour day, quota ores equal to partido ores?

All shouted, "Sí!"

Romero de Terreros had resolved it himself. He was carried away. "Take out for partido as much as you want, not just the two sacks but half the mine, and I will divide it with you without qualm!"

The men thanked him repeatedly for his magnanimity. They began to leave, "with God." The hot-headed boss had been brave, resolute, generous. The strike would have ended there, Real del Monte's greatest capitalist having proved himself a splendid arbiter. For the majority of workers, the strike was over. The next day's shift was full. However, a few pikemen leaders had lingered and were present when the peons came into the gallery, claiming their four-real daily wage. But this Terreros refused to discuss. And so the remaining pikemen proclaimed solidarity with the peons. "There was accord," they said, "but not with the peons, and now none of us will go below."[33] For these men the strike continued, with deeper bonds of anger among men who could not afford to lay off but who refused to work because of a principle of solidarity they had defined by themselves, for themselves.

What changed rational, patient, rowdy nonviolence into murderous rage? On Friday, August 15, 1766, the workers of Real del Monte viciously stoned to death district magistrate Miguel Ramón de Coca and the foreman of La Joya, Manuel Barbosa. Such an act might not have surprised the timorous royal officials, but there is nothing in the chronicle that would predict such violence.

This is perhaps because one factor of the work force has been neglected for a while—the recogedores, with their force and brutality sanctified by law and custom. Miguel Santos, from experience, had told Pedro Romero de Te-rreros that the problem of recogedores was second only to partidos in Real del Monte. The boss had answered characteristically: "The recogedores are not servants of the owner, though he pays them a wage, but rather are meters out of justice, allowed and held necessary by the laws."[34] Recogedores were management's legalized solution for the chronic lack of labor in the mine—force. Miguel Santos had posed the working man's compelling horror: what happens if just having left a full day's work in one mine, the recogedors round him up to work another twelve-hour shift in another mine? Romero de Terreros counselled—reasoning with them. The notary wrote down that self-satisfied little phrase, "all were convinced," but he was quite, quite wrong.[35]

August 15 is special even today, for it celebrates the taking up bodily of the Virgin Mary into heaven and gives the name La Asunción to parish churches in Real del Monte and Pachuca. In 1766 it was a day of what peon Juan González called "the awkward resistance of the workers."[36]

The morning began with payday. The Dolores divided without incident, but at the San Cayetano, La Joya, and Santa Teresa there was trouble. No one had to mix except well-known strike leaders. When it was the turn of Juan Diego de León, Juan Luna, Nicolás Luna, and Paulino Bustos, timekeeper Lira, who liked his miners to come to the table humbly, hat in hand, told the known dissenters that their partidos had to be mixed with the quota. The workers protested because no one else had had to do it. Angrily, they refused mixing and walked out. They sought out Pedro Romero de Terreros at La Palma, but he brushed them off: "He who wants to carry out the whole mine whould be content with what they give him, and he who doesn't like it should go home."[37] Juan Diego de León clutched his head in despair, and Terreros called guards to detain him. He escaped, cursing, and hid in a ravine until the crowds dispersed. His companions went free.[38]

That feast day the priest of Real del Monte had preached one of his elo-quent sermons, and he came out into the churchyard to face a distressed crowd' The workers were irate: "No more mixing!" "They must divide the partidos as before!" "The way the boss and the royal officials have resolved it is not good enough!" "Be it silver or tepetate, we will not tolerate mixing!" "We demand the partido of custom!" A miner and his wife moaned, "All the Real is a crying towel," and the woman wept when the priest spoke comfort to her. One witness recalled that the priest was known for his humanity, affability, and his measured words. But this time, when he warned the workers that to touch a mine or its structures was to oppose God, the king, and the public welfare, and when he reminded them to divide fairly, the sacks had to contain equal ores, voices interrupted him angrily: "Even you seem to have gone against us and for the boss!" "Use up the Sacrament, for today the Real will be demolished!" Touched, he promised to speak to the boss on their behalf. Even though it was raining, he called for his sedan chair and set forth to San Cayetano. He took with him the workers' demand for the release of the hostages, and brought back management's new strategy for divisions: with mixing, the miner takes the best ore; with no mixing, the miner gets the worst. At about one o'clock the priest returned, promising that at four Romero de Terreros himself would supervise the division. He gently recommended that the miners go home for dinner. The strike was telling on the workers, "You probably have something to eat at your house, and we are dying of hunger." The priest put his hands in his pockets and gave them all his money. It seemed, for an hour or two, that the priest had defused their rage with his understanding, by defining the conflict specifically as a quarrel over mixing in a situation where the miners felt they were getting none of the good ore, and by arranging what might have been a third arbitration attempt.[39]

About three o'clock, however, three recogedores captured a group of workers in the ravine and drove them with whip and lash to sign up for work in the mines of the Veta Vizcaína. By the time they arrived at La Joya and San Cayetano, a crowd, waiting for the division, had armed themselves with the people's classic ammunition, sticks and stones, and they took off after the press gang. The recogedores disappeared through the crowd; the captives, freed, did not work that night. No one worked in the mines that night. Miguel Sánchez explained, "The main cause of the riot was the recogedores."[40] And Miguel Sánchez was right.

Romero de Terreros, the administrator, and the district magistrate (who just happened to be there) were in the gallery of San Cayetano, about to take a break. A girl was preparing hot chocolate for them. They were discussing an incident that had occurred that morning at La Joya, when a miner (Juan Diego de León) had protested the mixing of ores and sought out Terreros at La Palma to complain. He had not been calmed or convinced by the information that all had been agreed to the day before. Terreros had ordered the grievant to be beaten for insolence, but he escaped. At the same time other workers had muttered that the hostages should be freed because the puebles were full. Suddenly, they heard a commotion outside and cut their conversation off. Terreros and the administrator fled to hide in the fodder. District magistrate

Miguel Ramón de Coca did not make good his escape. Workers broke into the gallery, found him, and saw him hit a worker with a stick. Then, they began to stone him. Someone shouted. "This one in the name of the crown of the Virgin!" A woman, they say, shied the last stone. Someone set fire to the hay.[41]

Old deputy Antonio Pintos, from his sickbed in his nearby house, heard the workers yell, "Down with the deputy!" "There is no justice, nor do we want any!" "The war won't stop!" and that hallmark of community rebellion in the Spanish heritage, "Long live the king! Death to bad management!"[42]

About three-thirty the priest came running, hatless. A stone found its target, felled him, and injured his leg. Amid "infinite rocks" he stretched out his arms, and on his knees in the mud he pleaded with them to stop, using images of agony a thousand years of religious devotion had laden with meaning: "By the stripes of the Lord, by his precious blood and passion, by the anguish of his mother." At great risk he entered the gallery, then sent two miners back to the church for the Host. About half the crowd went away, still angry. The rest knelt before the Sacrament, shielded from the drenching rain by a canopy. The priest rescued Terreros and the administrator, thrust candles in their hands, and sent them in procession safely back to the sacristy. He sent his sedan chair for old Antonio Pintos, who had observed from his house. The old deputy swore that the priest had saved him, too: "If there are mines and a Real del Monte, it is because of Dr. Díaz." Juan Yedra, a member of the barra that had organized the legal protest said, "If the priest had not worked day and night to contain the rioters, there would be no Real del Monte or mines in the Veta Vizcaína." A Spaniard summed it up, "His pleas staunched their fury."[43]

Before he left his house, the deputy had ordered onlookers to take the district magistrate next door. Miguel Ramón de Coca was still alive. His body was unhurt, but his skull had been completely crushed by a score of rocks and a blunt instrument. His nose was broken, his forehead and eyes cut, his lower lip and his left cheek split, his bottom teeth knocked out, his upper jaw broken. He died the next day, with his boots on, and was buried in a Franciscan habit. Two days later, because the two bloodletters who had examined him were not certified, two surgeons dug him up, officially counted his wounds, solemnly pronounced him dead, and buried him again.[44]

Father Inquisitor Melchor Velasco rallied a few workers to put out the fires of San Cayetano, but he was powerless to turn the crowd. Agitated workers fell on the Santa Teresa, but the hated timekeeper, Francisco Lira, had escaped to safety. They went on to La Joya, where that morning the disputed division had created another victim of the system. Searching for the hated Cayetano Celis, they were met with armed force by the mine foreman, Manuel Barbosa, who drew his pistols and, when they did not fire, pulled a knife. Miners stabbed him with his own knife and stoned him. He was in a coma by the time his rescuers carried him to safety. His arms were bruised from hand to shoulder on the left side. His breastbone was crushed. His lips were cut, his nose bruised, and his left ear flattened. The right side of his head was caved in. His wounds were mortal, but it took him an agonizing four days to die.[45]

Men, women, and children broke into the two-room jail of Real del Monte and released twelve prisoners (two debtors, one drunk, a besotted wife-beater, one lacking in respect for his father, one who quarreled with his wife, one accused of cohabitation, and the rest "other"). About three hundred or four hundred people walked down the mountain, taking care to shy stones at the store of administrator Marcelo González and the Pachuca house of Romero de Terreros. About fifty broke into the Pachuca jail, freed the four envoy-hostages, and refused to leave until the other prisoners had been let go. (Seven men escaped who were jailed for having difficulties with women—two had abducted their fiancees, four committed fornication, and one cohabited. Two were thieves who had stolen swatches of linen and wool from a store. One was accused of murder. One was disorderly. Two had been jailed by managers for crimes against the refinery of Santa María El Salto— one robbed the safe and one talked back when he was fined for an infraction. The rest found themselves there for unspecified reasons. The women prisoners did not escape because the jailer had locked them in the chapel.)

When the people of Real del Monte had accomplished their mission of rescue, cowering townsfolk heard them repeat the cry "Long live the king. Death to bad management." Franciscan monks calmed the crowd and guided them out of Pachuca. About midnight they returned to Real del Monte, perhaps still intent on burning the mines, but in the cemetery they found the priest with the Sacrament. He eased the crowd and sent the men home to bed. Soon after midnight, Pedro Romero de Terreros, wrapped in a cloak he had borrowed from the priest, and his men mounted their horses and rode the long trail to what turned out to be his long exile in San Miguel.[46]

From Pachuca messengers rode posthaste to Mexico City and to surrounding villages to call up the militia. Francisco Lira had gasped that both the boss and the district magistrate were dead and the mines burned. On August 16 royal treasury officials in Pachuca welcomed 330 armed men, on foot and on horseback, from Atotonilco el Grande, Cempoala, and Tulancingo.[47]

On the Veta Vizcaína the drainage works had been stopped, the cables cut, the apparatus blocked. The drifts were empty of people. The next morning at ten o'clock the priest saved the mines from deluge when, out of his own pocket, he paid whim operators, bailers, and laborers in advance to repair and undertake drainage operations. For the next few days the priest attended payday partido divisions, calming workers even when mixing was directed.[48] There were "a thousand alarms" and scares. Armed workers and their friends and families, four thousand strong, roamed the mountains in packs, eyeing the militiamen from afar. Roads were besieged, and townspeople feared that if the men of Pachuca were to march up the mountain, Real del Monte would be destroyed.[49] The royal officials were afraid the workers could not be contained: "The terrain of Real del Monte makes it impossible to crack down on them and even more so when bands of workers are going around armed. It will require more than twenty men and campaign artillery to overcome their resistance. On watch, they crown the hills, surveying what passes on the royal road."[50]

Francisco de Gamboa, the royal arbitrator, arrived the evening of August 27 to find peace. He was accompanied by the company of grenadiers from the America Battalion (officers and twenty-five riflemen). The mounted Dragoons of Spain (three officers and thirty cavalrymen) had lagged from fatigue and a lack of horses. They arrived the next day. Roving bands of workers and their fellow travelers were lured out of the hills on the promise of understanding from the viceroy. Not a shot was fired.[51]

One of Gamboa's first acts was to send a hundred militiamen from Actopan to quell a rebellion in their native village. From twenty-one miles away, five hundred Indians and mine workers of Santa María threatened with drumbeats, white flags, and whistling to stage a riot which authorities "knew" would ally them with the strike in Real del Monte. There probably was never any real connection, but had there been, the strikers would have been drawing on a new constituency, the villages from which they came. Actopan joined with Real del Monte and Pachuca would have roused two districts, not just two mining towns, and might have sparked what they used to call a "mass strike." But Actopan was calmed by a display of force, and Pachuca was occupied. And, to tell the truth, no one in Actopan ever figured out why Santa María had rebelled.[52]

The viceroy's promises to the strikers were published on August 18 in

Real del Monte, Pachuca, Pachuquilla, and Actopan. He gave his word that the troops would not be used against workers. He urged people to leave the hills and return to work with "submission, quiet, and repentence" and, once there, to work harmoniously with the bosses. Gamboa promised to treat workers' grievances with respect if they were equitable, reasonable, in conformity with the law, and presented peacefully. However, if workers did not return to the mines in twenty-four hours, they would be pursued and punished as "enemies of the fatherland," "rebels," and "traitors to His Majesty." Gamboa estimated that two thousand people came out of hiding to hear him in Real del Monte.[53]

Privately to the viceroy, Gamboa expressed his apprehensions. Thousands of people, "hardened and bold," were hiding out in the high country. Narrow mountain paths would not allow troop pursuit. The fugitives were, he said, "depraved. But necessary. Without them there can be no mines." That paradox he resolved, saying, "My principal guide will be prudence, moderation, and gentleness, for without them there will be no peace and no mines."[54] The lure worked. The strike was over, and the next day, shifts were full. On August 23 Gamboa published another proclamation to deal with returned workers on their own turf. The people were forbidden to bear arms and to assemble peacefully. Street meetings were forbidden. Drunks would be arrested, as would idlers or loiterers. Dr. Díaz prompted Real del Monte to greet Gamboa enthusiastically, with fireworks.[55]

Francisco de Gamboa had a long and distinguished career in the high royal bureaucracy of New Spain, no mean accomplishment for a colonial Mexican. His work on the Ordinances of Mining, published in 1762, won him an international reputation. He was the most outstanding Mexican jurist in the empire, one of the best mining jurists in the world. The viceroy who instructed him had been pressed by Romero de Terreros to force workers back on the job, but he was sympathetic to the workers' grievances. On the other hand, he was aware that crown revenues from silver, 100,000 pesos a year from the Veta Vizcaína, would suffer unless production resumed.[56] The viceroy clearly had both vested and labor interests in mind for resolving the problems of Real del Monte. His concern and his appointment of Gamboa as arbitrator gave recognition and legitimacy to the strike.

Gamboa's first direct act favoring workers occurred before he had talked to any. Hoping to convince the strikers of the "sense of justice and equity" inherent in the royal legal system, he fired administrator Marcelo González and timekeeper Francisco Lira. The recogedores who had so infuriated the crowd on August 15 had quit, intimidated. Gamboa named Bernadino Díaz, who had served the Marqués de Valle Ameno in Real del Monte for sixteen years as administrator of mines, to replace González. Bernadino Díaz, a Spaniard, was a man the workers liked and respected and whom Terreros trusted.[57]

Gamboa stayed at Romero de Terreros's house in Pachuca (Terreros, of course, was not there) and at the priest's house in Real del Monte, where he conducted a sort of open house for workers. He sought information from as many different sources as he could: from the boss, royal authorities, townspeople, the priest, other mine owners in the region, and from the workers themselves.

Gamboa's goal was social order and full work crews. As New Spain's most experienced mining expert, he brought to the bargaining table commitment to the principle that work customs themselves could best solve the problems that existed between workers and management in any mine. His strategy was to calm terror with terror, by making the soldiers visible everywhere, and to find the truth in the testimony of workers in their own voices: "The principal measure I took to prevent recurrence and provide an antidote was to listen affably to the workers about their complaints, the insults they have suffered, and their grievances."[58]

Gamboa conducted seven open meetings at the Santa Teresa between August 29 and September 13. Management was represented by the new administrator, foremen, timekeepers, scale men. Terreros, invited, refused to attend. Labor was defined as all those who fulfilled the functions of a shift. Of twenty-seven pikemen and peons selected as spokesmen for their fellow-workers, nine had signed or affirmed the July 28 grievance. Four had acted as spokesmen before Pedro Romero de Terreros. About three hundred workers attended the sessions. Gamboa kept his promise: he heard prolonged discussion on every single point the workers had raised in their petitions.

The first and most important problem, for both Gamboa and the workers, was "the equal, just and equitable division of the partido."[59] In order to observe it, mixing was acted out in the gallery of the Santa Teresa on August 26. Eight sacks, collected by four pikemen for the quota, were compared with their four partido sacks. The workers all agreed that the quotas were not of the same quality. Then two sacks from the quota were mixed with two from the partido. Gamboa remarked that it was not fair to workers to produce something that was half-good and half-bad, as what it really meant was that the owner was left with seven parts bad and only three good. He recommended, instead, that the partidos be mixed with all the quota sacks.

Pikemen told him they did not like to mix it all because the method was so unfair. Dispatchers put the good ores in a pile in the middle and made workers collect their partidos from the edges, which meant that workers were left with the worst. To top it off, workers were exiled from the gallery when the mixing was done. Timekeeper Francisco Lira and scale man Ignacio Pérez confessed that workers were shut out, but it was necessary, to keep them from stealing.

Gamboa was enraged. He called the procedure "a notorious iniquity." He spoke for justice: "It is beyond all reason and justice . . . workers have the right to be present to watch the mixing and to choose their partido from any place they like."[60] New administrator Bernadino Díaz said he had used a version of Gamboa's method in the San Vicente mine without any quarrel or difficulty with the workers.

Gamboa pondered out loud the difficulties of adjusting differences in ores. If good were substituted for bad without the workers' consent, it was unjust to labor. But what about the owner? He must have justice, too. Gamboa concluded that whatever proportion of bad ores the owner took, the worker should take, too. (The notary observed that no matter how many times Gamboa explained this one, the workers never seemed to understand it.) There was no question in Gamboa's mind, there would be no discussion. Mixing was the answer. Mixing was absolutely essential whenever ores were found to be unequal. "There is not nor can there be any other more natural or generally acknowledged solution than the mixing and stirring of the quota and partido."[61]

On September 2 Gamboa's method of mixing was demonstrated with four sacks of quota and partidos from three pikemen and a peon. The ore was mixed "to everyone's satisfaction" and heaped into four mounds. The workers, present the whole time, indicated what they wanted from where. Gamboa repeated the divisions at all the working mines until "all were satisfied." The notary concluded, "*All* were content with the method."[62]

A sack of ore was, in general, worth about 20 reales. If, as workmen charged, the size of the quota bags were increased, the boss would earn more and the worker would have to labor longer and harder for less. The demonstrations with ore sacks were awkward and inconclusive. Workers told Gamboa that while previously sacks had weighed a hundred pounds, the size had been increased to 175, 200, and even 250 pounds. Gamboa had two sacks weighed and found them to contain 146 pounds and 196 pounds; another quota sack weighed 147 pounds and a partido sack, 172 pounds. Gamboa said that the problem was that the sacks were not all the same size. Timekeeper Francisco Lira contradicted him: all the sacks were the same size and even with damp ore, none had ever weighed two hundred or more pounds. Lira pointed out that this was a fine example of the workers' tendencies to lie. Someone might infer that management, in control of the ore sacks, might have tried out larger bags and then retired them. Two peons continued to insist that they had worked five and six days just to complete the quota. Although the problem of too-large bags had been insisted upon in both grievances, Gamboa concluded that the workers' complaints were unfounded. [63]

Gamboa came to believe that peons had more opportunity to steal ore than anyone else in the mine. Ore sacks closed with a loop fastener and were supposed to be loaded full. But peons were expert at opening the sack and skimming off ore for themselves. Gamboa pointed out that this practice stole from pikemen as well as management. He decreed that pikemen should turn over their sacks to peons in the presence of the gang captain or the mine foreman. If, in the gallery, sacks were found topped, the peon must contribute ore from his partido to make it up. No one objected, and all peons present agreed to do it. [64]

The peons had been totally ignored in the talks, had taken a principal part in the strike, and seemed to be losing in arbitration until their pay was considered. Both Pedro Romero de Terreros and administrator Bernadino Díaz insisted that three reales a shift was ample reward for peons and manual laborers. Four reales, paid in Guanajuato and on the Veta Vizcaína, was excessive, they thought. The viceroy wrote that when Pedro Romero de Terreros took over the Real del Monte mines, he tried to lower the wage to three reales, and no one came to work until he raised it to four. On the other hand, the viceroy and Gamboa believed that since four reales had been paid at Real del Monte from "the remotest of times," to cut that traditional wage was both unjust and inhumane. Gamboa had to use all his powers of persuasion. Finally, sighing over the great expenses of mines and adits, the owner reluctantly, grudgingly, gave in. The peons had won their wage. [65]

The timbermen appeared before Gamboa with an ancient petition that surprised everyone. On May 1695 the carpenters of the Veta Vizcaína went to Viceroy Conde de Galve in Mexico City to protest wage cuts. They demanded a peso a day and a portion of ore that did not have to be shared with management. At that time they said the custom had been observed in Real del Monte since 1624. The viceroy confirmed the practice and said, "May the old customs be observed and complied with." [66] But the old custom had been lost, and Gamboa told the timbermen that with their peso wage they might take out a sack of partido, if in their work they found a reef of ore that had to be removed. Of course, Gamboa admonished them, their partido had to be divided with the boss. No one objected. At this point all present became fascinated with the rules for dividing a bonanza, where a sack of ore could be worth as much as sixty pesos. In general, the worker was given one-sixth to one-tenth of the ore and, if there were more silver in it than ore, one-twentieth. Bonanzas were not mixed.[67]

Gamboa read a draft of the ordinances which had resulted from his arbitration to seven hundred workers in the great gallery of the Dolores in September 1766. Although privately he had said that many of the miners' complaints had "no substance,"[68] in fact his ordinances granted workers' demands: the sack size, the responsibility of management to provide candles, sacks, and proper tools to get the job done. Asking a fee for partido sacks and "mixing in the dark" were absolutely forbidden. Alms to co-workers were voluntary, and there was a check on employees who, as Gamboa observed, "left the poor workers with only half a sack of partidos."[69] If smiths, whim operators, or dispatchers took more than the worker intended, they were to be treated like thieves. Miners were advised to fill each shift and were prohibited from working two consecutive shifts. Stiff fines were set for stealing ore, tools, and black powder, and both the worker and the person who bought the stolen goods were liable. Barras who filled their quota sacks with rubble would be punished. Peons were told that if they topped their loads, they would have to make it up from their partidos. Sack size was officially limited to 125–150 pounds. Bailers were promised four reales for their six-hour day. Mixing was mandatory if ores were unequal, and Gamboa's technique was prescribed. The key to unequal ores was fitted to the role of workgang captain, and workers were promised support from royal authorities if captains allotted work unfairly and with favoritism. The administrator was charged with choosing the most expert and competent captains and foremen to assign tasks and set quotas for pikemen. Recogedores were exhorted to stay away from miners who had just worked a shift and to treat the workers they rounded up well; workers were enjoined to respect recogedores as authority figures doing important work for the mining enterprise as a whole. Most important, the miners' inalienable right to partidos, which had never officially been questioned in this strike, was sanctioned and reaffirmed, a royal mandate for a practice heretofore unremarked by the law. Everything the workers asked for in their petitions, they received in arbitration. The notary observed that the workers present heard the new ordinances and "consented, praised, approved, and ratified."[70]

Compared to the treatment of workers in the United States more than a hundred years later, Gamboa's Spanish rule seems stunningly flexible and understanding. He even seemed to distinguish strike from uproar, though he believed that how grievances were expressed was a question of manners: "Though they may have just grievances about their interests and vexations, they should express them without violating reason and other people's rights. They should not stir up these hostilities and insults to justify their rights."[71] But while his approach to workers was demonstrably mild and fair, his approach to strike leaders was savage.

It got to be savage because of fear. Within the context of what had happened in Real del Monte, the most pervading emotion of the authorities was terror of murderous miners. Gamboa himself had rescued the royal authorities, whom he found cowering in the churches of Pachuca. Gamboa confessed to the viceroy his most serious problem: "to apprehend the ringleaders requires great prudence, sagacity, and finesse so that they do not stir up the others again, which would result in a major work stoppage in the mines and drainage works."[72] The attitude of Pedro Romero de Terreros also demanded action. Although Gamboa assured him that all was quiet, Terreros feared and hated his enemies too much to leave the haven of San Miguel. Gamboa was afraid that he would withdraw from the Veta Vizcaína. He asked the viceroy to "console and hearten" Romero de Terreros, so that he would return to work. What would most hearten him, Gamboa thought, was to see the ringleaders cruelly punished: "if an exemplary punishment is not made, neither he nor anyone else will want to expose themselves to the risks of dealing with insolent men."[73]

Though royal authorities had been given the names of forty or fifty suspects and had transmitted them to Gamboa, no one knew who had killed the district magistrate or the foreman. The viceroy and Gamboa had agreed that a general pardon would be good bait to allay the suspicions of the guilty and to lull the concern of the rest. Gamboa suggested that authorities round up the "traitors" in one night and jail them in Pachuca so that the next day he could release the pardon in Real del Monte before workers became aware of what had happened. Then there would be no sympathy demonstrations, no mass movement to free the prisoners.[74]

On September 8 Gamboa informed the viceroy of a new plan. He had been taking the names of everyone who came to work, and on that list were many "ringleaders." He proposed to publish his ordinances in the great gallery of the Dolores, a cavern that would accommodate two thousand men. He would read the workers' names aloud quietly, directing each to leave as he was pardoned. The forty leaders would be left until last, when everyone was gone. Grenadiers would guard the single entrance. The culprits would be seized and flogged with two hundred lashes each. Militiamen would force them to walk to Pachuca, where their statements would be taken in jail.[75]

Could a man flogged that viciously walk anywhere? Gamboa's bright idea was never tested. By return post, Viceroy Marqués de Croix cut short his fantasies. In a tone of indignation he commanded Gamboa to return immediately to Mexico City, before anyone was punished and before he published his ordinances. The viceroy sounded fair and pro-worker and affected the pose of a humane European beset with unjust colonials:

> It seems that in these dominions humanity is unknown. For the convenience of a single individual they trample, they violate, and they tyrannize the disadvantaged, who, content with their pitiful daily wage and the few easements that the law provides, would be satisfied because they do not aspire to more riches. You and everyone else knows the irregularity and almost tyrannical despotism with which mine workers have been treated.[76]

The viceroy accused Pedro Romero de Terreros of unjust labor practices. Why, he demanded, had Gamboa not investigated the "repeated and never-mentioned violence" of the recogedores, hired only to whip men to labor "without any hope of collecting wage or partidos, which both king and custom favor?" He admonished Gamboa, "Concentrate on the violence the workers have suffered and which made them desperate." The viceroy knew why there was trouble in Real del Monte: the workers had finally rebelled "as a natural result of . . . repeated extortion."[77]

Gamboa, presumably chastened, peacefully and without guile read a general amnesty to the "multitude" on September 13. The military was then deployed, the grenadiers and fusiliers left for Mexico City. Thirty cavalrymen and two officers of the Dragoons of Spain were ordered to remain in Pachuca and ensure that any disturbances of the peace were met with firmness. No troops were stationed in Real del Monte because the waters and rugged terrain made horses ineffectual. In spite of the reprimand, the viceroy welcomed Gamboa to the capital and praised his efficient and seemly conduct.[78]

What was to be done with the ringleaders was worked out in Mexico City to the satisfaction of both Gamboa and the viceroy. No one could catch runaways in the mountains of Real del Monte. To arrest the strike leaders as a group would surely incite a riot. The best thing to do, the authorities reasoned, since most of the suspects were still free, was to arrest them one by one for crimes (committed or contrived), crimes like drunkenness, disorderly conduct, fighting, homicide, or warrants from other towns. Then the "criminals" could be speedily delivered to Mexico City to be given their just deserts. Suspects might be smoked out by alerting other mining Reales (Zimapam, Taxco, Chontalpa, Tehuilotepec, Temescaltepec, Saquilpan, and Guanajuato).[79] Thus no indictment was even framed to accused men of organizing the strike, but if they could be apprehended in a totally unrelated incident, they would be presumed guilty of treason. Many suspects ran away. Notices sent to other mining areas brought no results. Only a few of those suspects ever appeared in the criminal records of Real del Monte again.

The strike at Real del Monte was organized by "inside agitators," the workers themselves. In arbitration with one of the most famous jurists in the land, they won everything they asked. The viceroy himself had sympathy for them and made his influence felt on the side of labor. For a few months there was tranquillity on the Veta Vizcaína. Romero de Terreros stayed away, but there were no disputes over mixing. Gamboa had brought back a hundred years of peace by restoring just practices to payday.

But, even so, the calm did not last. When the action came, it was organized, intense, raging. The workers of Real del Monte, armed with stones, rebelled again. But it was not against management. This time they fought against their own comrades.

!¡

CHAPTER 6

Direct Action: October 1766–February 1767

Just after sunset on October 12, 1766, gangs of workers were roaming Real del Monte on the eve of the official posting of Gamboa's Ordinances, rejoicing and exulting in a hard task done. The workers claimed victory with, said a disapproving official eyewitness, "the grandest huzzas and effrontery."[1] They even asked to celebrate the proclamation with masks. There is a euphoria in taking political action, in bringing people to pressure a turn for the better. When the system negotiates, accepts, moves, accommodates, it stimulates hope, as if change were possible. This is, perhaps, the legacy of the strike that came closest to the workers: an increased self-confidence in defining their own problems and organizing their own solutions. What was a new consciousness for workers was perceived by the authorities as their old insolence, their crass impudence. The authorities' perspective tended to magnify incidents and generalize isolated events into proof of recurring conspiracy. But it was not really like that. The truth is that miners talked back, miners fought back. They talked back to management; there is nothing strange in that. But they fought back against workers, and that, indeed, is different.

Real del Monte assimilated Gamboa's Ordinances, proclaimed by town crier and posted in the mine galleries, with joy, innocent of the unease that comes from the realization that what is swift to put down on paper above may take some slow and uncomfortable accommodations below. Their gains had yet to be tested.

An incident occurred in the mines the next day. It was not, as might be supposed, a quarrel over mixing or unequal ore sacks of the kind that had convulsed the Real in August. Rather, it was a dispute over the *solution* to those problems, that is, who should captain the barras. The third ordinance of Gamboa reads, "labor and management depending on the competence and ability of the mine foremen and captain-taskmasters to distribute the work crews with a perfect understanding of ores and work, owners should choose them from the most practiced, accomplished, and experienced workers."[2] Gamboa had explained to the viceroy that captains had sole power to set the work load, to allot the workers' space and time, and to decide which rock face should be worked and how much the partidos should be. If equalizing quota and partido ores was the goal, then only a good, experienced captain could find ways of effecting it. Only the captain could assure a good day's work from men who might rest, talk, fool around, or sleep underground. It was crucial that, in order to command such great authority below, the captain must be observant, fit, fair, and above all, know what he was doing.[3]

The incident in the great gallery of the Dolores on Tuesday, October 14, 1766, was first provoked and then resolved by mine officials, the timekeeper, the mine foreman, and the guards. About eight or nine that morning some forty or fifty men surrounded the pay table to sign up for the day shift at La Joya. There was no trouble until the managers named the captain of the work crew. The workers were incensed with the choice. He was, they said, a *pepenador*, used to pounding rocks and sorting ores above and, the workers insisted, useless below because he was not an experienced pikeman. The workers refused to go below without a qualified captain. The timekeeper assented nervously and sent for the captain of their choice. When he came, workers signed up and went below.[4]

Principle was clearly articulated by both management and labor. The workers cited Gamboa. An experience at the Santa Teresa the previous day had inspired them. The labor version of that incident was that workers had deposed their captain and chosen another without punishment. They had formulated the rule themselves: *"Pikemen had the ability to appoint or remove captains to their satisfaction."*[5]

This was taken as a declaration of war on privilege by the administrator, and he treated the incident as if it were a case of lèse majesté. The workers had intentionally acted to abrogate the right of an owner to name and remove captains, a right belonging solely to management and unlawfully seized by labor. The timekeeper went even further when he called the incident "this revolution."[6]

Was there intimidation? Did the workers get their way by force? The managers at the table had trembled with apprehension. They said that they were sure the workers were about to riot. The timekeeper and the foreman said that they feared for their very lives. The formal charges, written by the old deputy, expressed their perception: "they picked up rocks and took up the wedges that were on the table, threatening the managers with them if they did not do what they asked."[7] But only one witness, the foreman, said the men picked up rocks. None of the other management witnesses saw anyone pick up rocks, and their colleague, a dispatcher, specifically testified that *none* of the workers had picked up any rocks. All of the defense witnesses also denied having anything to do with rocks. Two of the leaders admitted that they had seized a pike, to complain because it weighed less than one and a half pounds, and some wedges to show that they were only three inches long, too little to do the job. One defendant said with a grin that the pike had no thrust and was good for nothing but cutting the hand, which it had done to him. Management insisted that workers had seized the tools to threaten and intimidate. Workers said only two men had picked up tools, and they sought merely to prompt those in charge to obey Gamboa's Ordinances and to issue only tools fit to work with. The tools in question should have been withdrawn and repaired for use another day. Gamboa's Ordinances indeed said "It is the obligation of owners to distribute the proper pikes and wedges for the work."[8]

All the workers and their witnesses, questioned separately, denied that there were any threats to kill or to injure or to riot. The dispatcher said he saw two men handle the pick and wedges, but, he continued, they did not threaten anyone, and no one else did either.

A defense witness tried to clarify the workers' tactics. Gamboa, in an open meeting, had told them never, under any circumstances, to leave their work; if they had a difference of opinion or a complaint, they should ask for what they wanted. So, at La Joya, fifty workers with a single voice had done just that. In doing so, they had reaffirmed their faith in the process Gamboa had taught them.[9]

Conspiracy. Did workers plot and plan secretly to commit the "crime" of deposing their captain? The deposed captain said he had warned the *rayador* that this was going to happen, for he had heard second-hand of a plot to reject him. The malcontents were overheard at a baptism held at the house of the successful captain's daughter-in-law, or perhaps it was when they were drinking in the cemetery after Gamboa's Ordinances had been posted. The informer said he had seen two of the principal defendants in the cemetery, and they were discussing the ordinances and wondering why the Santa Teresa could replace its captain and not the La Joya. All of the principals denied there was any plot or any meeting, and, except for the grandfather who became captain, none of them had even heard of the baptism, much less attended it.

Another phenomenon that convinced management was that after the shouting was over, only fifteen pikemen had gone down La Joya that morning. The timekeeper knew because he had counted them. He was certain that the rest had gone away because they had come to the mine just to make trouble. When they had their way, they left. The workers who had gone below did not know how many they were, but they assumed that it was a full crew of twenty-four and that the rest had left because they were not needed.

One small voice indicated that the miners were chastened by the confrontation and inspired by peaceful protest. On Thursday the managers named the deposed captain, once again, to go below. This time workers acquiesced, though they intended to complain to the royal authorities afterwards. No one spoke to him during the hard day's shift; all worked as he ordered. But when they came to the surface, the three leaders were arrested. [10]

Authorities feared another storming of the jail in Real del Monte. They noted with apprehension that workers were roaming the hills; they feared that workers had set a watch to free the prisoners when they were transferred to Pachuca. There were no disturbances of the peace, but when the defendants had served a month and a week in jail, two detachments of dragoons from Pachuca came to escort them down the mountain. The transfer was effected, of course, without incident. [11]

Administrator Bernadino Díaz asked that the three convicts be processed to the fullest extent of the law: "I accuse the three of criminal acts. They conspired in a premeditated act as leaders of other pikemen to remove the authority and command of Captain Tovar and put Cordero in his place. For this I pray you to condemn them to the greatest and gravest penalties." [12] Díaz maintained that they must be severely punished as an example to the rest. They had challenged authority, they had used the "rights of labor" to defy management, and they did it in a loud and disorderly manner and with malice of forethought. Díaz knew details that no one else knew: the deposed captain *was* an experienced pikeman; he had served with Díaz as a pikeman in the San Vicente for the Marqués de Valle Ameno. However, daybooks for 1757 for the Marqués de Valle Ameno listed him as a *pepenador*. [13] Díaz insisted on the principle. Even if he had not been experienced, the fact that the captain was named by the owner or managers was enough: "It is not indispensable to have been a pikeman, because though the captain sets the tasks and the quota, he doesn't do it on his own but on the orders of the foreman."[14]

Díaz also knew what really happened at the Santa Teresa. A captain did not show up on time; another captain was selected; but when the first one finally arrived, he went below with his men. There was no riot, nothing illegal happened. Managers named a new captain, then removed him. There was no crime. At La Joya, however, there was a show or threat of force, there was a conspiracy, and when workers defied authorities and named their own captain, a crime was committed. Díaz concluded that all the testimony of the defendants and defense witnesses was untrustworthy because, as companions in crime, they had all lied.[15]

Francisco de Gamboa judged the case from Mexico City. For the defendants he pointed out that the truth was, there were no scuffles, injuries, or homicides. For the prosecution he agreed that the prisoners had terrorized the managers and forced them to do their will. Mexico City agreed with management: deposing a captain was a reprehensible and criminal action of fraud and contempt against the company. Since the accused had been in jail since October, they were not flogged. Each of the three leaders was sentenced to a four-year exile from the Real. If they returned too soon, they would have to serve eight years at hard labor in a fortress.[16]

None of the three workers convicted had any official part in the strike in August. They did not sign or affirm the grievances. They had never before served as spokesmen for their fellow workers. All had been in jail before: one for a debt, one on a warrant (issued by the priest) that accused him of fornication, and one on a complaint filed by the woman who later changed her mind, said yes, and became his wife.[17]

In Real del Monte, the problem of the recogedores remained without solution, for what would have been needed was a radical change in both law and practice. To workers, recogedores represented an unfair, brutal activity which was always an insult and a challenge. To management, recogedores were legal and absolutely essential to the economic development of the mines, the industry, and the kingdom. On November 4, 1766, recogedores of Romero de Terreros brought their captives to sign up for the dry diggings in the Santa Teresa. Opposing views suddenly faced each other physically. A crowd of fifty protested their heavy-handed tactics, and soon two hundred gathered to demand that the recogedores be fired. Administrator Bernadino Díaz defied the crowd. But when the brief reached Mexico City, Gamboa did not support him. Gamboa instructed Díaz to fire all those recogedores and hire new ones. He fired the new district magistrate for failure to provide sup-

port when it was needed. Gamboa suggested a new solution: all *españoles* in
Real del Monte and Pachuca would, when problems arose, be responsible for
forming a posse that would take arms and pacify disorderly mine workers.
The fine for failure to sign up was two hundred pesos. In this incident royal
authorities accommodated and gave workers what they asked for. But the
forces of order started to count on grass-roots support. Labor would be disci-
plined and chastised with all the armed force people in the community
would muster.[18]

What caused the working people of Real del Monte to gather once again in
angry crowds a month later were the recogedores, not of Pedro Romero de
Terreros but of another mine owner in Real del Monte, don Manuel José de
Moya. Moya, in the 1760s, owned the mines of Morán, Santa Bárbara, San
Nicolás, Candado, and San Miguel. He rented the refinery of La Puríssima
Concepción from Pedro Romero de Terreros on a six-year lease for 600 pesos
a year. He made good on promises of bonanzas for the royal treasury. He,
too, complained loudly about the lack of labor in the area. And because he
was a mine owner with a legitimate claim and some history of success, he had
the right to employ recogedores to solve the problem.[19]

On the day of San Andrés, November 30, 1766, the villagers of Cerezo,
on the road to Morán, resisted the recogedores with shouts and stones. They
even ran the press gang down a ravine. The captive workers were freed. Cerezo checked the roundups of Morán several times.[20]

Real del Monte took its turn on December 22. Workers threatened the
recogedores, threw stones, and freed their comrades. Authorities were deeply troubled by the "bold insolence and continual complaints of their dis-
graceful conduct."[21]

The viceroy responded with a proclamation. His *bando* of January 4,
1767, reiterated the ban on drinking, gambling, frequenting taverns, and
assembling in the cemetery. Workers must submit to recogedores. Fishing
for the leaders of the strike, the viceroy ordered them punished by two hundred lashes and eight years of hard labor—unless they turned themselves in.
But, the authorities despaired, such was "the unrestrained and incredible
conceit and arrogance of that seditious plebe" that no one turned himself in,
and some even tore down the viceroy's proclamations from the five official
places they were posted. All the next day miners went two by two and three
by three into the house of the priest of Real del Monte. In the afternoon they
publicly stoned some recogedores. The priest, for his peaceful counsel, got a
name for himself as a pro-worker conspirator. But nothing was done to protect the men of Real del Monte from the recogedores of the Morán.[22]

In January 1767 the recogedores of Morán pounced on Real del Monte. They rounded up some miners who had worked the night shift, some who were just coming to work, and some who were going to the gallery for the division of partidos. The workers protested at once, peacefully but adamantly. They told the press gang that they must not proceed because there was a serious labor shortage on the Veta Vizcaína: at San Cayetano, Dolores, and La Joya there weren't enough barras below to get the job done. Administrator Bernadino Díaz intervened and released the workers. The recogedores complained formally to Pachuca.[23]

The royal officials of Pachuca devised an ingenious solution. They would deputize twelve veteran pikemen from the Veta Vizcaína to assist the recogedores in making a better-informed and more effective sweep. Why pikemen might take such a job is easy to understand. It paid twenty pesos a week.[24]

Two of the newly sanctioned deputy recogedores had affirmed the July 28 grievance. One, with other well-known strike leaders, had walked out on the unjust mixing procedures at La Joya on August 15, 1766. Four had been selected as "intelligent and capable" by their fellow miners to present strike grievances to Pedro Romero de Terreros and Francisco de Gamboa, and they had eloquently made their position known. The best known of the new deputies was Miguel Sánchez. Workers dubbed them the "twelve apostles" and despised them as sellouts. Suddenly, recogedores were not just pests; they were "traitors" and "executioners."[25]

Thus the provocation in February 1767 was much more than the usual resentment at being shanghaied. This time the workers were betrayed by some of the very leaders who had emerged to proclaim the strike. There is a real fury to this last great *tumulto* of the era. The strike made its farewell appearance in a "multitude of stones."

On Saturday morning, February 7, 1767, a mestizo pikeman (authorities said he was a known bully) swaggered into a store in Real del Monte and boasted to the shaken storekeeper, "Wait and see what will be offered tomorrow to the recogedores of the Morán.[26] Saturday afternoon the full crew of deputies and recogedores rounded up eighteen workers. The captives seemed in good spirits. When their wives came with their work clothes, they refused to take them, laughing, "This afternoon we'll see a comedy, and then we'll wait for the evening performance."[27]

The workers were marched out of town. Feeling safe, the recogedores dismissed five of the deputies, who went home. About seven o'clock the press gang met a great crowd lying in wait for them as they moved through Acosta Pass at the foot of San Andrés Hill. Workers whistled from the heights, shouted mightily, and threw a rain of stones. Thirteen of the captives broke free, and some joined the men on the hillside. Only five captives were enrolled at the mines of Morán that night. A deputy said that a worker had had his skull cracked. The recogedores identified Teodoro Cervantes, an inspired rock thrower, and arrested him later in a tavern. If he really had organized the episode, Cervantes never said so. He did not remain in jail twenty-four hours.[28]

That same Saturday night an incident, entirely unrelated to recogedores, occurred in the gallery of the La Joya. A peon, Juan de León, challenged the man in charge of partidos, protesting, "They took away my partido because it was not gathered from one spot but rather half from one spot and half from another."[29] Angrily, he pushed the manager in the chest. When he and his brother met after work, they agreed that they had to do something.[30] The officials swore that the brothers lurked outside the mine waiting to stone them. No stones were ever thrown. No such confrontation ever took place. When at last they went home to eat, their brother-in-law, convinced they were in the wrong, said, "Boys, don't get into trouble, for God's sake."[31]

The authorities were also concerned because they said that the León boys had worked a full twenty-four hours, against Gamboa's Ordinances. Two other peons explained how that was possible. They maintained that the ordinances pertained only to pikemen. Peons stayed below because if they did not bring up quota and partido in proportions exactly corresponding to the ratio set, their own partido would be taken away. Another peon explained, "It is true that no one is permitted to work more than twelve hours, but the demand to take out ore for profit made me do it."[32] This evidence is part of the scanty information pertaining to how Gamboa's Ordinances were dealt with by mine workers. But more to the point is how their brother-in-law admonished the mine workers. "You'll pay," he said. And they did.[33]

On Sunday afternoon, February 8, 1767, mounted recogedores and eleven apostles captured sixteen workers. They encountered a superbly orchestrated resistance. At the western edge of Real del Monte, they found some five-hundred workers lying in wait and a "multitude of stones." Nervously, they let the prisoners go and fled down another path, only to find another angry crowd. They ran to the road to town, but it was blocked with workers, whistling and shouting "embarrassing obscenities." A place called Carretera was jammed with people throwing rocks. They backed into the main square of Real del Monte to find another crowd. A deputy was knocked down by a stone. The recogedores fired three blunderbusses and cleared a way out across the plaza and down the streets. A deputy, hiding in a store, observed their escape. "At five o'clock the three recogedores came galloping on their horses, pursued by a deluge of people."[34] A young recogedor recalled the flight out of town: "We ran a thousand dangers and were stoned from every street."[35] The recogedores finally found a passage in the ravine near the Santa Teresa, and at last they escaped to Pachuca.[36]

A twenty-two-year-old recogedor from Actopan lamented, "Wherever we turned there were more workers with more stones. It seemed as if all the workers in the Real were rioting. Yet we mistreated no one and gave none of them cause."[37] The recogedores felt innocent because they had not beaten anyone or flogged them as had happened the year before. But the truth was, all the recogedores were from out of town. They could not appreciate what the enlistment of skilled pikemen as deputy recogedores meant to the community of organized labor in Real del Monte.

Workers and townspeople turned from chasing men and horses to stoning houses. A man who heard the noise said the rocks sounded like hail on the roofs. Five deputies' houses were severely damaged. Miguel Sánchez's house was not touched. He had not participated in either Saturday's or Sunday's roundup. He was home recuperating from knife wounds he had received from a worker who had refused to let himself, his friends, and a lawyer from Mexico City be taken to the Morán.[38]

At ten o'clock, in the dark, crowds stoned the house of the old deputy district magistrate. They broke into the jail and let the prisoners go. The door and a part of the stocks were found the next morning in the river. With a pike someone tore the viceroy's order from top to bottom. Well into the night they arrived at the Morán and stoned whims, pulleys, stables, doors, and roofs until they broke. They threw stones down the shaft of one mine until the workers were forced to leave. The inspector of the Santa Bárbara was a terrified Creole from Mexico City. He saw workers shouting and throwing stones from the path above and the road below. He was hit in the chest and begged the men not to kill him because he was "only a poor stranger trying to earn a living."[39]

They let him go. He saw workers smash the door and ransack the administrator's office. One man, quietly breaking and entering, stopped to light a candle before the image of the Virgin of Guadalupe. Then they all dispersed because they thought the soldiers were coming.[40]

The next day, mountains of stones lay around everywhere. Pedro de Leoz, on the job, conducted precise little inspections of property. In the jail one window showed the marks of eighty-three stones and some blows from an axe. The doors had gouges hewn out, and a wall was damaged. In the entry of the house of the deputy district magistrate there were seventy-seven marks from stones and eleven left by sharp instruments. The roof was damaged, the door splintered, and the living room scored by rocks.[41] At the Morán, Leoz found the walls of the gallery dented by stones. The timekeeper's table had been slashed with an axe and sharp instruments. At another mine the door, whims, and roof of the stables were smashed. In the administrator's office one wall had marks too numerous to count, and the other showed the effects of 120 stones.[42]

Authorities believed that the crowds had almost destroyed the mines of the Morán. They feared the "final, total ruin" of Real del Monte. Unfortunately for the prosecution, not a single person had been caught in the act of rioting or fomenting a rebellion. In the world of the managers in Real del Monte, where a concert of labor was so feared, no conspiracy was ever discovered, not even one ominous chat in the graveyard. Men, most of them framed, were severely chastized, but how the community organized its resistance was never ascertained.[43]

Arrests were made because of hearsay and from one deputy recogedor's recollections of glimpses made in the dark. With no list of real suspects, the authorities set out to trap some. They were frustrated at every turn. "It is incredible," said Pedro de Leoz, "that all being in the same neighborhood, no one recognized anyone."[44] When royal authorities issued a warrant on February 13, 1767, it was a license to falsely arrest people: "It is easier to free an innocent man than to apprehend a guilty one. Instruct officials in Actopan, Tetepango, Cempoala, and Atotonilco el Chico to detain strangers dressed like miners."[45]

Antonio Pintos, the old deputy district magistrate, was pleased that he and a posse including the commissioner of the Veta Vizcaína, recogedores and their deputies, and loyal businessmen, had apprehended the "prime movers" unaided, that is, without the intervention of the military.[46]

"Unaided," they caught poor Felipe Estrada, a forty-one-year-old mestizo pikeman who had not worked for a year and a half because he suffered debilitating pains in the chest and lungs. He knew he would never work again, but he loved to go to Mass on Sundays and walk in the plaza. He was arrested during his promenade.[47] They locked up a twenty-two-year-old pikeman who had been in Pachuca recuperating and had come back to work because he needed the money, even though he was not yet well.[48] They confined a nineteen-year-old Indian pikeman from Cerezo, although he said he was home with his wife and five children.[49] They seized a young Creole who swore, "I only leave my house to go to work and leave work to go home." They arrested a mestizo pikeman who had been at home with his family all day and all night and who protested, "I don't go to taverns, I only go to work."[50] They picked up a young mestizo who came in tired from walking all the way from Sultepec. Corroborating testimony proved conclusively that he had gone to bed, not out.[51] They apprehended a peon who had spent the weekend in Pachuquilla and who had not returned to Real del Monte until the Monday after the tumulto.[52] They took from his family a mestizo pikeman who had been shopping with his wife and a peddlar Sunday morning. He was home before the crowds gathered. He said, "I have always been quiet and peaceable. I leave the house only to go to the mine. . . . If they picked me up, it was because they were going around picking up everything in front of them."[53] Authorities also brought in the known drunks, bullies, and "unquiet spirits." In short, they rounded up the "usual suspects."

In Pachuca the royal officials freed four of the accused: poor Felipe Estrada, so ill from silicosis; the peon who had spent the weekend in Pachuquilla; the Indian pikeman who had been recuperating; and a miner who had worked all night at the Santa Teresa. In Mexico City Francisco de Gamboa released two mestizo pikemen: the one who said he was "quiet and peaceable" and the one who stayed home and never went to taverns. He also let the Negrito Elías go free. He judged that although the recogedores said a Black captained the men who took the captives from them, there was no positive identification and no reason to charge this particular Black man.[54]

Only ten of the suspects had been in jail before, and the only one authorities mentioned was the ore thief. But there were others. A real difficulty for these workers was relating to women. "I made my wife jealous, and she locked me up." "Every time we have a quarrel, she puts me in jail" (three men). "I was caught dallying in the woods." "I was put in jail for fornication, but then I married her" (two men).[55] Five men had been detained previously for fighting, some with rocks. And one said he was apprehended in a tavern while he was listening to a guitar.

The wide sweep of February 1767 carried along with it a few individuals who had participated in the strike and in other incidents. And they received the stiffest sentences.

Only one strike leader was in custody: Juan Diego de León, who had circulated the July 28 grievance and had tagged the envoys to Mexico City. On February 8, 1767, de León had been at his *comadre's* house, reading a play. Pedro de Leoz concluded that de León had been implicated in the riot, not because he had been seen but because he did not denounce. it. Witnesses described de León as a good, sober, competent pikeman. When he was jailed, de León explained that he had been arrested "because the foremen have it in for me because I tell the truth" and because he had had a falling out with the boss, who must have asked his men to seize him. Gamboa sentenced the twenty-five-year-old mestizo pikeman to eight years' exile, the first four to be spent at hard labor in Havana. The viceroy commuted the sentence to a concurrent four years' exile and hard labor in Havana.[56]

Two other Leónes, *castizos*, twenty-three and twenty-five, had worked as peons in the mines. Juan pushed the scale man of La Joya in the chest on Saturday night, and he and his brother Manuel threatened to stone him for unfairly taking away his partido. No stone was thrown in the incident, but Leoz was convinced that the León boys were defiant, dangerous, and lacking in respect for authority. The peons had no part in the tumultos against the recogedores. Their father had locked them in the house on Sunday night and would not let them go out. Juan de León confessed another reason for not participating: "The riot was not directed against the managerial staff in the mines but only against the recogedores."[57] The brothers revealed they had been a part of the crowd on August 15, but only because other workers threatened to kill them if they did not join. Gamboa imposed the same penalty as for Juan Diego de León, and the viceroy commuted their terms to four years' hard labor in Havana.[58]

The harshest sentence was given to a twenty-five-year-old peon, "Guadiana." He was accused of killing the district magistrate Miguel Ramón de Coca on August 15, 1766. No one had seen him do it, but five deputies testified that his guilt was "common knowledge." He consistently denied it. He had been in the gallery that afternoon, but only to search for his little sister, who had been serving chocolate. Guadiana said he was an Indian and was treated legally as such; but Pedro de Leoz insisted, "He is demonstrably a mulatto." The viceroy sent Guadiana into exile for ten years, the first four to be spent at hard labor in Havana.[59]

Accused of the same crime, killing the district magistrate, was Coyote, a twenty-five-year-old mestizo. His only accuser was his mother-in-law. No one saw him do it or heard him boast of it. The viceroy sent him into a six-year exile, the first half to be spent at hard labor on the fortifications of Vera Cruz.[60] His alleged accomplice, a Creole pikeman, had been freed of suspicion of being involved in the February 8 incident. He was accused, however, of being a notorious drunk and a "scandalous provocateur." Among all the suspects, he alone had a criminal record: he had been jailed for robbing ores, breaking the head of a miner in a fight, and amassing debts. He was never sentenced. He died in jail in Mexico City in May 1767.[61]

Four Indians, two Creoles, and one mestizo (working as three pikemen, three peons, and a manual laborer) had nothing in common except that the cases against them were not proved beyond a reasonable doubt. They were given the lightest sentences: all to serve double time at hard labor in fortresses or sweatshops. One of these men was the nineteen-year-old father of five. Another was the man from Cerezo who went out only to work.[62]

Gamboa and the viceroy agreed on the fate for fifteen workers: six years of exile, the first three to be spent at hard labor in the fort of San Juan de Ulúa, Vera Cruz. Nine of these men were mestizos, two Creoles, two mulattoes, and one castizo. Most worked as peons, though three were pikemen, one a chandler, and one a drainage worker. Two had resisted arrest or the recogedores. Four told stories subsequently refuted by witnesses. Five were "known drunks" or "scandalous provocateurs," and one was the bully who, by boasting to the storekeeper, informed authorities that the riot had been plotted in advance.[63]

Indians, also, were harshly dealt with: two pikemen, a bailer, a peon, and a manual laborer. One said he stayed home with a boil, and no one saw him outside. Two were known for their prowess in escaping press gangs. Another's story was all too typical of this criminal investigation. The pikeman said he had gone to work at the Santa Teresa, but there weren't enough peons to go below. He left the mine, went to the tavern, had a medio, and went home to bed. Incredibly, the timekeeper at the Santa Teresa testified, "His statement is false. No one by that name worked Sunday night."[64] Gamboa's original sentence was two years of exile. However, the viceroy commuted the sentence to *six* years' exile, the first year and a half to be passed in Vera Cruz at hard labor.

Sentencing of the men, involved or not in the February 8 incident, was harsh and swift. However, the death penalty was not imposed; no spikes impaled the heads of the activists. In the troubles stirred up when the Jesuits were expelled, such cruel punishments were imposed on protesters by Visitor General José de Gálvez, who thought the "vile rabble" needed a lesson. But the psychopath "butcher of Tierradentro" never reached Real del Monte.[65] No such punishments were imposed on the men of the Veta Vizcaína. Labor was precious in New Spain.

There was only one formal appeal. Officials of the village of Tetitlán said Marcelo Estrada, twenty-seven years old, a bailer and an Indian, was a good worker, always paid his tribute, and was needed to support his dependents. Estrada was one of those rare people who knew his rights. Knowing that Indians deserved legal protection to be treated "with special commiseration and equity because of their misery and country ways, and their judgments should be mitigated."[66] He begged not to be sent to die in the fortress, "for if I die, my aged mother, [my] wife, and my small children will die, too."[67] Gamboa said he could not change the sentence and ordered him to start for Vera Cruz.

Marcelo Estrada was right. Indians in the Spanish world were very much like wards of the crown. The fiery propaganda campaign of Fray Bartolomé de Las Casas on behalf of Indians during the terrible and swift depopulation in the sixteenth century had elicited an extensive code of protective legislation in the Indies. In all of these 1767 briefs, Indians were offered the services of an interpreter, but in Real del Monte all free Indians in the mines were bilingual. A special "Protector of the Indians" was appointed, and all Indian suspects were represented by counsel. There were rules against harsh sentences. Gamboa himself said, "It is forbidden to exile Indians."[68] Yet in these cases, Indians were exiled. Indians were not supposed to work at hard labor on the fortresses, but all the Indians in this case ended up at the *presidio* of Vera Cruz instead of in the sweatshops the law provided.[69]

The theory of protection of Indians and the tactics of national defense created a dialectic where the legal and traditional rights of "God's Innocents" were sacrificed to the exigencies of Spain's military preparedness. The viceroy's commutations of sentences may be interpreted in the light of that contradiction. Viceroy Marqués de Croix was living in the hangover of the Seven Years' War when Havana, in 1762, was captured by the British. The viceroy's first concern was the defense of Spanish North America. He imposed the punishment of Havana on the "worst" criminals and also increased the labor force at Vera Cruz. The sentences served to punish the suspects and to provide for the national defense at the lowest possible cost. Hard labor in pestilential Havana and malarial Vera Cruz often turned a tour of penal servitude into a death sentence. Gamboa also believed in harsh punishments to deter workers in other mining areas.[70] The hard hand would crush rebellion, restore order, and inspire obedience.

The authorities' "mob-and-rebellion" perspective is easily understood. To men in charge, a riot was disorderly, irrational, defiant, and sometimes drunken violence. Those who participated were "criminals," "provocateurs." But what happens to these experiences if they are interpreted from the workers' point of view, by the light of a "different hue"? Their interpretation of "riot" was a value judgment, and it was never descriptive to begin with, except to catch the authorities' negative reactions. The concept "collective action" emerges to find a focus. The participants become members of a community. Their organized protest becomes "direct action."

Direct action is a way of claiming community participation and exercising political power collectively. People join together to choose a face-to-face confrontation as a means of articulating and defending their own rational special interests. This kind of rebellion is neither revolution nor the Apocalypse of class war. It is what we used to call in the 1960s a "zap action," a guerrilla tactic, planned but contained in time, confined in theme to a single issue.

In Real del Monte people hated and feared the press gangs. When their own leaders were co-opted as deputy recogedores, they resented and feared them even more. They could not use the non-violent, reform, legal tactics the strike had taught them. Press gangs were legal, so any kind of protest against them was illegal. Besides, the workers of Real del Monte wanted more than just to protest. They wanted to end press gangs forever. The authorities liked to talk about "rioters" and "rebellion" as if the "viciousness" of workers was inherent or a pathological allergic disorder which came from going down mines. What they never admitted was that it was a response, a reaction to the violence indwelling in the system. No one ever explained this contrary point of view better than Gandhi. He said it was government's repression, authorities' protection of legally organized violence, that was "lawless." Thugs are thugs, whether they are legal or not. Laws can be unjust and official at the same time. In this situation the criminal court system itself was organized not for justice but for repression. Gandhi might have read these briefs, for he said, "Sentences were passed unwarranted by evidence and in flagrant violation of justice."[71] This is how and why the mine workers of Real del Monte resorted to stones.

Afterwards, they demonstrated that they had learned the most important lesson a strike can teach a worker: an appreciation for what labor power is and what workers can accomplish if they withdraw it. Some did what they said they would do: "If our just grievance has no tangible result, . . . we swear that we will desert the mines and move where we can seek our living with more ease."[72]

An inspection in April 1767 revealed a 70 *percent reduction* in the work force of the Veta Vizcaína. Pedro de Leoz found only 87 barras where 311 had labored before: "Even though the recogedores took great care, they could not find more people. The lack of workers is visible and results in the nothing to which the work of the mines is reduced, prejudicing the royal treasury, the public, and the owner. . . . the [28] levels that have been made ready to mines are abandoned."[73] None of the workers on the payroll, despaired Leoz, seemed to know what they were doing.

An analogy with the "desert year" of 1732 may help make the point. In 1732 an inspection team found 130 barras at work; in 1767 there were only 87. In 1732 San Cayetano was working at a profit, but the rest were in ruins. In 1770 Romero de Terreros had only 3 mines producing ore: Santa Agueda, Santa Teresa, and La Palma. San Cayetano and La Joya were being drained, and the other mines of Romero de Terreros were stopped. In 1732, 13 mines were working, and 14 were ruined in Real del Monte. In 1770, 5 mines were working, 2 were being drained, 9 were stopped, and 14 were abandoned in Real del Monte. Despite the time and money and effort that had produced the bonanzas of the early 1760s, the mines of Pedro Romero de Terreros in 1770 were, authorities testified, once again a "desert." Only 6 were working according to ordinance, 23 were maintained by contrivance, and of the 133 mines of Real del Monte, Pachuca, and Atotonilco El Chico 97 were stopped or deserted. If the purpose of a strike is to shut down an industry, the men of the Veta Vizcaína made their point effectively and decisively.[74]

Official treasury statistics also show the consequences of work stoppage. They suggest that silver production fell in 1768 to a level lower than the "desert" José de Bustamante encountered when he and his associates took hold of the venture of the Veta Vizcaína in 1744. As a result of the strike and the aftermath of direct action, silver production in the Pachuca area declined by almost a half.[75]

The workers' strike was a success. Their direct action made its point and succeeded in the Veta Vizcaína even as it failed in the Morán. Some workers left Real del Monte. They did not have to sit and wait to starve. Wherever there was silver in New Spain, there might be work. Each mining Real was a world unto itself; blacklisting did not seem effective. When authorities tried to discover "criminals" in other areas, they failed. Some workers moved to Pachuca, Cerezo, Atotonilco el Grande, Atotonilco el Chico. Those miners who remained in Real del Monte worked for the company, worked for other mine owners, or went on their own to exploit what ore might be left in old mines. Some hid out in the mountains to protect themselves and lived the best they could. Workers won, they lost, they survived.

Authorities fumed and figured over one final enticing set of incentives— how to induce Romero de Terreros out of exile in San Miguel and back to the stopes of the Veta Vizcaína. The incentives they offered were great indeed, and Terreros emerged from this most serious labor conflict in eighteenth-century Mexico as a nobleman and the greatest capitalist in New Spain.

!¡

Pedro Romero de Terreros

Through it all, Pedro Romero de Terreros exiled himself in his refinery of San Miguel Regla, feeling himself a victim of the malice of his workers and the ineffectiveness of the authorities, and plotting his reward.

After his long night ride to safety in August 1766, Terreros stayed away from public life. He did not go to Pachuca, he would not go to Real del Monte. Though authorities asked him nicely and tempted him with honors, he would not go to Mexico City. He would not go anywhere. Authors who care have disagreed about why he stayed in San Miguel. Luis Chávez Orozco said it was because he was brooding a righteous indignation and was bent on displaying himself as victim.[1] Alan Probert reacted to this idea by evoking a kind of Red Scare to defend the owner's nobility of spirit: "Labor apologists blame D. Pedro for everything in their zeal to damn the capitalist system. They have been particularly critical of his taking refuge at San Miguel hacienda to look after his juvenile family, suggesting his absence merely denoted petulance."[2]

If attitudes are to be probed, it is not hard to find Romero de Terreros' own reasons for barricading himself away from Real del Monte. His workers, foiled at trying to kill him once, might at last succeed, killing him and leaving his children orphans. He feared for his life and their security. But it is not always wise to ponder attitudes overlong. It is behavior, after all, which provides the true grist of history. The fact is the boss did not spend all his time "feeling." Rather, with his wits and experience and single-minded determination, he set about making the most of his fortune: multiplying it through shrewd capital investments and applying it to exalt the honor and status of his family. The time was well spent. No individual in New Spain ever captured more status symbols or diversified his wealth through so many different economic ventures. The success was partially accomplished with rugged individualism, hard work, canny intelligence, application of the right resources at the right time, and phenomenal good luck. That concept has been defined: "What is termed luck is commonly the result of swift comprehension and firm grasp of opportunities."[3] And at each step the Spanish crown was both his right hand and his great benefactor.

Of all the status symbols in New Spain, a noble title best proved, now and forever, that a man had "made it." A title was a hedge against the charge of "nouveau riche." It testified that for generations the family had worshipped in the Holy Catholic faith, led a respectable life, and married only "nice" girls. A title conferred immortal respectability to its holder and his heirs. Thenceforth, he was a king's man of the highest repute. It was admirable to have a knighthood in a military order, as Pedro Romero de Terreros did in the Order of Calatrava, or to serve on a city council or as honorary peace officer as he did in Querétaro. It gave status a boost to marry into the nobility, as he did when he married the daughter of the Condesa de Miravalle. But to wield the king's own shield against suspicions that one was immersed in materialism to a fault, there was nothing like a noble title.[4]

And Pedro Romero de Terreros received not only one, he received three. In the midst of his sad exile from the mines, he was granted, in September 1768, the title of Conde de Santa María Regla. He paid ten thousand pesos to have it permanently exempted from the yearly noble tax of *lanzas*. At last he was a millionaire and more. His lackeys called him to breakfast as "Su Señoría." His clerks presented the paperwork to "Señor Conde." And then he wanted more. He asked for, and received in 1777, two more titles for his younger sons, Marqués de San Cristóbal and Marqués de San Francisco. If it is quantity that proves a man's worth, his family had the documents to insinuate that they were the bluest bloods in the kingdom of New Spain. Pedro Romero de Terreros could not buy everything for his children. But he did the best he could.

The dialectical dilemma of great wealth in colonial Mexico played itself out when the craving for status was satisfied, and the bills for the noble lifestyle began to drain investment capital. Families with titles were required by law to maintain conspicuous consumption commensurate with the honor of a title of Castile. Pedro Romero de Terreros had a head start. Along with the mines, adits, and tools of the mining enterprise, he had inherited from José Alejandro de Bustamante the beautiful house in San Miguel Regla and the town house in Pachuca. While his wife was still alive, he bought and remodeled a convent in Mexico City into an urban palace worthy of her. But even so, the costs of living were high.[5] The solution, the synthesis that reconciled investment for status with drain on capital, was entail.

If the title conferred dignity, entail was intended to assure the sustaining of wealth by assigning a fixed portfolio of assets to underwrite and perpetuate the noble life-style. So Romero de Terreros asked the king for, and received, three entails. Associated with the county of Regla were mines, refineries, the ex-Jesuit harvest haciendas, and great houses. All the mines of the Veta Vizcaína were included. The other entails were mainly rural, although one was assigned an income from pulquerías, shops, and town houses.[6]

Through it all Pedro Romero de Terreros preserved decorum and simplicity in his private life. Antonio de Ulloa described the Conde de Regla as the wealthiest man in the world in the 1770s. His clothes, deportment, table, and life-style were not ostentatious but rather as unassuming as those of a man of middling income. For fun, Ulloa said, the conde inspected his mines and the workshops of his refineries and gave liberally to charity. Though his possessions were "limitless," he was always modest.[7]

Pedro Romero de Terreros might have been in a sort of limbo in terms of his work as developer of mines, but not in his relations with Spain. His requests received priority in Madrid, and the affirmative responses of his sovereign were swift and sure. If the high councils of empire were trying to coax him out of retirement, they could not have done more.

It was not all for status, and he was hardly "in retirement." What he was putting together, there in the exile of San Miguel Regla, was the biggest real estate deal in the history of colonial Mexico.

In June 1767, the Jesuits were expelled from New Spain, and their properties, confiscated by the crown, were put up for sale to private enterprise. Pedro Romero de Terreros chose the most lucrative harvest haciendas which had belonged to the Jesuit novitiate of Tepotzotlán and the Jesuit College of San Pedro y San Pablo. Among those was the million-peso Santa Lucía, historically the greatest sheep ranch in America. La Gavia produced everybody's favorite clean white pulque as well as wheat and livestock. Jalpa, valued at half a million pesos, was considered to be the largest and most beautiful hacienda in the Valley of Mexico. All in all, there were five great properties with a purchase price of more than a million pesos. Romero de Terreros paid 700,000 pesos down in a complicated combination of cash and credit. After the death of the first Conde de Regla, Miguel Domínguez, who later gained fame as a defender of textile workers and husband of Insurgent heroine La Corregidora, thwarted the crown's attempt to collect another 999,000 pesos. The Conde de Regla had turned from lodes and stamp mills to ranching, grain and vegetable fields, and pulque production. However, most of the great haciendas he leased to tenants.[8] What land did best in colonial Mexico was to assure its owner a sure and generous supply of credit— whether he was in residence or not. For a man who was supposed to be sulking, Pedro Romero de Terreros was in fact, very, and profitably, and spectacularly busy.

He showered succor upon the crown itself. In 1767 he placed 400,000 pesos as a loan to aid Viceroy Marqués de Croix, and gave Viceroy Bucareli 800,000 pesos at no interest. Later some of these funds were used to underwrite the establishment of the Monte de Piedad, the national pawn shop in Mexico City, whose purpose was to "restore the dignity of the poor." Another 150,000 pesos bailed out the tobacco monopoly. In 1776 the Conde de Regla contributed to the national defense (in the war where Britain was the enemy, and France and the new United States were the allies) by raising 200,000 pesos, in cash and credit, to build a warship of eighty cannons in Havana. It was launched the year before he died. In his son's time the ship, "Nuestra Señora de Regla," saw action at the battle of Trafalgar (where France was the enemy and Britain Spain's ally). Pedro Romero de Terreros did not neglect God. His will listed more than a quarter of a million pesos donated for church work.[9] He backed what he believed in, God and the king, with almost as much money and energy as he spent on creating wealth.

It is only when this great burst of activity and generosity, occurring after the strike, is understood that we can responsibly return to explore the feelings of Pedro Romero de Terreros about his workers in the mines. Everyone else appreciated his efforts, everyone else applauded him, everyone else acceded to his will. His employees, uniquely, had tried to kill him. He survived because he was hidden in the fodder; he really escaped by "Divine Providence," because the priest saved him when his life was truly in danger. After August 1766, no one threatened him, no one singled him out as the enemy. But he explained it all in a sort of tragic misperception which was reinforced at every turn by the royal authorities in Pachuca: his workers were out to get him. Let us examine an incident that is clearly unrelated and perceive how he lost no time in relating it to himself.

A month after the August 1766 incident in Real del Monte, at the autumn equinox, there was trouble far away in the refinery of Santa María Regla El Salto. Though it had nothing directly to do with the owner, and everything to do with foremen, cruel punishments, and private justice, Romero de Terreros added it as a bead to his hoard of resentment, his rosary of griefs. The incident is worth considering because it was not what he thought it was.

The rowdy three-day incident began on September 21, 1766. Authorities interpreted it as another proof of workers' concerted efforts to harass Pedro Romero de Terreros and his managerial staff. However, the real historical precedent for the trouble at El Salto can be seen not in the strike of Real del Monte but in the complaints of forced laborers about the physical abuse Indian men had to endure at the refinery. [10]

The principals, labor and management, were all employees of the stamp mills. The leaders were all free men, men from Pachuca and Pachuquilla. There were strong precedents of prejudice. Management's patrician Peninsular contempt for Mexicans provoked workers' resentment at the pretensions of heavy-handed *gachupines*. The Spanish foreman of the stamp mill seemed to enjoy pushing workers around, for he extended his authority well beyond the tasks of ore grinding. On Saturday evening he came upon two dozen workers gambling outside the refinery and righteously broke up the game. Irritated, the men talked back. Bravely he drew his sword on the astonished card players, then took his pistol and fired at the feet of his "assailants." When they dispersed, his next encounter was with an Indian "lurking" in the patio. He locked the man up for the crime of waiting for his brother. There were past incidents of flogging, fining workers at payday, and imposing humiliating punishments for men caught dallying with women. There were grumbles and even rumors of workers who wouldn't half mind seeing someone give the foreman his comeuppance.

It was payday, early Sunday morning, when the Spanish foreman found a thief. Not a silver or mercury thief or a robber of tools or other such "criminals against the industry," who could be punished on the spot. This thief was a cape thief. The worker had not returned a cloak to the man he had borrowed it from. The foreman officially assumed his role as the deputized commissioner of the royal treasury office in Pachuca. Without any pretense of trial, the foreman seized the worker and tied him to the whipping post. After the first lash a watching woman began to yell in loud, vituperative outrage, and a crowd of about thirty supported her by throwing stones. The foreman, the gatekeeper, and the storekeeper ran to hide in the chapel and at last escaped, as so many authorities escaped in these stories, by Divine Providence. [11]

The incident at El Salto led to a forcible work stoppage but not to a strike. At the shift change, workers were turned away by the persuasion and intimidation of other workers, and for three days the refinery was idle. It was not a strike, because there were no labor demands about work or working conditions. They were not called to collective action because of the job; they were angry at the foreman. By Sunday afternoon what authorities called "an innumerable multitude" had gathered, scaling the wall, throwing rocks, banging at the doors. The crowd damaged none of the machinery and stole nothing—no tools, no silver, no mercury. Incited to riot, they sought only to punish those in charge. They stoned the buildings and yelled, "Death to the gachupines." Rumors of threats with flaming pine torches were allayed by the fact that no fires were set. By Wednesday everyone had returned to work. The lasting damage to the great refinery of El Salto remained only in the marks of stones. There was no damage to machinery; there was no loss; no one was hurt.

Francisco de Gamboa convicted sixteen people. All were condemned to exile and hard labor. One woman was remanded to the protection of a shelter for women. The other, who had been an equal participant and whose language was so foul strong men blanched before it, was also condemned to time in a shelter. [12]

Gamboa did not rebuke management directly, but he rooted out the practice of private justice and private jails. Only royal authorities could try and could sentence culprits, and then only after an official investigation.

The only link between the tumulto at El Salto and the strike was the owner, and he was an indirect link. But to him it was obvious. All the troublemakers were his employees. All the workers involved were demonstrably not docile, subservient, and obedient. He felt personally assaulted—again. Authorities acted on the premise. Escapees from El Salto probably hid in their homes in Pachuca and Pachuquilla, but no one searched for them there. Pedro de Leoz rode straight for Real del Monte. That he found none of the culprits is irrelevant. This is how authorities wove a network of conspiracy that never really existed, a fabric of fear like the emperor's new clothes.

Reconsider the riots that occurred after the strike of August 1766:

September 21, 1766	riot at El Salto
October 14, 1766	nonviolent protest at the Dolores
November 4, 1766	nonviolent protest against the Veta Vizcaína recogedores
December 22, 1766	riot, with stones and freeing of workers, against the Morán recogedores
January 1767	nonviolent protest against the Morán recogedores
February 7, 8, 1767	violent riot against the Morán recogedores (with property damage)
after that:	not a single incident or act of protest or violence in Real del Monte

None of the incidents subsequent to the strike threatened Pedro Romero de Terreros; the workers never mentioned his name. Violence was directed only against those applying unjust, unwarranted force brutally and directly. But authorities linked them all together, and the owner read into the events proof that his workers were out to destroy him.

Pedro Romero de Terreros might have, probably did, pardon his assailants as individuals in his prayers, but what he really wanted was a collective vengeance, to make his workers suffer as they made him suffer. He found his champion in Pedro de Leoz, mayor of Tulancingo and special royal investigator. There was peace in Real del Monte from 1767 to 1769, partly, I suspect, because Pedro de Leoz left town to persecute the Windward pirates.[13] But when Leoz returned, it was revealed to him that the peace in Real del Monte was only a mask. (There had been, of course, no further violence, not one rebellious incident since February 1767.) It was revealed to him that under the calm churned malevolent rebellion. There were traitors and unquiet spirits to be crushed. Leoz helped Terreros find surcease from fear by seeking to allay his every suspicion. Were there suspects still at large? Find them and banish them. Did motives for discord still exist? Root them out. Leoz was a frequent visitor at San Miguel Regla, and so much were he and Pedro Romero de Terreros in accord that it is impossible to tell which idea was whose. But it is certain that Leoz said publicly exactly what Romero de Terreros wanted to hear.

How did Pedro Romero de Terreros feel? He was *angry* at how things were. He maintained that his mines had been ruined by the "hostility, ferocity, and insolence" of his workers. Mexico City had been influenced to do nothing because of rumors of mismanagement "without basis and without truth."[14] He hated the way Gamboa had resolved the dispute. He deplored the lax discipline in the few mines still working. Leoz said in his report: "The management and methods used today are contrary to the conde's orders. All his experience and knowledge of mining oppose them."[15] He wanted to pay peons and manual laborers three reales, not four. He wanted to punish anyone who resisted the recogedores with two hundred lashes *and* eight years' hard labor in the fortresses. He *liked* the old system of mixing. When miners were allowed to select the portion of the mixture they wanted, they always took the best and robbed the owner.[16]

The answer? To abolish partidos entirely. Leoz said, "Before anything else, it is indispensable that the word "partidos" be eliminated at the root and never be uttered in the mining industry again."[17]

In a way Leoz's brief against partidos is a sermon on how to reform, from above, men who are vicious, murderous, lazy, incorrigible thieves. Workers should not live where they pleased because the barrancas were "so far from judge, God, and the law."[18] They should not drink, play cards, or frequent taverns. They should never question a command; if they did, the law and the soldiers should make them regret it. They should not be allowed to choose where they were to work because they would avoid the dry diggings and thus cheat the owner. They should work contentedly for their wages. Only radical means could restrain workers who were "all consumed with trying to rob their owners." Only abolishing partidos could transform their crimes into hard-working sobriety.[19]

Partidos, Pedro de Leoz began his official tirade, were "the perdition of the industry, the moth of investment capital, and the mother of all vices."[20] They were "insufferable," "irrational, unjustified, illegal, and pernicious."[21] Partidos made men greedy, made them thieves who would steal from the company, from the king, and from God. Greed made workers insolent and disrespectful.

Leoz moved on to new heights of passion when he said that without partidos the mines would be more healthful. High risks did not justify the reward of partidos. The work of the mine was not dangerous. Mining, he said, was no harder than being a muleteer, no more tiring than being a reaper; yet these workers did not get shares. The sailor on the high seas, the soldier in battle, the peon in a black powder factory ran more risks than the miner, and they did not get shares. Of course, the work of an ore refinery was healthful too, but even if it were harmful the smelter and those who worked with mercury settled for their two-and-a-half reales a day in wages, and they asked for no partido. Leoz had a fine flair for drama. He insisted that the owner ran more risks than did the miners. The work of miners was the same, risks or not, and Taxco and Zimápam did not pay partidos.[22] (Leoz neglected to point out that every other mining Real in New Spain did.)

Without partidos all evils from robbery to drunkenness to rebellion would be expunged. Miners, for their wage, would bring up four bags of ore a shift. If more bags were filled, the owner would take all the ore, and the worker would be paid extra cash. The owner would pay pikemen and carpenters four reales and peons, manual laborers, and drainage workers three. Independent ore refiners would be driven out of business. The owner would also employ forced Indian labor. As recompense for all he had suffered, Romero de Terreros asked to purchase mercury from the crown at cost. Since the price of mercury had, in 1768, been lowered 25 percent for all refiners, the crown never granted Pedro Romero de Terreros the privilege enjoyed in Taxco and on the Morán.

Pedro de Leoz's mandate for change was reported directly to the Attorney General José Antonio Areche, and Areche counseled the viceroy of New Spain. Areche was positive, impressed, and instrumental in furthering Romero de Terreros's cause. Vigorously, Areche endorsed every point in Leoz's argument.

Areche's brief shows clearly how the Bourbon efforts to stimulate economic development skewed governmental perceptions away from the old-fashioned sense of proportion and towards entrepreneurial monopoly. Leoz was "modern," Areche said. "Gamboa's Ordinances have proved quite useless."[23] Miners did not deserve the "unmerited piety" with which Gamboa had treated them. They repaid him with hostility, obstinance, and incorrigibility. They had learned nothing from his clemency. They would have, should have learned from swift punishment and the death penalty, as the people of the Provincias Internas had learned from José de Gálvez. The ringleaders of Real del Monte should not have been shipped out to Havana; they should have been executed.[24]

Areche did not trouble to disguise his disdain for workers, even as he confessed their power. They were vicious, lazy, rude, malicious, and irrational. All they wanted to do was work a day or two and "eat grossly the rest of the week."[25] Areche believed that the strike had raised the consciousness of workers. They had united to resist, and now "they dare to think their united forces have made them respectable and fearsome."[26] In our time it may be difficult to discern class war in events that occurred so long ago. But Areche saw it in the attitudes of workers at Real del Monte: "Ultimately, they harbor in their gut a mortal hatred of owners and management, who, well aware of their vices and habits, live in mortal terror."[27] Areche, Leoz, and Romero de Terreros harmonized their prescription in a coda: abolish the partidos and punish the unquiet spirits still in Real del Monte. Only then would there be peace and submission.[28]

Areche sent his resolutions to his great friend, Visitor General José de Gálvez, reminding him that the Conde de Regla was the "finest miner in the kingdom," who worked not for his own self-interest but for a posterity in which his mines would be a permanent source of wealth.[29]

Although in 1769 Gálvez had decided that partidos should be left alone,[30] Areche and Leoz changed his mind. Besides his proficiency in executing pious people, José de Gálvez had a real talent for co-opting other people's ideas and writing them as his own. Although he confessed that he had been so busy that he had learned nothing of mining, he drafted a new set of mining ordinances to replace Gamboa's, and they guaranteed Pedro Romero de Terreros almost everything he wanted. There was one innovation, pikemen should be paid six reales a day.[31] Gálvez counseled the viceroy to reward the Conde de Regla for his wealth, his intelligence, and his genius. Partidos must go, forced Indian labor and soldiers must be summoned.[32]

Viceroy Marqués de Croix passed the draft ordinances to the executive advisory committee of the Audiencia, but they were never promulgated. His successor, Viceroy Bucareli, found the draft in a file cabinet and assumed that Croix had let it go because his counselors had given him conflicting advice.[33]

Pedro Romero de Terreros did not give up. In September 1771 he wrote to the king himself. He confessed how "melancholy" he was. Although he was spending a thousand pesos a week for the drainage of the Veta Vizcaína, he could not make a profit because of the "hostility, ferocity, and vengeance" of his workers. Before he could consider returning to work, he made it clear he must have "remedies." "Criminals" must be flushed out and driven from Real del Monte itself. Force alone could influence his workers. His mines must be filled with docile Indian labor forced in from surrounding villages. Only if he obtained these remedies would he resume his personal supervision of Real del Monte and invest the capital necessary to rehabilitate the industry.[34] The riots had seared his soul with terror; now it was time for the workers to be terrified of royal authority.

Viceroy Bucareli knew that no other fortune could be induced to take the risks in Real del Monte. Manuel José de Moya had tried and was failing. The viceroy told Spain there was another looming problem. In time Pedro Romero de Terreros would divide his fortune among his seven children. Then no one in New Spain would have the capital to bring silver out of the Veta Vizcaína.[35]

Bucareli moved to smooth his path by authorizing the use of terror against the men of Real del Monte, not to prosecute them but to threaten into exile those who had for so long troubled the reverie of the Conde de Regla. The secret list, compiled by Pachuca and added to by Mexico City, enumerated about eighty names, including "Fulanos" and "the brothers ———." No list of crimes was appended, no systematic effort made to establish who was where. One principal striker was on the list, envoy Juan Barrón. Seven affirmers of the July 28 grievance were named, but no one knew where all of them were. Seven spokesmen for pikemen and for peons were named. One affirmer and one spokesman, apparently distrusted by both labor and authorities, can be identified as deputy recogedores in the riots of 1767. Four other rioters from 1767 were accused, but three of the four had "whereabouts unknown." The rest of those named were called *reos* (offenders, culprits). They were the "usual suspects" of the district of Pachuca and Tulancingo: men swift with stones or knives, bullies and brawlers, the insolent, offenders against the institution of marriage, pot companions, thieves, fornicators, "ravishers," rowdies. No warrants were served, no investigation charged, no trial held.[36]

At first the exile of the "proud," "disrespectful," "idle," and "ungrateful" was set at ten leagues roundabout Real del Monte. When the royal officials of Pachuca pointed out that the distance would not purge the refineries, it was extended to twenty leagues.[37]

On July 26, 1772, the viceroy's proclamation was read in the plazas: anyone named by the list had one week's grace to remove from the mines, towns, and refineries and to send himself into exile. If he refused or returned, he would face an automatic penalty of five years' hard labor in the presidios. For a week deputies observed, then they reported that none of the accused was to be seen in Real del Monte, Pachuca or Omitlán. Only in Atotonilco el Chico a miner who had suffered a fall at work could not be moved. On March 1 the royal authorities of Pachuca told the viceroy that the Reales had been scoured of "unquiet spirits" and disturbers of the peace. The region, at last, was "tranquil."[38]

On March 1, 1772, Captain Agustín Callis (Compañía Franca de Voluntarios de Cataluña) marched out of Mexico City with a detachment of infantry: two lieutenants, two sergeants, thirty-six soldiers, and one drummer. In Pachuca they picked up five cavalry from the Dragones de México. The viceroy thought, because the terrain was so rugged, soldiers would be more effective than cavalry for apprehending those who might try to hide or return. Foot soldiers and horsemen arrived in Real del Monte on March 4. The royal officials of Pachuca had rented a large house for them and furnished it with beds, mattresses, and sheets and provisioned it, the bills paid by the royal treasury of Pachuca.[39]

The viceroy's orders to Captain Callis defined the means to keep the peace. The soldiers should treat miners with moderation, though they should not be too friendly, and should guard against provocation, discord, and disputes. Requests to take arms against working men should be obeyed when they were given by the royal officials and district magistrate of Pachuca or by the Conde de Regla. The area was to be surveyed by day and night patrols. Arms and ammunition should be kept in good condition, and discipline maintained by frequent inspections and reviews. No soldier might sleep outside the barracks, and all should strive for behavior that would be considered respectable and above reproach.[40] The troops saw no action, never fired a shot, and remained comfortably lodged in their house. For the first time there were troops stationed in Real del Monte; for the first time the military was ordered to give priority to the task of disciplining industrial labor and their disorderly families and neighbors.

Pedro Romero de Terreros was pleased. The soldiers were at ready, the Real was purged of reos, the right to compel Indian villagers to work on the Veta Vizcaína was reaffirmed. In 1773 Viceroy Bucareli sent him a present, and Romero de Terreros replied, "I cannot but give you my tribute of thanks . . . you have me enslaved with so much favor."[41]

Favor, but not every favor. Pedro Romero de Terreros had wanted, demanded, the abolition of partidos. He had received the support of official investigator Pedro de Leoz, Attorney General José Antonio Areche, and Visitor General José de Gálvez, subsequently an influential member of the Council of the Indies in Spain. In opposition Viceroy Bucareli adamantly refused to alter the traditional system of incentives for labor. His reasons reveal some of the abiding ideals that justified the Spanish imperial system. Once again a viceroy stopped to consider in New Spain the way things were. Bucareli decreed that the partidos would survive, and he explained why:

> I hold as one of the principal maxims of good government not to change old customs when they are not harmful or when they have established themselves as good and of considerable utility. The practice of giving partidos to workers in the mines is, I understand, almost as old as the mines themselves and is so universal in the kingdom that there is scarcely a Real where they do not exist.[42]

Adhering to tradition meant reestablishing the possibility of the greatest good for the greatest number. The viceroy would not tolerate the idea that the price for developing industry must be paid in high unemployment and the end to competition. If the partidos were abolished, a multitude of independent smelters would be ruined and with them the common people and the poor who sold them ores. The big refiners would thrive, the rest would suffer. Since partidos, the most usual form of mine wages, were widespread in New Spain and had not provoked any disturbances with workers anywhere else, Bucareli concluded that partidos were not the problem. Only Pedro Romero de Terreros had difficulty with labor. His predecessor, José Antonio de Bustamante, had responded to the complaints of his workers peacefully, by paying partidos. No other Real had ever experienced so much labor agitation.

Why Real del Monte? Bucareli believed that discontent had come both from the "depraved fraud" of the workers and from the excessive punishments and manipulations of disbursements by management. If tampering with the partidos had caused Real del Monte so much trouble, abolishing partidos might cause what Bucareli called a "general revolution." Though some miners were probably vicious and bold, the viceroy was sure that "there are probably many honorable ones with large families." Without the partidos even decent men might join a "flood of bandits." Although the Conde de Regla had the vast resources of an opulent fortune to pay high wages, most mine owners in New Spain relied on partidos to reward labor. Many mine owners with great expectations paid partidos, but not cash wages, both workers and owners hoping for a bonanza. Small owners provided tools and candles, workers provided labor, and they shared the profits. If partidos were abolished, Pedro Romero de Terreros would be satisfied, and the majority of mine owners in New Spain would be ruined.

The viceroy, with the blessing of the Spanish crown, reaffirmed the kingdom's protection of working men by decreeing that Gamboa's Ordinances, so sensitive to the special interests of workers, were still in effect. By retaining partidos, heretofore an extra-legal privilege, now a royally endorsed entitlement, workers would benefit and the competition of small refiners would be assured. Pedro Romero de Terreros could have his troops and exiles and his forced Indian labor; but he could not expand his enterprise at the expense of labor or other sectors of the industry. The essence of this aspect of Spanish rule was protection and proportion, a balancing of diverse interests so as to conserve the weight of their separate integrity. The Conde de Regla could have everything he wanted until what he wanted threatened to unbalance other interests of labor and capital. This is why the viceroy and the king denied him new ordinances which would have abolished partidos. Partidos persisted at Real del Monte for another one hundred years and more, through Independence and the nineteenth century. What the crown had rescued was the principal wage system and profit-sharing mechanism for industrial labor in New Spain.

These are the policies that brought peace to Real del Monte. There was one more. Before Pedro Romero de Terreros returned to work, he had contrived one more "remedy:" the removal of one more "unquiet spirit"—the priest of Real del Monte, who had saved his life.

CHAPTER 8

The Priest

There is a very human story to the aftermath of the strike at Real del Monte, and it chronicles the disgrace and exile of the workers' favorite priest from the parish church. It reveals Pedro Romero de Terreros's cold vengeance and tells how bureaucrats in Pachuca and Mexico City imposed their authority to impugn and submerge old Christian concepts of the duty of the clergy to support and succor ordinary people. In this case the Catholic Church in Mexico knew and told the truth, but religious authorities did not dare to defy the secular government. It is a story of charity, dedicated service, small town scandal, malice, and, in the end, bitter injustice.

Dr. José Rodríguez Díaz came to serve as rector of the parish church of Real del Monte in 1756. The good reports of his ministry stressed "the great love and respect with which all his flock venerates and respects him."[1] He went about his duties with dedication, compassion, and zest. One friend remembered him as quiet and reflective: "He lives in his house with books in his hands."[2]

No one denied that he was an inspired and eloquent preacher, who exhibited "Christian zeal" in the pulpit. The priest who replaced him said, "in this ministry no one can equal him."[3] He gave the sermon once a week, then assisted his curates in the ceremony, and sang Mass and preached on all high feasts. He left the sacraments of the townsfolk to his four curates. He did not say Mass every day, and when he did, it was in the early morning. He said Mass in the mines occasionally and visited the sick and took extreme unction to the dying himself. His congregation thought he was, in everything, an exemplary pastor.[4]

All his supporters praised him for beautifying the church. He bought a new organ; clothed the images sumptuously; decorated the sanctuary with jewels, ornaments, silver and gold trim; and provided the baptistry with a new font and the two unmatching church towers with bells. A presbyter testified that this had cost Dr. Díaz 3500 pesos of his own money.[5]

Dr. Díaz was not just the respectable businessman's priest. In his fourteen years as minister, he had built up the congregation to include mine workers, smelters, craftsmen, merchants, doctors, foremen, manual laborers—most of the people who lived in that town. A sixteen-year-old surgeon testified that he was especially good with youth and children. He distributed eight pesos a week to the poor in the cemetery on Sunday and, as the Bible directs, gave away more secretly. He administered all the sacraments to the poor and married them, baptized them, buried them, fed and clothed them free. He paid the way of poor children to attend his catechism classes in the cemetery. When the price of corn went up to four pesos, he bought out the supply of a storekeeper and sold corn to the people at three pesos. He was cherished because anyone, rich or poor, young or old, man or woman, could talk to him easily, find a sympathetic listener, and take comfort from him. As time went on, he found a concern for prisoners and visited them in jail, counseled them, and assisted their families. Even in his role as ecclesiastical judge, he was, his flock said, benign, sagacious, humane, and moderate in his verdicts. The old deputy district magistrate summed it up: "The priest is, and has been ever since he came, the father of all."[6]

Influence is an ability to sway people, to persuade them, to use the esteem others feel to stimulate them to change their behavior. But that is not what Pedro de Leoz meant when he condemned the priest's influence over workers, saying that Dr. Díaz "permits his flock to live without reins." He dispassionately confessed that he had a personal reason for vengeance, "When the workers stoned my house and I called the dragoons, the priest publicly made fun of me."[7] In working out his long investigation, Leoz revealed what he meant as influence and stacked the questions for the witnesses. "Did he influence the workers? Or, at least, give them justification? . . . Didn't he always dominate the hearts of the workers? Didn't he pardon some criminals?"[8]

Because the authorities defined riot as "mob" and inferred that the "rabble" would not have moved without pressure from the outside, they came to identify the priest as "agent" and cause for the tumultos. From Leoz to the royal officials of Pachuca to the powers in Mexico City, Dr. Díaz's "influence" over workers came to mean collusion, conspiracy, and if not leadership, then guilt by association. That is what Francisco Lira, timekeeper of La Joya, meant when he testified that the priest "influenced and has continued influencing and sheltering the workers."[9]

The royal officials of Pachuca really did not need to investigate. They already knew all the answers. "The leaders of these events were inspired by the parish priest, who, making them reflect on the scriptures, came to the conclusion that while their just desires were not attended to, they did not have the obligation to obey the foremen or even the owner of the mines."[10]

When the viceroy passed on the indictment against the priest, the Archbishop of Mexico was surprised. He said that he had heard only good reports of Dr. Díaz. The priest had done a good job, and he had fulfilled his mission when he calmed the riots and prevented greater damage to the mines. A man of the cloth in the Spanish world was protected by the ecclesiastical *fuero*, a code and court of law. The archbishop was supposed to be the final arbiter of the behavior of his priests; and he found no fault in Dr. Díaz. But the immunity of the clergy was long undermined. The viceroy simply insisted, without explanation, that the priest be separated from his parish forthwith. With no further protest, Archbishop Lorenzana directed Dr. Díaz to leave the church he had served faithfully for fourteen years. Dr. Díaz sensibly protested that to pay the penalty before he was tried or found guilty was unjust, but neither church nor state listened to him. After trying to explain that Leoz's charges were "full of hatred and passion,"[11] he, like the toughs of his parish, went into exile. When he went to Mexico City to prepare his defense, the viceroy would not allow him to remain in the capital.

It was hard for townspeople in Real del Monte to understand what the priest had done wrong. Influence over miners? Of course he had. He pacified a crowd that had tasted blood and calmed them more than once. He turned the anger of the crowd in the churchyard to a request he himself had carried to Pedro Romero de Terreros. He kept angry miners on the side of the law by counseling them to present a petition of grievances to the royal officials in Pachuca. And on the day after the riot, when no one would work and people roamed the mountainsides, he persuaded drainage workers and manual laborers to repair ropes and whims to prevent the drifts from filling with water, and he had paid their wages himself. He was, many said, a peacemaker, and they respected him for it. A priest concluded, "He is a brave man who has the esteem of his flock."[12] And, not the least, he had, at great risk, saved the life of Pedro Romero de Terreros and his men.

The power of Pedro Romero de Terreros in this mining town cannot be exaggerated. He had more money than anyone in the region. He was the largest employer. He had the ear of authorities in Pachuca, Mexico City, and Madrid. If he had pulled out his investments, Real del Monte would have been left to smaller capitalists and the tender mercies of Moya and the mines of Morán, and Moya went bankrupt in 1773. If Pedro Romero de Terreros had spoken on behalf of the priest who saved his life, Dr. Díaz would have gone free. But in his circuitous way, he condemned him. He wrote the viceroy:

> In the private dispatch in which Your Excellency instructs me to inform you of the conduct of the person you mention in your letter of the ninth (which, with all due respect I received today) . . . I cannot express what deep anguish in my heart it costs me to say . . . I know with the certainty acquired from being there, and afterwards confirmed by infallible hearsay [*de infalibles oídas*], and in the pain of my heart I repeat it, that he did have influence . . . I have [also] heard from dispassionate persons that he has not been what he should have. [13]

The boss never mentioned that the priest had saved his life and his men and his mines, or that he had worked tirelessly to arbitrate and restore peace in a dangerous situation. The viceroy, of course, understood his use of the word "influence" to mean a culpable role in fomenting sedition and riots in Real del Monte. Did the forgetful millionaire ever remember to return the priest's cloak he had borrowed for his midnight ride to exile?

It may be that Romero de Terreros had another grudge against Dr. Díaz. The priest of Pachuca thought so. He said they had quarreled over parish funds for the slaves of La Palma. But more likely Romero de Terreros resented the many times the priest had interceded in the miners' behalf. Since Leoz had come to the conclusion that the partidos caused riots, and since the priest had encouraged workers to negotiate the partidos, it was easy to condemn Dr. Díaz after the fact. Retroactively, with all the new assumptions, they decided that he had aided the cause of turmoil. The royal officials of Pachuca gave their judgment:

> informants have no doubt that the increase of insolence among the workers is the work of Dr. Díaz and that it was the cause, at least indirectly, of the eruption, for he approved of their grievances, judged them as very justified, influenced those who led them, and helped them with money and efforts. All of this gave pride to the boldness of these ignorant commoners, and the casualties followed. [14]

It was clear to everyone that Pedro Romero de Terreros was actively engaged in ridding the Real of the priest. The administrator of La Palma said it bluntly: "The Conde de Regla has his sword unsheathed and has told the viceroy if this investigation was not conducted correctly, he, in spite of his age, would go to Spain."[15]

Previously, in August 1766, Pedro Romero de Terreros and his men had, in fact, accused the priest of inciting the riot. Francisco de Gamboa reviewed the evidence and concluded that the charges were fabricated from gossip. He was shocked and rebuked the authorities for the ease with which they accused a man of the cloth. He absolved Dr. Díaz and told the viceroy: "The priest, although he did counsel the workers to seek justice by complaining with grievances, cannot be called the inciter of the riots or the cause of the homicides. He is a cultured and cautious subject; he calmed the workers . . . and contributed a great deal to the pacification and the positive results of my commission."[16] But by 1770 Gamboa himself had been exiled to Spain (though he served there with honor as *oidor* in Barcelona) to punish him for defending the Jesuits. Without him "infallible hearsay" concocted an indictment that presumed the priest guilty and ran him out of town before anyone could protest.

Men who later spoke on the priest's behalf represented the *gente decente* of Real del Monte. They were important in that small town, and they not only defended their priest but in doing so revealed the occupations that such a place appreciated. There were twelve merchants, nine independent smelters, seven clergymen, two mine owners, a silver merchant, two surgeons, a druggist, a pulque guard, and Real del Monte's ex-deputy district magistrate. All were Mexican Creoles except for ten merchants born in Spain. A mulatto master tailor also tried to vindicate Dr. Díaz.

The hostile witnesses were the Conde de Regla and his employees—José Marcelo González, ex-administrator of the Veta Vizcaína; Agustín de Subira, administrator of La Palma; Francisco Lira, timekeeper of La Joya, and the Spaniard Gregorio López, new administrator of the Veta Vizcaína. Then there were the new royal authorities—Joaquín Alonso de Allés, new district magistrate, and his deputy, Rosendo Francisco del Campo. Loudest was Manuel Rubí de Celis, who blamed the priest for dispossessing him of the deputy's job. Pedro de Leoz, the royal investigator and prosecutor, and José Antonio Areche, attorney general in Mexico City, were implacably hostile. The priest of Pachuca was also an unfriendly witness. Realizing the prejudice, the defense protested in November 1770 and asked that no testimony be admitted from any of Pedro Romero de Terreros's employees, but it was too late.

Neither defense nor prosecution called on workers for their version of events. But a few mine workers betrayed their priest and, as suspects, made the question of his influence as relevant in 1770 as it had seemed in 1766.

Gamboa had not charged the strike leaders in 1766. The envoys, freed by the crowd after a week's imprisonment, had remained free. In July 1770 Pedro de Leoz was empowered to round up the old conspirators. He netted Juan Barrón. Since there was no charge against him, Leoz let him go. The authorities noted an ominous clue: Barrón asked about the priest, and the priest put in a good word for Barrón. [17]

Another leader (affirmer of the July 28 grievance), Juan González, returned in desperation to Real del Monte because his wife and children were gravely ill. The priest had buried his son free. Agustín Subira said that the priest had been protecting González for a long time. Dr. Díaz had told González to hide from Gamboa and then from Leoz when he came to investigate the tumulto of February 1767. He had, at that time, given González six pesos to go to work in Guanajuato. [18]

Subira had misrepresented the facts, according to eyewitnesses. Pedro de León (a smelter), Juan Yedra (member of the barra that had sent the envoys to Mexico City), Francisco Quintero (a young surgeon), and Francisco Escobar gave another version. On Easter Sunday, April 27, 1770, Juan Gonzélez met the smelter in the churchyard before Mass. The smelter told the distraught miner that it would be better if he left town. Then González went to Atotonilco El Grande, where the priest had gone to escape unpleasantnesses with Leoz. González woke the priest to tell him that Real del Monte was up in arms and that Juan Barrón was under arrest. The priest prodded, as he always did, "What does your conscience tell you to do?" When González insisted on advice, the priest said, "If I were you, I would go someplace where no one knew me." But González did not heed him. Rather, he appeared a week later at La Palma. He told the startled smelter, who was there, that Agustín Subira, the administrator, had called him in and told him that since the priest was implicated in their going to Mexico City, González would be pardoned. The smelter advised him that Subira's word was not enough: he should go to work and the next day throw himself on the mercy of Pedro de Leoz. [19]

González and Juan Yedra turned themselves in at seven o'clock the next morning. The surgeon maintained that Leoz had pardoned them. González and Yedra then went to the house of the smelter for breakfast. Yedra said González rejoiced and said he felt as if he had been "born again." González told his companions that Leoz had directed him to leave town without even going home first, for a warrant would be issued for his arrest. Yedra concluded his statement, "I went home and never knew what road González took."[20]

Leoz maintained that he had never promised González anything and had not let him go, but the truth was, González was gone. The priest and the archbishop both protested that González had implicated the priest in order to save himself, but Mexico City continued to wonder.[21]

Another prisoner, "El Zapatero," sentenced to two years of exile for his part in the August 15 and February 8 tumultos, told authorities that he had broken his exile because his mother told him that a miner's wife told her that her husband and brother-in-law had come home safely on the word of the priest. The prisoner had worked eleven months in the village of Mestitlán. Then he became ill and worked six months at the refinery of El Salto.[22]

The priest's enemies continued to work overtime. Manuel Rubí de Celis concluded, the priest "is the principal reef on which the circulation and current of His Majesty's interests founder."[23] Without the priest as their protector, miners would think only of their work and be more obedient. "He is or was the root and origin of the former revolts and harassments of this Real."[24] Pedro de Leoz added, "The priest protects the principal prisoners."[25] Dr. Díaz defended himself wearily to the archbishop: "If I did give a safe-conduct, it was only when there was no crime."[26]

Townspeople were uncomfortable with the authorities' investigation. They protested that workers everywhere sought advice from a parish priest and held him in high regard. Some of them said why. In Real del Monte the priest was able to influence the people because they knew he esteemed them, loved them, and beyond all doubt, respected them.[27] In eighteenth-century Mexico an educated man who respected workers, appreciated them, and, when their troubles ignited, tried to guide them away from violence without asking them to compromise their concerns, was most rare. Predictably the authorities wanted him out. Pedro de Leoz said, "Let us not lose the opportunity to clean Real del Monte of this pernicious moth."[28]

Authorities clinched their argument by saying that Dr. Díaz was too friendly with miners. He shared their company too eagerly. The royal officials of Pachuca explained it to the viceroy:

> He dealt with them in a familiar manner, with visits, at fandangos and public diversions, and it made him so liked by those people that even today he is so much in command of the goodwill of Real del Monte that anything that is stirred up against the priest is to them most hateful. Their passion is so blind that witnesses have refused to see what they could not have ignored.[29]

Workers liked their pastimes, and so did the priest. There was not doubt about it, Dr. Díaz loved cockfights best. He made long trips to Tulancingo, Mexico City, and nearby towns to cheer, as he cheered in Real del Monte, in the cockpits and in the streets. He even carefully nurtured his own fighting chickens at home. The authorities were especially shocked by his relish for cockfights at night. But they suppressed the fact that he gave up the chickens in 1768. Apparently, he and a dear friend quarrelled over a bet. The friend was deeply troubled and stayed hurt. The priest was so conscience-stricken that he made his confession to the archbishop. After that, Dr. Díaz gave away his fighting cocks and only watched the mains from balconies.[30]

He also loved to play cards day and night. Authorities frowned on the fact that he played with workers. Friendly witnesses assured them that he played with all kinds of people, nice people, too, and often at home.[31]

The subject that stirred authorities into a frenzy was women. Pedro de Leoz claimed that he "tolerated concubinage." Manuel Rubí de Celis licked his lips over the "carnal affections" the priest must be having in his own house. Pedro de Leoz charged that he was immorally involved with a mulatto girl of fourteen. The new deputy said that everyone was aware of "the passion of the priest of Real del Monte."[32]

Women are, and were, after all, the majority, and they entangle themselves in many kinds of relationships with men, complexities that cannot be unraveled in a sentence. There is, they say, in the Hispanic world a deeply rooted jealousy that Spanish-speaking men feel when they see women under the influence of a priest. In our time a priest in Arizona said that priests have a fascination for women because they are men of mystery, otherworldly.[33] Is that fascination also because, in those little villages, priests are the only men who listen and take women seriously? Or maybe it is simply because they are kind. Dr. Díaz had no *barrangana* at Real del Monte; there is no reason to suspect he ever broke his vows of celibacy after he became a priest, but he did share his house with a number of young women.

The relationship that gave the authorities palpitations was one that involved a fourteen-year-old mulatto girl, Lugarda Pozos. The priest visited her often, and she ran freely through his house with the other girls. He took her on trips that lasted a week or more to see cockfights in Tulancingo and Mexico. When he danced with her at a fandango at Tulancingo, people talked. Manuel Rubí de Celis was talking about that dance when he said, "He has courted her publicly." The district magistrate threatened the girl's father with exile unless she stopped seeing the priest.[34] He even forced the family to move. After that, some said they continued to meet, some said they did not. All the witnesses who had been on the trips and promenades said her

family was always present. Her father, a master tailor, said with great dignity that he and his wife had accompanied their daughter on the outings. The
archbishop's investigator did not help much when he explained that the
priest had frequented the houses of two other girls, who subsequently made
honorable marriages with two of the most distinguished men in the territory. And, he made his point, "malicious gossip even saw wrongdoing in
that."[35]

Living with the priest in his house were two women, Ignacia and Bárbara,
the younger eighteen. There was no scandal about them; most people
assumed they were the priest's nieces. But they were not his nieces, they were
his daughters, born to his passion before he became a priest. The
archbishop's man knew the truth and explained that they had gone to live
with their mother, who had made an honorable marriage in Mexico City.
Also living with the priest was a fourteen-year-old orphan named Rafaela
Montalvo. When she was a toddler, her mother died in Pachuca, and she
became the priest's ward. The royal officials "knew" that Rafaela was the
priest's mistress, but people who knew her protested that she esteemed and
loved the priest like a father. The archbishop's man said sharply, no one
would dare imply anything improper between them. Even Augustín de Subira, no friend to the priest, said, "I never heard Rafaela was his concubine
nor do I presume that she was."[36]

Another group of women the priest sheltered were runaway wives. It was
his belief that such women needed a refuge, a safe place to stop and think and
sort out their lives. The old deputy testified that the priest always tried to
reconcile the couples and counsel them, saying "Daughter, was any crime
committed? What does he say? Does your conscience chide you?"[37]

Manuel de Rubí accused the priest of indulging in "carnal affections" with
these distraught wives. When Joaquin de Allés was deputy district magistrate, he stayed in the priest's house and was bothered that the rectory was
turned into a shelter for women. He chided, "People said he only took in the
pretty ones." Allés was caught between the priest and his superior when the
district magistrate accused his own wife of "persistent unchastity." When
she ran away, he was furious. At his insistence, Allés locked her up. She
escaped to the priest; Allés put her away again, but she escaped. Finally, she
was captured and sent to a shelter for women.[38]

When Allés became district magistrate, he took the runaways from the
priest's house. From then on, if there were women in trouble, he punished
them without therapy: unmarried women were sent into exile, and wives
were sent home. He told the priest in a friendly but firm way not to take in

any more women. Manuel de Rubí speculated that this order had come about because the priest had molested them. Even unfriendly witnesses balked at this calumny. Agustín de Subira said the district magistrate had admitted that he had been misinformed. The archbishop's investigator was indignant and ruffled: "All these accusations are false and without evidence. Actually, I left Pachuca saying the district magistrate's intentions were not honorable."[39]

Finally, what else made Pedro de Leoz think that the priest had "tolerated concubinage"? Dr. Díaz baptized illegitimate children or acted as their godfather. The deputy said he himself believed that women who sinned should be exiled; but when he exiled them, they kept running back to the priest. He did admit that the priest often saw to it that women either married later or mended their ways. The priest of Pachuca summed all this up when he said, "Here people talk a lot."[40]

As the investigations went on, passions ran so high that the most minute and mundane activities were scrutinized. Once when the priest's brother sent shrouds from Querétaro, the Father Guardian of the Franciscans in Pachuca claimed them and made a scene when he found out that Dr. Díaz had given them away to the poor. When the niche for Our Lady of the Rosary was finished, the priest arranged a celebration of religious plays in the cemetery although the people had been officially forbidden to assemble.[41] Some lamps were missing from the church, and though a man had been arrested as the thief, the priest was blamed for taking them. The archbishop's observer concluded that the accounting books proved that church ornaments and funds were in order. Dr. Díaz, plainly, was not guilty.[42]

From summer to fall 1770 Manuel de Rubí said he was persecuted by "secret agents of Dr. Díaz," who, disguised with hats pulled over their eyes and bandannas, or perhaps it was sheets, threw stones at his house and at his person and yelled obscenities at him. Eight cavalrymen patrolled Real del Monte to calm his fears, but no connection was ever found to implicate the priest.[43]

The irregularities in the case are troubling. "Infallible hearsay" wrote the prosecution's script. No defense briefs were presented, there was no cross-examination. Four lawyers were appointed to defend the priest, but none contributed anything but their silent presence at interrogations. Only Dr. Nicolás de Velasco, named by the archbishop to observe and protect the ecclesiastical *fuero* rights, set pen to paper on Dr. Díaz's behalf. The priest did choose his own defense witnesses, but the prosecution discounted them as prejudiced. Prosecution witnesses lied. Another example: Agustín de

Subira said that a widow had told him that when her husband died, the priest took from her the keys, title deeds, and coffers of a laymen's church organization (the *cofradía* of Our Lady of the Rosary) and pocketed the money and sold one of its ranches. The widow indignantly denied it, "What Subira said is false, all of it."[44] This was an investigation, not a trial in court. There were summations from the archbishop and his man, but the final sentence came from Mexico City's attorney general for civil affairs.

The archbishop's investigation by Dr. Nicolás de Velasco declared the proceedings improper: "The charges are based on a kind of defamation of character (easily come by in Pachuca). They were hastily done, and no care was taken."[45] Nothing illicit was found in the priest's relationships with women. There were no mentions of midnight visits or unchaperoned behavior. Nothing was improper in his relations with Lugarda Pozos or Rafaela, either. The truth was the archbishop knew that his "nieces" were his daughters and that they had left the Real to live with their mother, who was respectably married. One of the runaway wives had indeed accused someone of improper conduct, but it was the district magistrate, not the priest. Dr. Díaz used to go to cockfights, but he reformed. There was no evidence of any other wrongdoing. The priest's role in the riot of August 1766 was to stop it, not to start it: "All who saw the uprising of 1766 believe, because they were there and experienced it, that Real del Monte owes more to Dr. Díaz than to its discoverers because he was able to preserve it after the uprising."[46] If he had done no more than save the life of Pedro Romero de Terreros, it would be enough to clear him of the charge of "influence." The priest had not freed any convicts, but Velasco was troubled that Juan González had never been found and cross-examined and that Pedro de Leoz, who let him go, had denied it. Velasco told the archbishop that the prosecution used rumor and hearsay, *vagas voces*, instead of facts.

In Mexico City Velasco's statement was considered partial. The idea that the priest had suffered defamation of character was turned against him. Attorney General Areche concluded, "This in itself warrants his separation from Real del Monte, since a priest should not have a bad reputation among his flock, nor can he be useful among his enemies."[47]

Dr. Velasco protested, "I learned and became convinced that if Dr. Díaz suffered personally from some vice, it was not in his ministry nor did it involve his flock."[48] The archbishop wrote his reaction vigorously and forcefully. There was no evidence to charge the priest, he said, and much evidence to acquit him. His recommendation was pious, just, and unavailing: "The innocent must not be condemned."[49]

Mexico City began the sentencing by trying to get right with the ecclesiastical fuero. According to law, secular authorities might not indict priests or condemn them. The brief, then, was simply to "inform" the archbishop. The fact that Dr. Díaz had already been relieved of duty and exiled was not mentioned. The fact that Pedro de Leoz and his informants were directly contradicted by the defense witnesses was dealt with. Areche made it sound simple: "The priest's witnesses may tell the truth; Leoz surely does."[50]

The attorney general was not completely insensitive to the defense. He conceded that nothing illicit had been proved in the priest's relationships with Lugarda Pozos or Rafaela. However, he added quickly that it was very wrong of him not to say Mass more frequently, and perhaps it enabled him to see Lugarda Pozos.[51] Areche was also persuaded that the priest had not organized the workers to strike. He made a point of mentioning that the priest had indeed calmed the rioters and happily freed Pedro Romero de Terreros from the bloody hands of his enemies.

Everything else Dr. Díaz did, however, was wrong and immoral. It was wrong to give "forbidden plays" in the cemetery and to provide benches from the church for the people to sit on. It was wrong to play at chickens and at cards, scandalously, at all hours. It was wrong for him to come to Mexico City to arrange his defense, even though the archbishop had not forbidden it.

Areche thought that the fact that a priest had daughters was reprehensible. He wrote, "It would not be strange if this minister retired because of that weakness."[52]

The priest's "main fault" overshadowed any questions about cockfights or women. Areche concluded that Dr. Díaz's most reprehensible activity was his influence over workers: "he fomented the miners' unjust claims about partidos; he influenced them to put them forward, and he aided them. . . . The claims doubtlessly made the greedy spirits of this barbarous people insolent, and the favor that they won increased their presumption and arrogance and gave them the boldness to use force and violence."[53] It had taken Leoz and Romero de Terreros four years to pinpoint and publicize partidos as the main cause of the troubles in Real del Monte. Yet only one of the post-strike incidents was provoked by partidos. The question of partidos had been articulated, presented, and resolved nonviolently. Almost all the other regions of New Spain paid their miners partidos, and they had no problems and no strike. Partidos were never abolished in the eighteenth century at Real del Monte, and when they withered away more than a hundred years later, they did so without a word for or against them. The authorities and the owner lost the war on this subject, but the church lost its case, and the priest was never reinstated. Dr. Díaz was condemned to the loss of the living and to spend the rest of his life in exile from the region twenty leagues roundabout Real del Monte. Areche said he would assure that the priest "would never again exercise any influence in that mining town."[54]

The story ends with a whimper. In January 1771 Dr. Díaz wrote the archbishop a sad letter of resignation: "My time in Real del Monte has broken my health, and my residence there has been difficult."[55] Unable to ride a horse, he walked to a ranch near Piedras Negras where he collapsed from a hemorrhage of his bleeding piles. He was supposed to go to a new church in Jalapa, but in February 1771, the viceroy freed him from that obligation and allowed him free travel in New Spain as long as he did not return to Real del Monte.

!¡

CHAPTER 9

An Interpreting

Ask yourself, what is this thing in itself, by its own special constitution? What is it in substance, and in form, and in matter? What is its function in the world? For how long does it subsist? —Marcus Aurelius, *Meditations*

The mode of production of material life conditions the general process of social, political, and intellectual life. It is not the consciousness of men that determines their existence, but their social existence that determines their consciousness. At a certain stage of development, the material productive forces of society come into conflict with the existing relations of production or—this merely expresses the same thing in legal terms—with the property relations within the framework of which they have operated hitherto. From forms of development of the productive forces these relations turn into their fetters. Then begins an era of social revolution. The changes in the economic foundation lead sooner or later to the transformatin of the whole superstructure. —Karl Marx, "Preface to a Critique of Political Economy"

Most conclusions smooth the themes and tie up the loose ends. Here, however, besides those concerns, several propositions continue unresolved. In history techniques of dealing with values in the past are seldom discussed. How values arise, how they mediate, and how they operate specifically in a conflict are topics central to this study. Further, there remains a compelling problem: how can a strike happen without a labor union or an enabling ideology derived from workers' previous experience? Under what conditions do workers become strikers?

In this study four kinds of data are examined: (1) the actual experiences of Real del Monte workers, (2) principles selected from Marx (for general labor theory), (3) conclusions from the work of E. P. Thompson (for the social history of workers engaged in their long struggle to develop the working class), and (4) an experiential field theory worked out by American behaviorist psychology. Miners in Real del Monte made their own strike. But to show how takes some explaining.

In the eighteenth century Real del Monte staged an industrial strike without knowing what a strike was. Workers were aware neither of the experience of strikers elsewhere in the world nor of the prescriptive enthusiasms of anarchism and socialism, which first brought the call of labor unions to Mexico more than a hundred years later. How this strike happened in 1766 is not easy to imagine. There were no outside agitators, no apostles of labor to illuminate for workers what they were doing and advise them how to change it for the better. It was an unexpected strike, apparently rising out of nowhere, called a "passing strike" or a "partial strike" because it had no labor union and because its influence dissipated as it disappeared.[1] Where does a strike without ideological or organizational precedents come from? E. P. Thompson observed wryly: "Even sympathetic observers write about miners as if their solidarity sprang from some sub-intellectual sociological traditionalism, a combination of the muscles and the moral instincts."[2]

The truth is there is a bridge that connects muscles to morality, and it is not sub-intellectual at all. It is called *learning*. Workers did not need a teacher, or a human nature born vicious, or deeply repressed instincts of freedom to bring about their strike. They learned from experience. They were taught from an "instructional social environment."[3] They added to old repertoires of strategies, actions, and reactions, or they innovated new ones. Within the conditions of their life as agents in industrial relations they discovered behaviors useful not only for conforming to work patterns but also for fighting back. What was learned would be appreciated as useful and relevant if what they tried obtained for them what they wanted, or part of it, even if what they wanted varied: food in the mouths of children, a clever escape, a fair payday, a just distribution of wealth, or the old-fashioned reward of vengeance.[4]

The most complex and useful instructional environment in Real del Monte for a strike was work, and more than anything else work experience enabled miners to find their role as strikers. Many work activities were carried over to strike-making directly. The grievances were fair work practices proclaimed. A barra, the basic unit of labor in the mines, met inside and outside work and began to spell out the basic grievances as well as to elaborate the organizational patterns the strike followed. One barra contacted others, these barras roused the shifts or *puebles*. In spite of the great variations among workers, it was pikemen and peons who began the strike, the same pikemen and peons who worked together below. At odds at first, they reconciled their differences and supported each other, the gulf between skilled and unskilled bridged by unity. No authority ever figured out how the riots of February 8–9, 1767, were orchestrated. Yet at every turn, press gangs were met with whistles and catcalls. The language miners used at work to warn of danger and to communicate changes in the job had been transformed to the language directing control of counterattack. Finally, there was the solidarity itself. The mode of cooperation in the work day is in itself a productive force. In division of labor, where tasks are specialized, work rehearses men in cooperative efforts and develops mutual loyalties. Norman McCord writes that in mining the dirty, unpleasant, uncomfortable jobs and the constant presence of danger tend to make workers especially sensitive about the rewards they have come to expect: "Where a man is asked to risk life and limb in such conditions, it is perfectly comprehensible that grievances can be felt very strongly."[5] Feeling resentful, men seek to escape or resist. If changes have specific consequences that can be felt immediately, the situation may change quickly and dramatically. The repertoire of cooperation that had been tested and found useful in the workplace was martialed to confront the new situation of antagonism.[6] The capacity to rebel was in their hands, but only hope and help enabled them to strike.

The work of mining defines "down to earth problems."[7] All the grievances targeted problems of *change*, yet all assumed continuities of accommodation to the industrial system. Workers did not claim possession of their tools. They accepted the separation and only asked that management do its share by providing equipment free and in good condition and lighting adequate to last the shift. The long work day, the deplorable working conditions, the fearsome risks and loathsome occupational diseases were mentioned, not to ask for alleviation but to back miners' claims to their customary partido and all it promised. The changes the workers of Real del Monte specifically objected to were pay cuts, a speedup, and harassment by the managers.

The road to the strike was a long one, and the series of changes gave workers time for an almost remedial course on how to perceive injustice and express resentment and how to plot a way out. While the pay cut for the peons was drastic and sudden, the problems of pikemen centered around a long series of alterations of the pay system. The loss of reward was bad enough, but managers' manipulations and aggressive behavior helped transform the antagonism of individuals into the just demands of a group called "labor" against unjust and brutal men in authority called "management."

Within the vision of workers on the Veta Vizcaína was a practice common to small mines all over New Spain: the day's ore haul was shared one-half by the worker and one-half by the boss. As mines were rehabilitated and productive techniques specialized and integrated, management began to set quotas. Mixing of quota and partido was instituted. If quota and partido were unequal in value, the ore was split, mixed, then divided. There was little complaint. Workers adjusted peacefully, if restively, to the new system: "in the end we all suffered it, as all miserable people do, for fear of this powerful man and believing the evil would end there."[8] But innovations in the system did not end there. Quotas were inexorably increased to three to one, then four to one, and increased again by issuing larger quota bags and smaller partido sacks. Mixing was arranged so that miners picked out the worst ore from the edges of the pile. At last these miserable pickings were guaranteed by banning the workers from the gallery when the mixing was done. If they had pried out amethysts or filaments of pure silver or rich ore, they lost their chance to find them again in the pile. At payday managers took more than their share of "alms," sometimes leaving a worker with only one-third of his share of the partido. All in all, the rewards of work at Real del Monte were, within the span of a year or so, cut again and again—and again. Workers felt not so much robbed as drained, and in the August 1 grievance they wearily concluded, "we benefit nothing."

Of all the conditions favoring the development of the collective action of labor, Real del Monte's past and present tolerance of irregular management practices was unique in New Spain. While other mines giving partidos might institute mixing, none forced miners to divide in the dark or from the barren edges of the pile. Francisco de Gamboa, who knew all the mining centers in the kingdom, and who counted on work customs to adjudicate disputes, called the innovations at Real del Monte "iniquitous." His was not the only indignant voice. Village Indians, forced to the mines, complained of unbearable working conditions, pay pared for "compulsory charges," denial of portal-to-portal compensation, and brutal treatment from the managers. From rural Mexico to industrial Real del Monte to Mexico City itself, the charges of irregular practices were compelling enough to persuade even viceroys that the trouble prodding workers to defiance was serious. Personal animosities in the mines exacerbated workers' antagonism, and the managers who insulted them, beat them up, and cheated them shaped the strike at every turn. Management failed at labor relations at Real del Monte and proved itself injudicious, if not arrogantly simple, when it failed to predict that workers would become indignant enough to protest. But what workers did do next was beyond prediction, for in Real del Monte in 1766, they went to the law.

The institution of justice was plain to everyone in the area: the royal officials of the treasury office in Pachuca were the designated magistrates of the Veta Vizcaína. However, there was no recollection anywhere that workers had ever presented a grievance to them before. And while workers do not need a teacher to tell them what their grievances are and how to organize a work gang for the job or for political action and what the merits and mechanics of a work stoppage are, men do have to have instruction in how to behave within a judicial system and how to use the rule of law to their advantage.

Counsel came from the rectory. The most extraordinary man in Real del Monte was the priest of La Asunción, Dr. José Rodríguez Díaz. He was a man for whom miners and townspeople alike felt *cariño*, as John Womack has translated it: "they liked him, admired him, held him in high but tender regard, were devoted to him."[9] Dr. Díaz was deeply involved with his parishioners, so deeply that he talked with miners at work and at play and cared about them all around their lives until they trusted him and discussed their problems with him and listened to what he said. And what the priest did, in all this talking, was to suggest to someone like Nicolás de Zavala or Domingo González that they should submit a written list of grievances to the royal treasury officials in Pachuca. Perhaps he gave them money to buy a fold of stamped paper from some bureaucrát to write it on. The strike leaders were literate, and presumably they could have written it themselves. The priest did not write it nor did he recommend that anyone else do so.

The priest's contributions were great because he showed them a legal way to petition that was an alternative to violence. He continued to act out nonviolent alternatives in front of their very eyes when he served them as mediator with the boss, when he pacified the crowd, and when he worked to save the mines from inundation afterwards. That the strike was a strike and not just a riot has much to do with the inspiration and example and compassion of the priest of Real del Monte. His enemies knew it, and they were successful in persecuting him out of the Real. They charged: "he fomented the miners' unjust claims about partidos; he influenced them to put them forward, and he sided with them. . . . The grievance doubtlessly made the greedy spirits of this barbarous people insolent, and the favor that they won increased their presumption and arrogance and gave them the boldness to use force and violence."[10] They were correct to say he supported miners and influenced them to make a legal protest to Pachuca. But he worked so that they would turn away from force. He urged them to pursue legal, nonviolent means. He took the side of labor to management and to royal authority as if workers' grievances carried weight equal to profits. Pedro Romero de Terreros never forgave him for it.

How Nicolás de Zavala chose the man to transcribe the miners' grievances for the royal officials is not certain. Antonio Núñez de Lovera could read and write and had the legal experience of being a scribe at the treasury office. He was known as a friend of the priest. Lovera did much more than draft the original resolution of July 28. In his fear and pessimism that the royal authorities would do nothing, he let slip that it would be better to find a lawyer and go to Mexico City. As it turned out, the royal authorities in Pachuca did accept the petition, but they tarried and observed the situation and failed to reconcile anyone.

To carry grievances to Mexico City and to present them directly to the viceroy confirmed this struggle as an authentic, recognized strike. The delays at Pachuca made the daring tactic worth a try, and though the priest tried to stop them, the envoys carried a new grievance, drafted by a lawyer, and submitted it to the viceroy himself. Heads of state in Mexico still have hours open to hear complaints of citizens, and it is possible to walk right in without an intermediary. Mexico City moved, treated antagonism as if it were responsible protest, as if labor and management were equal contenders with equally valid interests. Because of this interview with the strike leaders, because of pressure from Pedro Romero de Terreros, and because of reports of the violence and homicides on August 15, 1766, the viceroy sent his most distinguished expert and jurist on mining to the mountain. Francisco de Gamboa conducted an arbitration that, day after day, assured workers that they were being treated as equal partners in the industrial enterprise.

The community of miners provided both numbers and direction to the struggle. Working men had the strong support of the women they knew. Workers found their crowds swelled by parents, wives and children, brothers and sisters, kin, neighbors, compadres and comadres. Communities knew that workers had a stake worth fighting for. Miners earned double and more the pay of agricultural workers or of the militiamen or soldiers sent to control them. They ate well, as Areche pointed out. While they worked and lived in terrible conditions, there were compensations in the pay and in the living. They built their hovels in remote areas that offered them protection against recogedores. In town they lived in their own *barrios*. They seemed to control the rhythms of their work and leisure, and they liked living with their own kind, "with their own manners and customs, which again encouraged communal action in defence of their interests."[11] Authorities, in disapproving of workers' life-styles and in trying, unsuccessfully, to burn them out, testified to the reality of miners' satisfactions. Whether for collective action or "lawless habits of life,"[12] the daily routine in the neighborhoods of Real del Monte profoundly affected miners, strikers, and rioters.

Collective action in Real del Monte, almost always, took the form of direct or ricocheting effects of counterattacks against recogedores. Complaints that miners took peacefully to managers or royal authorities often brought workers relief, but recogedores were prescribed by law, and the best that could be expected was a lecture to recogedores to minimize violence while they carried on with their work. That is, there were peaceful protests, but nonviolence did not stop the press gangs. On the other hand, no man needed lessons in stone throwing. Workers had plenty of practice on each other in the taverns. Miners had tried collective action with stones in 1755, when the men of Real del Monte successfully and exultantly chased the workers from Guanajuato off the mountain. Men often used stones to free their companions from the lassos of a press gang. Not always, but sometimes, they succeeded. Stoning was a practiced art and favorite tactic in Real del Monte. Usually, this kind of violence took place outside, where men could duck and run away. On August 15, 1766, there were thousands of participants, and the arena was inside. Two men trapped in the galleries were killed. It seems strange that no one died in the "deluge" of rocks on February 8-9, 1767, but once again the combat zone was outside. Violence showed its vestiges only in battered houses and the marks of rocks on walls. It may be, too, that since workers were out to discipline workers, they did not want to kill them but rather to give them a hard lesson that would drive them back, alive and chastened, to the mines where miners belonged. There is no question that violence shaped some of the behavior of the era. It killed the district magistrate and the foreman. It brought soldiers to Real del Monte. The terror affected management and authorities for years afterward and wrote the script for their vengeance. But it was nonviolence that Gamboa stressed, and his arbitration rewarded not rioters but strikers.

Forged from work and wrought in struggles were the experiences that came to distinguish the miners of Real del Monte as a special interest group. "Interests are what interest people, including what interests them nearest the heart."[13] Their grievances were expressed "in contraries" to the actions of management. The ensuing tensions proved beyond a reasonable doubt that a labor system of values was in conflict with a management value system. The resulting struggle came to be experienced as awareness. It is in this sense that "consciousness is a social product."[14] A conflict of interest is a conflict of values.

Values attest to human satisfaction.[15] When we read about them, they almost seem like a typology, for those that last persist in form even under distortion. But they are not static figures. Instead, they are part of an ongoing system of positive reinforcements. People talk about them to explain why they find doing things worthwhile. Values are never "frozen," "backward," "archaic." If values are long-lived, it is because they have been part of a living, relevant source of satisfaction, because they have given meaning to the blood, sweat, and tears of human effort. When people no longer prize them, the system no longer works and the values are extinguished. When the elements of a situation are maintained and the solutions to problems continue to be tried, the satisfaction of solving them, or trying to solve them, will also continue to be valued. If the behavior is rewarded, more or less or sometimes, the behavior is strengthened and the values persist. What are called "traditional values" continue and have continued to pay off. When conflicts come, values are maintained as goals, and ways of defending them or maintaining them are devised anew to meet the changed situation.[16] There is no "dead hand" of the past but only the living hands of men in struggle.

Most radical of all the ideals put forth by the strikers was their insistence on social and economic justice. *Workers should be cobeneficiaries in the industrial enterprise:* "it is a precept in all systems of natural, divine, and secular law that there should be a just proportion between labor and profit."[17] Miners defined the best means of guaranteeing proportionate profits as the traditional wage distribution of the partidos. Manuel Cordero, their lawyer, translated their experience into principle: selling ore was no more useful, necessary, or important than wresting it out of the rock face. If the state rewarded owner over laborer, protected boss over worker, government was unjust. Through the eloquence of their counsel, workers cried aloud against their exploitation. They blamed the boss and the state, and Manuel Cordero made it memorable: "He wishes to tyrannize over us through the very indigence and poverty he sees us in. This is an injury and affront to all humanity and society. It runs roughshod over us. It requires that we, the most unhappy members of the body politic should be born to serve society, the sovereign, and Don Pedro Romero—but not they to serve us."[18]

The men of Real del Monte were strikers. They were vehement against an unjust economic system. They were passionate about their ideals of proportionate profit, the dignity of the working man, and their right, united, to oppose an unjust system. In this context it was as if they had uttered the first syllable of a social revolution. E. P. Thompson has reflected on a similar situation. The Luddites in eighteenth-century England were not, he concluded, a reactionary movement but rather a *transitional* one. They linked the tensions of their present to a past solution that became a future hope: "they contained within them a shadowy image, not so much of a paternalist but of a democratic community, in which industrial growth should be regulated according to ethical priorities and the pursuit of profit be subordinated to human needs."[19] Protesting profiteering, claiming their fair share, speaking as working men for working men, organizing to resist, clamoring for economic justice, the men of Real del Monte declared their values, which, like the ideals of the English Luddites, "trembled on the edge of ulterior revolutionary objectives."[20]

A student of rebellious villages in eighteenth-century New Spain found not only no social revolution but no revolutionary ideas: "Late colonial villages suffered material distress, but it was not the kind of pervasive, dislocating threat to their existence that might have promoted a concept of struggle between classes and orders and united villages in regional insurrection."[21]

Mines are different. A "concept of struggle" surely existed and played itself out in Real del Monte. Such a concept of struggle, trembling on the edge of revolutionary objectives, does not need a single pervasive, dislocating threat or an extended impact in order to be. In fact, the notion is backwards. Very simply, "Class struggle is prior to class." "Class does not precede but arises out of struggle."[22] As coral grows for eons before a reef appears above the waves, so interest groups must engage in conflict long before they succeed in creating a class. The realization that economic situations can be controlled by workers because they have been successfully dealt with in the past is a marker of class-building consciousness. Workers, perceiving the antagonism, define their own interests against those who oppose them.[23] Real del Monte strikers distinctly used working class values to defend their working class interests: their relationships were formed by work within a set of industrial relations; they articulated their interests in their own terms; they were aware that their insistence on benefiting from their own labor challenged management's right to profits; they struggled to oppose and defend; they perceived that management was pitted against them; and they remained purposeful agents.[24] Very importantly, they were aware of the significance of their own labor power. Both grievances threatened that if workers' just complaints were not rectified, they would leave the mines. Withdrawing labor power was their ultimate weapon.

"Men make their own history, but they do not make it just as they please."[25] To make a strike, "irregular practices" changed the productive relations of work. At Real del Monte workers taught themselves how to deal with the changes and came to be aware that they had become a unified interest group. There was no "class," but there were working class values and the solidarity to defend them. Class consciousness developed with the strike. In Real del Monte workers defined class struggle — in their own terms.

It was not contagious. There was no silver industry in New Spain. Each Real was its own industrial enterprise, controlled by its own rules and traditions. If antagonisms existed in other mines, they must have subsided before the workers had time to pursue the course of resistance that transformed Real del Monte workers into strikers. To my knowledge no other silver magnate was repeatedly charged with "irregular practices." There was no "brotherhood" of silver miners. The mode of production was atomized. Except at the highest, most removed functions of the mint in Mexico City or the treasury in Spain, there was no integrated enterprise. Each producing area was separate, distinct, and isolated from all the rest. Each was a castle of production. And among them, for a short while, only Real del Monte was a citadel of class consciousness.

Besides the fact that there was no integrated industry, no understanding among silver workers, and no transforming industry-wide change in the mode of production, class consciousness, even in Real del Monte, stopped developing for another reason. In Real del Monte workers fought the class struggle — and won.

Once workers' grievances were channeled legally, the way was easy. There were libraries full of labor legislation in Madrid and Mexico City. Spain's first protective legislation about hours, working conditions, pay, and rest for men, women, and children was codified in the Laws of Burgos in 1512–13. Hundreds of years of laws and practices to protect Indians meant that the Spanish government had not only the power to intervene in capital enterprises, which it surely did, but it also had the moral imperative to look after working people. The burning zeal of Father Bartolomé de Las Casas in the sixteenth century was not enough to save the millions of Indians who died. But it wrote the book on the crown's Christian duty to labor. In the eighteenth century, when the horror of depopulation still haunted authorities, it was enough to guarantee a serious hearing for Indian communities forced to labor. In the 1750s Mexico City heard the complaints of Indians compelled to serve time on the Veta Vizcaína, and the authorities respected the old principle: *the need for labor is matched by the need of labor for good treatment.*[26]

The heritage of concern for labor and the precedents in law for its protection made Manuel Cordero's task easy when he wrote the August 1 grievance (Appendix 2). The laws had been written for Indian labor. The problems of free workers, most of them not Indians, had simply to be defined as analogous to the work and injustices of Indians. All the lawyer had to do for his free worker clients was to argue their interests in their own terms, emphasize their complaints, then suggest a reason why they had never been heard from before. It was because they were too poor and miserable to seek their sovereign's protection. That very "poverty" and "misery" qualified them for royal concern. Cordero's grievance translates what appears to be a petition of class struggle into a statement of workers' special interests aimed directly at the charitable commitment of the crown and at an acceptance into the system of conflict resolution and protective legislation that were markers of Spanish imperial government. In principle these were the demands that trembled on the edge of revolutionary objectives. But in the Spanish empire, they sounded familiar, a bid for recognition from a government that had, for more than two hundred fifty years, recognized workers as a legitimate interest group.

In short, the history of Spain in New Spain created a chance that these miners would win a fair hearing. So Cordero showed the moral basis of how free men contract their labor, how they had fallen victim to the obsessive profit motive of the industry, and how their government had failed to rectify the imbalance: "In these matters a pact or convention between those who make the contract makes the law. Each one may make covenant with the employer for the salary that seems proper, and the employee will decide yea or nay. But this cannot happen when the employer takes advantage of the indigence of the employee, knowing he has no other job to maintain himself, nor can it happen when the rule of good government is not as permissive an authority for the man who hires out his particular labor as it is for those who hire."[27] Then he showed how free men are not just a factor of production but equal partners in the industry itself. That they were not treated as equals or paid as equals was obvious. The fact that the employer had taken unfair advantage of free men because of their poverty sounds like a call to revolution. But it wasn't. It was rather a time-honored formula to oblige the crown to intervene on the workers' behalf.

> There is no more necessity or usefulness in the extraction of metals . . . than there is in maintaining so many men in his work force. This is what we are arguing here. He wishes to tyrannize over us through the very indigence and

poverty he sees us in. This is an injury and affront to all humanity and society. It runs roughshod over us. It requires that we, the most unhappy members of the body politic, should be born to serve society, the sovereign, and Don Pedro Romero—but not they to serve us. At least we are satisfied that is not the attitude and pious will of His Majesty the King.[28]

Within the context of Spanish imperial experience, accepting the labor of free men as an important interest group and the conviction that this group deserved to prosper justly from their work was not revolutionary at all. It was simply a small adjustment, a reform effort hardly demanding at all. In fact, all the crown had to do, with a few strokes of the pen, was to send Gamboa to the mountain. It did not even have to pay for his lodging there or for the wages, room, and found of his escort. The boss paid.

Justice and tradition had persuaded the crown to take the workers' side. So did silver production and profits. Workers were as valuable as the God-given ore and the investor-given drainage projects which allowed the exploitation of the lodes. Labor, in fact, was much scarcer than silver. The fact that there was a shortage of labor in the mines of New Spain cannot be emphasized enough. That the Real was also a royal protectorate helped the workers' cause immeasurably. A strike threatened to cut mining revenues abruptly, and even the possibility of a drop in royal revenues prompted officials to action.

Francisco de Gamboa's arbitration in 1766, the revelation of a kind of royal justice that allowed workers to win, diverted the flow of workers' class consciousness into the mainstream of royal patronage. The main reason that class consciousness at Real del Monte dissipated is that workers received just about everything they asked for. Harassing managers were summarily fired. The speed-up was slowed and regulated; pay cuts were revoked; wages were paid fairly; and, for the first time, the right to partidos was placed in writing, pledged by Gamboa's ordinances. Labor compromised on mixing, and the method was "universally conceded." Almost at a stroke Gamboa had stripped away all the "irregular practices" the miners had organized to protest. The instructional social environment that had created the strike was turned back to the country rock of work. The citadel had fallen—not to force but to mediation, conciliation, and acceptance.[29]

The conflict at Real del Monte confirms Lyle McAlister's conclusions, and his is still the most thought-provoking analysis of Mexican colonial society in relation to social change. McAlister explained that there were interest groups in New Spain and that the crown had many different techniques to reconcile class conflicts. This is why "social unrest took the form of drives to improve the status of the individual and the group, not efforts to change the system."[30] At Real del Monte more can be verified than the generalization: the process by which this occurred can be observed in detail, in a case study.

Mexico City did send soldiers, the epitome of force, but they never killed anyone. They never hurt anybody. They patrolled the area, but they never took arms against the workers. They must have emanated some sort of terror, or Bucareli would not have sent them and Romero de Terreros would not have been so insistent that they be stationed permanently in Real del Monte. It is surprising. The soldiers not only never opposed the workers but at least once leaped to their defense. On February 22, 1769 (that is, two years after the great riot of 1767), four dragoons of the Regiment of Spain heroically confronted the recogedores of the Morán and freed twenty workers of the Veta Vizcaína. Moya, miffed at the loss of profits to himself, His Majesty, and the public interest, demanded that the dragoons be arrested. And they were.[31] Even the application of military force against workers was not predictable.

Another kind of force that Gamboa, Romero de Terreros, and the authorities counted on was the power of exemplary punishment. But the situation was so tense in Real del Monte in 1766 that Gamboa and the viceroy feared that to arrest the criminal strike leaders would be to incite the whole Real to riot once again. This kind of expedient moderation came to be interpreted as weakness. Pedro de Leoz and Attorney General Areche prided themselves on using a hard hand against the suspects rounded up after the riot of 1767. As it turned out, more of the unimportant innocent suffered punishment, and only one of the committed and nonviolent principals of the strike was caught. There is no evidence that harsh sentencing ever deterred anyone. What did deter them and what sent them away from the Real was not punishment but betrayal.

In February 1767 the men of Real del Monte went to battle not against management of government officials, for those scores had been settled. They fought against their own strike leaders and their own comrades who had sold them out to become part of the universally hated press gangs. Pedro Romero de Terreros never intervened, even though another mine owner was depleting his labor force. Perhaps from his solitary confinement in San Miguel he thought it served his workers right. How any royal official could devise a plan to take labor away from the most valuable mines in the area, and from the most important mine owner, is hard to fathom. It is easy to understand how workers sold out. The job of deputy recogedor would double and triple their wages each week. It is also easy to understand the real fury of miners against men who had publicly spoken for their interests and then publicly and contemptuously and with force betrayed them and enslaved them to hard labor in mines where everyone dreaded the cold water. The riots of February 1767 were the last, furious articulation of unified workers at Real del Monte. When the noise of the rocks turned to silence, the events subsided to individual memories as people began to desert the Real or make accommodations for staying. Martín Luis Guzmán implied that the Mexican Revolution died in a "fiesta of bullets."[32] The strike at Real del Monte died in a "multitude of stones."

Its memory, though, was long-lasting in law and in custom. Investors drew on Real del Monte's legacy to reform the management of capital in colonial Mexican mines. In the years that followed, the pressing problem of mine owners was to obtain funds for development. The man of vision was José Alejandro de Bustamante, who in 1748 conceived the grand idea of consolidating capital in a bank dedicated solely to mining investments. The last great silver family banker, Manuel de Aldaco, had died, and the era of private capitalization that had brought Pedro Romero de Terreros to Real del Monte was over. In 1774 Juan Lucas de Lassaga and Joaquín Velázquez de León proposed a bank and more. They wanted a guild of mine owners and investors, a central court of law to ajudicate disputes over claims, and a technical school for aspiring young men who would administer mines in a progressive way.[33]

Ordinances for the new mining guild, drawn up in 1778, showed concern about what had happened in Real del Monte. The principle was reiterated: the environment made the rules and they were sacrosanct. That is, no owner in New Spain could alter, for any reason, the pay system established by the customs and traditions of the Real. If the customary wage was four reales, the owner must pay it. If the custom was to give partidos, workers would take partidos. The rules of the work of mining must not be disturbed by irregular practices. Compulsory alms were forbidden. Ore thieves, though they might be seized and bound in the gallery, must be brought to the royal justices for punishment. Recogedores remained. Forced Indian labor might be employed, but such Indian "volunteers" had to be treated well according to the stipulations given for their protection in the Laws of the Indies.[34] The official promulgation from Spain added a rule from Real del Monte: mixing of quotas and partidos must take place in the presence of the worker.[35]

Authorities had reflected upon the "unquiet spirits" of Real del Monte. In 1774 a decree sternly reminded priests that the ecclesiastical fuero would not protect them from secular prosecution if they were charged with inciting to riot. Passing around "seditious papers" would be punished as premeditated malice. All taverns and card games should be shut down after a commotion. The military would guard the jails and use force only against those who sought to free the prisoners. Ringleaders would be prosecuted; followers would be pardoned by His Majesty.[36]

Under ordinances there was industrial peace at Real del Monte all through the rest of the eighteenth century and the wars of Independence. When British investors and management assumed the lease of the Real del Monte mines in 1824, Mexican workers demanded to retain their partidos. At each confrontation the British lost and the partido was saved. In 1827 regular Mexican army troops had to be sent because the British feared that working men in militias would go over to the strikers. The conflict was resolved when workers were given their customary wages of four reales and partidos, an issue of tools and candles, and the hiring of men as individuals, not in gangs. In 1840 and 1841 the Mexican government refused to send soldiers, and the workers won their claim of the partido, the privilege cherished as a sacred, social compact at Real del Monte. Workers won partidos after struggle in 1845, 1848, the 1870s, 1880s, and 1890s. This is to say that Real del Monte battled for its partidos for a hundred thirty years after the initial strike of 1766. But in the end, though it lost every direct confrontation, the British company gradually introduced Cornish tutwork and altered the instructional social environment of work at Real del Monte forever.[37]

Mexicans today are more aware of the contributions of Pedro Romero de Terreros than of the legacy of his workers. Less rich than the Mexican Conde de la Valenciana, less a mining genius than the Aragonese José de la Borda, less innovative than the Mexican José de Bustamante, the Spanish Conde de Regla is still perhaps the greatest entrepreneur in Mexican colonial history. Like a canny businessman, he seized on other people's ideas and, with applications of money and energy, made them work. He grasped the principle that to control an industry one must hold power over all its constituent parts, and so he owned mines and muleteams and refineries, stockfarms and harvest haciendas to provision them, and retail stores to sell equipment and surplus products. If churches, convents, and monasteries were the banks of his time, he cultivated relations with the bankers. He understood that in the world of eighteenth-century New Spain to command credit meant to control land, and he acquired from the sale of Jesuit properties some of the grandest and most beautiful haciendas in all New Spain—and never moved in. His generosity to the poor made him well known in his time as "father of orphans." His continuing contributions to the crown made Spain think of him as the most loyal of subjects, one to be rewarded over and over. He cared for his many children as best he could, and while I do not see them as very happy because of it, he left them well provided for. As an immigrant youth, just before leaving Spain, he promised Our Lady of Regla to exalt her name if she helped bring him success. Both fulfilled their obligations. He died in the odor of sanctity, which Ricardo Palma once described as smelling something like roses and lemon verbena.[38]

Pedro Romero de Terreros was, then, a great man and a dedicated and brave, if bad, boss. Wage cutting was his specialty. Part of his enormous fortune was created by the forced labor of Indians whose only crime consisted of being born poor into villages where labor had been doing something else for centuries. Another part of his capital was generated through the agency of recogedores, who flogged miners, and anyone else with two feet, into hard labor down a dark shaft. It is plain that he himself insisted on lowering the customary wage of peons and manual laborers to three pesos: he tried it in the 1740s, again in the 1760s, and was still all for it in the 1770s. He learned to be adamantly anti-partido. He sanctified his grudges, and he ruined the priest who had saved his life. How much he was aware of the goading harassments of his managers is impossible to say. He was a "modern" man, and the stubborn defenses of labor proved to him that workers were vicious obstacles to economic development. Only the power of the state stopped him. Viceroy Marqués de Croix, well aware of his many contributions to church and state, called Pedro Romero de Terreros a tyrant and a despot, whose extortion of labor at Real del Monte had initiated such violence that the workers were driven, in desperation, to defend themselves.[39]

This story has dealt with "the other side" of colonial industrial relations. Workers have been discovered in that light of a different hue, labor history. The conclusions are not the same as the managers and authorities wanted to hear, though they have presented their case in its original vehemence. This Mexican strike was legitimized by Spanish imperial conciliation, and together workers and viceroys checked the excesses of the tide of Bourbon modernization.

Spain used its vast power to assimilate and co-opt what in other societies might have been considered revolutionary demands to recognize the rights of labor and to reallocate the priorities of profit. Unity of workers, proportionate rewards, and fair wages were, in the Spanish world, inherent in the definition of social justice for labor. The state chose proportion, providing for each interest group its share of the good of the whole.

Spain's support of workers in a very serious industrial dispute with one of the richest men in the kingdom of New Spain is surprising. That Spain's vast repertoire of protective legislation for Indians was used to back strikers' claims must be unique in the history of free workers. Although most strikers in industrial cultures languish inarticulate, Mexican workers defined their struggle "in their own voices" because Real del Monte's notaries thrust what was almost a microphone into the labor disputes. Labor history, with what seems to be its intrinsic behaviorist base of psychological theory, can explain what has been inexplicable before: how spontaneous strikes arise and how men innocent of unions organize themselves to resist exploitation.

And what is left is men at work and in brawls and people at play and at home and workers in the mines, in jail, in negotiation, purposefully doing what they determined to do. Their resistance made its mark in their time. In our time what happened at Real del Monte is a chapter in Mexican history that reveals the dignity and determination of men who wanted to work for a just reward, demanded the rights of labor, organized their strike, and won it.

The Struggle Continues: 1985

Mexican Miners
Demonstrate
in the Nude

Pachuca, Mexico

About 3500 miners protesting lax safety standards and a lack of clothing and equipment dramatized their plight with an hour-long demonstration in the nude, it was reported over the weekend.

Dressed only in hard hats, boots, belts and an occasional neck scarf, the miners of the Compañia Real del Monte y Pachuca, in the mineral-rich hills of central Hidalgo state, staged the protest Friday at the mine, the newspaper *La Jornada* reported Saturday.

The demonstration by the nude miners, whose photographs were splashed throughout the newspaper, persuaded the mine owners to open negotiations with the protesters, *La Jornada* said.

From the *San Francisco Chronicle,* May 27, 1985, United Press.

!¡

July 28, 1766, Grievance

In the city and mines of Our Lady of the Assumption, Pachuca, [Monday], July 28, 1766, before the treasurer and accountant, judges and royal officials of the royal treasury of this noble city and judges of the Veta Vizcaína, this petition is presented.

The workers of the mines of the Veta Vizcaína, belonging to Don Pedro Terreros of the Order of Calatrava, themselves residents of Real del Monte, who sign below, those who know how, as the law directs, before your honor we appear and declare:

Being pikemen, we have been working these mines for many years with excessive toil and fatigue, in exchange for the only protection a pikeman has in a mine — the partido he may carry away from the daily task, which is and has been the only thing that permits miners to live in decency — not the wage, for that four reales can be spent in a day or a night inside the mine itself in eating and fortifying oneself against the toil and dampness of the mine.

The partidos in this lode have never exactly corresponded to the set task of the day. Before, the division was done after mixing up the ore, a means that though it is different from custom, we tolerated because the division was done fairly, and something remained for us, though not as much as if the ore were divided according to the old custom, where only that ore which the pikeman took out specifically for the partido was given him without mixing it with the ore of the task or using other means prejudicial to the miners. Then, they stopped the mixing and required that for every three bags gathered to meet the daily quota, one would remain to the pikeman for the partido. This, too, was against our will, but we acquiesced, and it has been like this for some time. Now, a few days ago, they have imposed a quota of four bags to one partido, but the partido must be mixed with the ore of the quota. This would be tolerable if the mixing and the division were made fairly, as God commands, so that the poor pikeman might profit from his labor, but by order of Administrator Don Marcelo González, the worker must empty the bags of the quota on the floor and then pour the partido bags on top; then he must go outside, without being consulted as to whether it is placed right or mixed well. Once the worker is outside, the men who do the mixing set themselves to take out the best ore for the boss, leaving the miner with the most useless and unserviceable rocks. The bag is then refilled, weighed, and divided.

In the division, the ore is not divided in half, but rather almost in thirds, the boss taking the most, more than half, and the pikeman receiving the least, more or less a third, and that turns out to be dirt and low-quality ore. At best, the pikeman may earn four or six reales. Before, with high-grade ore, he might make three or four pesos.

To this we might add that while before the bags were of a comparable size in the mines, today they are disproportionately large. Sometimes a poor pikeman has to work twenty-four hours straight just to meet the quota, which means he loses wages. If one earns only four reales from eight in the morning until eight at night, or vice versa, the one who spends day *and* night completing the quota for four reales has clearly lost another four reales. The main support of his subsistence, and here is where the partido fits in, is lost when the administrator is greedy and the miner has no recourse; he ends up with no partido to meet his own obligations, and yet he has to eat.

Thus, we have found ourselves wiped out, consumed, beaten. Everyone knows we have been experiencing just that.

The administrator has also ordered that we be given no more than three candles, which is the customary number each pikeman takes below with him, but down in the mine three candles barely last the twelve-hour shift, much less twenty-four; and so he must either leave the task without completing it or buy candles to finish it.

Rations of explosives have also been cut. They are not giving the pikemen the sticks of explosives necessary for the difficult jobs, nor are they issuing adequate tools.

So today all is done to profit the boss and to make the workers perish. For this reason we have been compelled to desert Real del Monte, but because we do not want to be accused of disloyalty to our king when we do not work the mines, we have not stopped work.

Now, weary and vexed because we cannot stand so much tyranny, we seek justice from you so that you will impose the remedy: commanding that they divide the partido according to the old custom, our portion to be only the ore that we bring out as the partido; that they provide us with regular-size sacks and with candles, explosives, and tools adequate to and fit for our tasks, without making us lose work time. This is just.

If our grievance has no tangible result, we will take it where we see fit, and if neither this nor that writ brings results, we swear that we will desert the mines and move to where we can obtain our sustenance with more ease.

Therefore, we make here formal and legal petition as our intention and obligation and deny [having done] anything injurious or hurtful.

We petition and implore your honor to dispatch justice. We swear on the sign of the cross, et cetera.

We do not know the correct form in which to sign our names.

We also say: the great act of justice will be for your honors to command them not to tax the partido, not to raise the daily quota, and to rectify the bad treatment we have received in said mine with Don Francisco [Lira].

Those Who Signed [with *rúbrica,* in order of signing]

Nicolás de Zavala	Juan Joseph Orizaba	Diego León
Domingo González	Florencio Garza	Manuel Santos Agiar y Saixos
Rafael Ramírez	Lonicio Jiménez	Pedro Agustín Martínez
Juan Antonio Velasco	Joseph Barbosa	Joseph Pintos
Miguel Rosales	Joseph Thomas Juárez	Juan Enrique

Those Who Affirmed [in alphabetical order]

Mariano Andino	Ignacio Castro	Joseph Oviedo
Lucas Angulo	Lucas Castro	Vicente Oviedo
Joseph Aniceto	Nicolas Castro	Francisco Pérez
Alejo Antonio	Cirilio Celis	Juan Perlín
Pedro Antonio	Juan Contreras	Miguel Puerto
Thomas Antonio	Nicolas Contreras	Pedro Puerto
Juan Aquino	Joseph Manuel Cortés	Juan Joseph Rendón
Ignacio Arellanos	Miguel Escorcia	Juan de Roa
Rafael Armente	Eusebio Escorcio	Matheo Rodríguez
Manuel Asencio	Julián Flores	Rubiales
Felipe Barbosa	Vicente García	Pedro Sánchez
Diego Blanco	Manuel Godines	Juan Manuel Joseph Santos

Joseph Blanco	Juan González	Manuel Santos
Paulino Bustos	Nicolás Guerrero	Pablo Benito del Valle
Antonio Cabrera	Juan Luna	Joaquín Villar
Eugenio Campos	Nicolás Luna	Niceo Viveros
Xavier Campos	Marcelo Miñón	Diego Xarillo
Joseph Matheo Caraza	Francisco Múñoz	
Antonio Carmona	Luis Ortega	

15 miners signed their names. 55 miners affirmed the writ. Royal officials signing: José Rodríguez Palacios and José Tineo. Notary: Francisco de Zevallos Palacio.

!¡

August 1, 1766, Grievance

Miners of the Veta Vizcaína. Grievances. Pachuca. Friday, August 1, 1766.
In the name of 1200 workers. To the viceroy:

Excellent Sir:
    The workers of the mines of the Veta Vizcaína, who sign (those who can)
at the bottom of this representation, for ourselves and for those who do not
know how, in the most legal form, without renouncing the right to litigate,
declare:
    That as the grievance sworn before the royal officials of Pachuca maintains
[July 28, 1766] . . . we find ourselves sorely afflicted and oppressed by don
Pedro Romero de Terreros, of the Order of Calatrava, owner of these mines.
We explained it to said justices, and still clamoring for the proper remedy,
we now present it in this document.
    The old custom observed between the owners of that mining *Real* and the
workers, principally the pikemen, was to designate a daily quota or task,
more or less large depending on the difficulty or ease of the ground which was
being worked, a quota that would be given to the owner for his profit, and to
the worker his daily cash wage. Once the quota was filled, the pikeman
would continue his work, and everything he could pry out and take out
would be divided equally between him and the company.
    Little by little, don Pedro Romero has been changing this custom. First,
he introduced the innovation that if the pikemen and other workers who
were permitted partido took out a number of bags that were better than the
quota, half of the one would be exchanged for half of the other. Once this
exchange was made, the partido, composed of those two halves, would be
divided. This change was hard to take, indeed, since it altered the deep-

rooted, firmly established custom of that mining camp. But in the end we all suffered it, as all miserable people do, for fear of this powerful man and believing that the evil would end there.

But we were deceived. Hoping to augment his estate, he ordered that our quota be increased exorbitantly, almost doubling the size of the bags, so that if before they had held four *arrobas,* they now hold seven or eight, some even ten, without lessening the number of bags required to fill the quota. As many are designated for the quota now as were then, when they were lighter, and without taking into account the difficulty or ease of the terrain. Thus, a poor pikeman, confronting a hard plane or wall, is wont to be interred in the mine caverns two, three days, and many times five or six, in order to be able to complete the quota. This is an injury that could be lessened simply by observing the difficulty of the rock face in the place where the worker is assigned and by making his quota proportionate to that, as authors teach us has always been practiced in all nations that have worked mines. They have the foresight and policy to designate experts, who, among other things they officially do, might resolve this.

Add to this that the partido has become so small that without taking into account either the increase of the quota or the [daily cash] wage of four reales, it is not enough even to feed the worker. This would be true for anyone who, like the worker, for reasons already mentioned, works two or three days in the mine. They have reduced the partido so that they allow only four bags of quota to one of partido, and that one only weighs six arrobas.

That lowering of the rate would be frightening enough if it were not for much more: when he brings the bag of six arrobas and dumps it on the floor of the gallery, he is commanded to leave the room, and, while he is outside, they pick the worst from the quota and divide it in two halves. Then they throw it in the middle and divide it, thus by a deceitful strategem really defrauding the worker of the partido he brought out.

The same thing happens to the miner's half. They take ore out for the smith or the dispatchers so that they may, in their turn, share it with the boss. From the miner's half they also take out the alms, except for those of the churches of San Francisco and San Juan de Dios, which are taken from the pile before it is divided. Lastly, they take out a handful for the rent of the bag which the company lends us to carry away the partido.

Every day we are paying the company. In a word we are contributing to a fund that permits don Pedro Romero to finance all the equipment his mines require.

The extortion does not stop there. They are not issuing the candles, blasting powder, and proper tools needed to complete the task they set for us. This obliges us to work twice as much, and the costs eat up all our wages, so that we find ourselves without anything to take home.

En fine, sir, if the mines are profitable, God intends all who participate to benefit. After the owner, it is especially for his instruments, however he obtains them. We workers who are the instruments have come to profit the least, for drained in so many ways of what is rightfully ours, we benefit nothing.

This injury, sir, is the injury of an entire people, more than 1200 men. We who have been driven out by these tyrannies have taken to the road to represent them before the authority of Your Excellency, for we fear that in Pachuca the royal officials' respect for the almighty owner will close the doors of the tribunals to us.

We ask that Your Excellency command said don Pedro Romero Terreros to give us all the materials we need for the workings of his mines—candles, blasting powder, and usable equipment; that peons and manual laborers be paid the customary wage of four reales, and not with the pay cut of one real which has been given them; that those pikemen and others who are engaged in taking out rocks or ore be assigned quotas in proportion to the difficulty or ease of the terrain, to which end there should be experienced men who understand and by whom they can be regulated and who can order that the partidos conform to the old custom: taking out all the workers' efforts will allow, judging according to the terrain assigned to him, ending up with the ore in the worker's hand, one rock for the boss and another for himself. By this procedure we can satisfy our necessities until the division takes place, for this does not occur right away. Let the division proceed without the haggling, mixing, and exchanging of ores that we have described.

Finally, let the poor worker who, either from fatigue from the task or for some other reason, could not gather a partido, let him keep the ore his companions gave him, let it not be taken away. Rather, after dividing with the boss, let him carry his half away. Do not allow the smith or dispatchers each day to take it away, or [management] to charge for the sack or to collect alms for which we do not want to contribute voluntarily. Charge the royal officials or the district magistrate to supervise and be vigilant and impose grave penalties for not abiding by these rules and, if the rules are infringed, issue a warrant approved by the treasurer so that all proceeds according to law.

Don Pedro Romero Terreros ought to give the worker everything necessary for working in the mines—candles, powder, good tools—for it is a matter of justice, not only because without these things the work cannot be done but also because the employee contributes only his labor and not the materials or tools needed to do it. They should be issued to him, not taken from a four-real wage. . . . Since the owner is the one who principally profits, it should be his obligation.

Let them be compelled to pay the peons, manual laborers, and other laborers the four reales that are customary, and not take one away, which is what has been done. That is also just. When there is no other test possible, custom should command because it is a precept in all natural, divine, and secular systems of law that there should be a just proportion between labor and profit. For this reason, those who weigh justice are repeatedly entrusted with that maxim.

It is frightening to read the expressions that authors use to explain the terrors of this work: the continual risks of losing one's life, smothered in a landfall, plunged down an abyss, breathing noxious fumes, contracting pestilential diseases; all of which, added to the nature of the work itself, commends labor enough; four reales is little reward for it.

In these matters a pact or convention between those who make the contract makes the law. Each one may covenant with the employer for the wage that seems proper, and the employee will decide yea or nay. But this cannot happen when the employer takes advantage of the indigence of the employee, knowing he has no other job to maintain himself; nor can it happen when the rule of good government is not as permissive an authority for the man who hires out his special labor as it is for those who hire. It is like that for those who work out of necessity. Because of the region where we were born, this is our trade; we cannot be deprived of it without injury. Every man has a right, according to his condition, to enjoy the jobs and trades of his native soil.

It is offensive to us that under the pretext of not adjusting those unfair wages that don Pedro Terreros has fixed for us, we are excluded from work because we will not accept them. This is especially true when we are compelled to work. As forced labor, our efforts are made for the boss. He, in turn, should be compelled to allocate the work of the mines to us. There is no more necessity or usefulness in the extraction of metals . . . than there is in maintaining so many men in his work force. This is what we are arguing here. He wishes to tyrannize over us through the very indigence and poverty he sees us in. This is an injury and affront to all humanity and society. It runs roughshod over us. It requires that we, the most unhappy members of the body politic should be born to serve society, the sovereign, and don Pedro

Romero—but not they to serve us. At least we are satisfied that this is not the attitude and pious will of His Majesty the King.

And so Your Excellency will appreciate the great anguish which we suffer in the workings of the best mine which Real del Monte has today, which is La Palma. They have brought other people there to toil, depriving us natives of the right to work it and share in its fruits. If there are rules to defend this, you can make others, no doubt better ones. It is not considered a good policy, referring to the troubles other nations have had, and such slaves are used only when free men are not to be had. If the anguish of the time does not prevent us, some call us free.

Thus, for all these reasons we should be allowed to work in the mines of Real del Monte and to be given the wage that custom has dictated.

Let the quota of the pikeman be meted out by the judgment of experienced men according to the difficulty or ease of the terrain. This is reasonable. To justify it, it is enough to say that this practice can be observed all over the world, wherever mines are worked.

Let the partido of the worker be whatever he can take out from the area assigned him. This is justified by old custom, for which, if Your Excellency deems it necessary, we can give the corresponding justification, as we can for the act of dividing itself.

Let the division proceed without haggling, mixing, and the exchanges we have described, knowing that the honorable interpreter of the ordinances [Francisco de Gamboa] will assent, saying, after considering the terrible working conditions of the mines, that he who works at this hard labor not only deserves the wage paid according to the custom and circumstances of the place but also that it would be incredible to expect workers to come voluntarily to work if it were not for some hope of gain. This may be accomplished by checking their robberies and compelling them to do their duty, or by paying more than the regular wage, as they do in some places. Or, after taking out the quota, which is the quantity of ore which must be turned over to the boss during the hours designated as the workday, by dividing what is left over into equal portions. This is the partido, and the workers' share is either sold to the boss or to some other refiner, whoever offers the best price. Thus it may be seen that this custom does exist. Let said Señor enforce its observance and enhance his authority. Since we have no other way to justify ourselves, our petition is enough.

It is certainly impossible for us not to defend our right to continue working in Real del Monte. After dissolving ourselves in sweat and watering the earth with it, we still have no relief. Without doubt, we will desert the Real, impelled by violence. It will not be easy for don Pedro Romero, without us, to find so many black slaves to work for him. When labor is scarce, the interests of His Majesty suffer losses, the public welfare is affected, and so is that same don Pedro, even when he does not take this seriously.

All these are the motives which irresistibly compel Your Excellency not to be indifferent but to make observance of this custom possible, be it for no other reason than the interest of the king's service.

Let not even one handful of ore be taken from the partido for the hire of the sack. That practice is contrary to the custom which dictates that the bosses will provide everything necessary for the work involved in filling the quota and the partido. When we pay for the use of the sack, it is an expensive and extra fee. . . .

Let them not take from us a portion for the smith and the dispatcher. We ourselves should not pay the employees. The alms should be voluntary.

In addition, we will spell these fundamentals out in more detail if this representation is not acted upon.

We beseech Your Excellency to provide and order as we petition, as a matter of justice.

We swear in the name of God on the holy cross, etc.

(Signed, with *rúbrica,* in order of signing):
Licenciado Manuel Cordero
Domingo González
Joseph Vicente de Villanueva
Joseph Manuel
Joseph Hesabino
Pedro Joseph Pintos
Joseph Antón Osorio

!¡

Developing the Mines
of the Veta Vizcaína

The three great problems of the mines of Real del Monte were labor (its scarcity and recalcitrance), water, and the amassing of capital enough to deal with deluge and mine buttresses and excavations.

The mines of Real del Monte were exploited in their shallowest levels in the sixteenth and seventeenth centuries with profit. But by the eighteenth century most rich silver ores could only be found in mines so deep in the earth that they collected groundwaters. Isidro Rodríguez de la Madrid, who claimed the Veta Vizcaína from 1721 to 1728, pioneered the technology of draining the waters of deep mines by means of an adit, a tunnel devised to dump mine waters into controlled runoffs. He started construction of an adit to the south of the lode and found water so abundant that workers hauled away rubble in canoes. After about seven years of applied effort and funds, he quit, 2933 meters short of the mines. As if flooding were not bad enough, the wooden scaffolding, so necessary to deep construction and excavation, repeatedly rotted away in the damp. Of the mines still working in 1766, Isidro Rodríguez de la Madrid, in the 1720s, deepened the shafts of the Santa Teresa to 197 meters, La Palma to 138 meters, Sabanilla to 165 meters, and La Joya to 153 meters. Only the Dolores was worked in the old ways, at thirty-three and forty meters. Since ordinances required only a depth of six meters and since the partial adit and 39 whims enabled him to claim fifteen mines, De La Madrid had clearly made prodigious efforts. However, ruin quickly followed his retirement. An inspection in 1732 described played-out mines *en borrasca*. The Santa Agueda had fallen to pieces. Water dripped from the ceilings, and *tepetates* buried the standing stone supports and the floors. The mine was closed as too dangerous to work, and so was the crumb-

THE VETA VIZCAÍNA AND ITS MINES, 1732–71

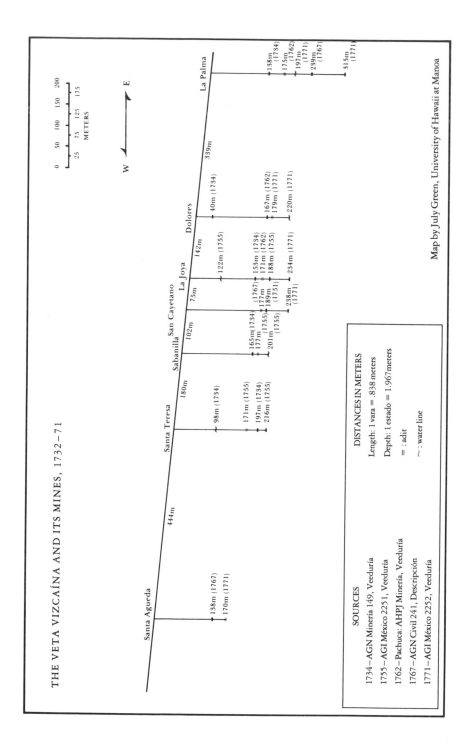

Map by July Green, University of Hawaii at Manoa

SOURCES

1734 – AGN Minería 149, Veeduría
1755 – AGI México 2251, Veeduría
1762 – Pachuca: AHPJ Minería, Veeduría
1767 – AGN Civil 241, Descripción
1771 – AGI México 2252, Veeduría

DISTANCES IN METERS

Length: 1 vara = .838 meters
Depth: 1 estado = 1.967 meters

= : adit
~ : water line

ling La Joya. The Santa Teresa needed scaffolding, La Palma was in disrepair. Only San Cayetano passed the inspection, in good condition according to ordinances. After Isidro Rodríguez de la Madrid gave up in 1728, silver miners worked for partidos only, exploited abandoned claims, sought other work, or, as their employers later believed, were mischievously idle.[1]

In 1739 José Alejandro de Bustamante made formal claim to the deserted Veta Vizcaína. He tried a different kind of adit to move waters from the drifts to a runoff in the southeast near Pachuquilla. The adit San Francisco and San Antonio de Azoyatla consisted of a double-decker tunnel, the bottom bore destined for water (1.2 meters wide and 1.8 meters high) and the upper one for ventilation (2 meters wide and 1.8 meters high). Begun in 1749, they were excavated to a depth of 275 meters by 1755, when their length reached 1006 meters northwest of Azoyatla. Because the results disappointed him, Bustamante gave up on what had promised to be "the greatest adit in New Spain." Pedro Romero de Terreros worked nine more years to the south and one year to the north, aiming at Omitlán on the Río de Carmen, but the adit never fulfilled its promise for the Veta Vizcaína. The Marqués de Valle Ameno and Juan de Barandiarán, sometime partners of Bustamante and Romero de Terreros, completed it to the Camino Real, made the crosscut at Acosta, and continued it to the Santa Brígida lode, where the new drainage system exposed veins of silver that made them money before Bustamante or Romero de Terreros had made a substantial profit.[2]

Bustamante also tried a north-south crosscut of the Veta Vizcaína at the Dolores. Santa Guadalupe—La Rica was the most successful adit in Real del Monte in the early days and the most expensive. Begun in 1743, its 1089-meter length took twelve years to build and by 1755 had cost 172,489 pesos.[3]

Adits and canals drained the mines themselves directly. The San Gabriel adit connected La Joya to San Cayetano, and others linked them to Sabanilla and Santa Teresa. Canals, constructed along drifts exhausted of ore, drained San Cayetano, Santa Teresa, and Santa Agueda into the principal adit of Pedro Romero de Terreros's Veta Vizcaína, Nuestra Señora de Aranzazú. In 1771 inspectors could and did walk the whole length of the Veta Vizcaína inside adits, from La Palma in the east to Santa Agueda in the west. This extensive drainage system pierced the mine shafts of the Veta Vizcaína at a depth of 171 to 179 meters.[4] (See Map 2.)

In 1759 the adit Nuestra Señora de Aranzazú crossed the Veta Vizcaína at a place between La Joya and San Cayetano. It crosscut the lode at about 170 meters, and its 2415-meter length stretched back to a place called Doña Juana or Melgarejo on the banks of the Río del Carmen. By 1755 Pedro Romero de Terreros had invested 22,996 pesos, but the prospects for this "principal adit of Real del Monte" seemed dim because the heading was still too far away from the mines, though it was discharging 2585 liters (13 *surcos*) of water a minute. Only in 1759, after it had joined the Santa Guadalupe–La Rica adit and the parallel mine adits, did it prove itself efficient in taking out "an abundance of water" and draining forty-two different levels. Inspectors in 1762 walked the adit and exclaimed over its eleven ventilation shafts and the solid wood scaffolding that supported the adit all along its length. They insisted that there was no mine structure in New Spain comparable to Nuestra Señora de Aranzazú. (See Table 1.) Pedro Romero de Terreros, counting the days, said the adit had been under construction for 23 years, 2 months, and 3 days, but he concluded that the effort had been worth it.[5] (For expenses, see Table 2.)

The water the adits Santa Guadalupe–La Rica and Nuestra Señora de Aranzazú took out from the mines was equivalent, miners said, to the work of forty whims. But it is a mistake to think that controlled runoffs solved the problems of water below. If they had, then the drainage works could have remained safely unsupervised for weeks or months at a time. In reality such work could not be abandoned for more than a single day without serious water damage to the mines. Adits also served as catchments, especially in the "sump" of the Veta Vizcaína, the San Cayetano–La Joya area. Every day, every night, water collecting had to be bailed out by hand, in rawhide buckets. Miners said it took eight whims to drain a shaft, and two to drain a level. Cranes, working on the spot below, were also used. Thirty-two whims operated in 1755 and 18 in 1771. To work them the owner stabled 300 horses in 1755 and 200 horses and 167 mules in 1771. A whim took eight horses, walking round and round a capstan in a two-shift period to lower the empties and wind up full buckets that bailed out 300 to 350 kilos of water in twenty-four hours. Other horses were saddled so that bottles of oxhide hung from each side. To drain San Cayetano, horses or mules went down and up the paths, in and out of the mine, in four six-hour shifts.[6] This is to say that by whim or by horseback or by crane, much of the water of the Veta was extracted bucketful by bucketful.

Most of the problems of water came from streams below, but storms took their toll. Manuel de Barbosa, then 38, reported the effects of a sudden summer hail and deluge of rain on June 17, 1755. The abundance of waters clogged drains, submerged drifts, and tumbled down the main shaft and a

TABLE 1: NUESTRA SEÑORA DE ARANZAZÚ ADIT

From Doña Juana (or Melgarejo) on the Río del Carmen to a place between the mines of La Joya and San Cayetano. Measured from ventilation shaft to ventilation shaft; converted to meters.

	Distance	
	Length	Depth
Doña Juana to the first ventilation shaft	190	18
first shaft to Escobar	54	9
Escobar to Camacho	206	23
Camacho to Aguas Calientes	98	26
Aguas Calientes to San Nicolás	62	29
San Nicolás to below San Andrés	73	43
below San Andrés to San Andrés	211	105
San Andrés to San Francisco	134	115
San Francisco to San Joaquín	117	122
San Joaquín to Sacramento	198	175
Sacramento to Trinidad	272	281
Trinidad to the crosscut of the Veta Vizcaína	560	170

Source: Veeduría General, September 6, 1762, Pachuca: AHPJ Minería. Inspectors claimed the adit was 2415 meters long.

ventilation shaft in San Cayetano. It destroyed the Sabanilla when water filled the main shaft up to the surface. Whims worked successfully to save the San Cayetano and the other mine it drained, La Joya, and the Santa Teresa. In the Sabanilla, however, "waters continued to bleed in" from above, while strong currents below made the work impossible as men tried to drain the mine from San Cayetano. Cranes did no good, either. After 1755 the Sabanilla was removed from the roster of silver-producing mines on the Veta Vizcaína.[7]

In 1755 Pedro Romero de Terreros told authorities that he had rehabilitated most of the Veta Vizcaína, brought seventy-two work sites into production, excavated three new adits, built three new shafts with seven whims,

TABLE 2: EXPENSES OF PEDRO ROMERO DE TERREROS, 1741–55

	pesos
Connecting works, Veta Vizcaína	476,221
Refinery Santa María Regla, El Salto	425,708
Adit Santa Guadalupe–La Rica	172,489
Refinery Hacienda Ixtula	170,666
Mines: Santo Cristo and Animas	88,753
Adit San Francisco and San Antonio de Azoyatla (incomplete)	72,078
New adit Nuestra Señora de Aranzazú	22,996

Sources: Pedro Romero de Terreros's report on his expenses since his partnership with José Alejandro de Bustamante in 1741. Bustamante died in 1750, and these documents support Romero de Terreros's claim to be sole owner in 1755. Pedro Romero de Terreros, June 19, 1755, AGI México 2251, fs. 98–99v, 55v–59. Not accounted for are the payroll or the costs of 133 Black slaves. Alan Probert says the slaves were paid three reales a day, and, over the period 1741–55, Romero de Terreros paid 29,197 pesos for their wages, lodging, and found (Probert, "Pedro Romero de Terreros—The Genius of the Vizcaína Vein," *Journal of the West* 14, no. 2 [April 1975], p. 71).

Accountants gave the sum of expenses as 1,428,906 pesos.

and positioned eight whims for the drainage of San Cayetano–La Joya. Some 670 meters of tunnels, shafts, and mines were being drained by adits. He had deepened La Joya 35 meters, Santa Teresa 20 meters, and Sabanilla 6 meters, and they had been flooded since the time of Isidro Rodríguez de la Madrid. Sabinilla, flooded after its inspection, had received a new shaft, gallery, ceiling, stables, sorting houses, and storehouses for fodder. In 1755 the marvel, after an investment of almost half a million pesos, was the refinery Santa María El Salto, built on a profoundly deep ravine, "where wild beasts used to roam" and where water fell off high cliffs in a long plume. To the inspectors the hacienda represented "grandeur" and an "invincible effort." They effused, "A more magnificent enterprise has never before been built," "nor has any single individual ever undertaken such a difficult task." In Pachuca and Real del Monte citizens praised Pedro Romero de Terreros for another effort, attracting nice people and vigorous small businesses to the region. Labor was impoverished, they said, but it was because working men were lazy and liable to all the vices.[8]

Though the inspection of 1762 focused mainly on the new adit of Nuestra Señora de Aranzazú, inspectors did manage to find other structures to crow about. Eight whims were draining San Cayetano without getting in each other's way, "something," an inspector marveled, "never seen before in this kingdom." The mine's retaining walls had been reinforced with rock and cement, and the shaft had been rebuilt since the flood of 1755. Beams were made of thick solid oak planks, six meters long. Both the mortaring and the woodwork were "magnificent," "costly and good." All the working mines were solidly structured. The only problem was the Dolores, where men were still digging down in search of ore because no silver had been taken out since 1754.[9]

The inspection of 1767 complained of lack of labor to mine and drain the twenty-eight working levels, but the most serious findings reported the effects of fire in the stopes. Fire in the ventilation shaft of La Palma had burned for a year and could not be extinguished. Santa Agueda was shrouded in smoke, drainage operations were stopped, and the waters were so interconnected that all the levees were inundated. La Joya, Dolores, San Cayetano, and La Palma were all being deepened, drained, and worked for silver. The scaffolding and drainage works were in excellent condition. Pedro de Leoz blamed the foremen, captains, partidos, drunkenness, and lazy, vicious workers for the drop in production and the labor shortage.[10]

In the 1771 inspection Pedro Romero de Terreros said that he was a hard-working and most industrious man. Asking the question "Have any of my predecessors done this much?" he answered "no." Nothing had deterred him from his appointed rounds of the Veta Vizcaína, "not the rigors of winter or the great heat of summer or the damp of autumn, and not the considerable discomfort that I have suffered in the last thirty years."[11]

He was not resigned to the labor shortage and complained bitterly about his inability to bring outside labor into his mines:

> If I desired to work these mines fully and take out the abundance of treasure they guard, I would realize this would require many workers, but to really do it, I would still need many more. At great expense I brought a group of workers from Guanajuato and subsidized them for some time in Real del Monte. Because they fled, I found myself with the same need for labor. I petitioned authorities to press neighboring villages to send me Indians as is provided for by the Laws of the Indies and the original claim to the Veta Vizcaína (approved by His Majesty). I have repeatedly sent petitions to the government, and in spite of this I have never been able to gain what I want.[12]

He concluded that there was a labor shortage because the workers of the Veta Vizcaína were lazy, vicious, and obstinate. He had hired anybody who asked for work, and the reason there were not more workers was that *no one else had come to seek work*.[13]

The contradictions of economic development on the Veta Vizcaína were plain to see in 1771. On the one hand, the mines were well constructed, well supported with wood and masonry, and, for the most part, adequately drained. On the other hand, only a skeleton crew was working. The main shaft of La Palma was sturdy. Wooden structures inside the mine had been replaced after the fire of 1766. A breast of silver had been exhausted and some levels were under water, but men were mining three levels, one 18 meters below the water line. Only 36 men were at work where 240 had been before. More stopes with silver ore had been exposed than could be mined. Santa Teresa was "perfectly constructed," but more *tepetates* than ore were being brought out. The foreman said that only half of the sacks contained silver ore. A new whim had been built, just to remove tepetates. Nine men were mining; six were draining, though 130 were needed, and 380 had worked before. Five work sites in the Dolores were being worked, but the rest of the levels were under water. Walls and dikes were in good condition. San Cayetano had a new whim for water, and the seven others were working well. Inspectors praised the two solidly-built galleries. Fifty or 60 men were dedicated to the drainage of adits and canals and the mining of some silver where 360 had worked before. La Joya was draining, and 36 men worked the whims and dispatched the water. Santa Agueda, scorched by fire in 1766 and filled with smoke and water for years, had 43 men mining and draining where 250 workers had labored before. Adits were well mortared, and their wooden scaffolding was pronounced good. Excavations deepened Santa Agueda to adits, San Cayetano to 238 meters, and La Palma to 315 meters.[14] With high hopes the administrator of the Veta Vizcaína asked for two thousand men to mine the ore and maintain the structures.[15]

In 1771 supplies were plentiful, attesting, inspectors said, to the generosity of the owner. La Palma had 107 wedges, 55 used picks and 55 new picks, 48 *barrena* levers, and a great deal of scrap iron for making tools. The Dolores stored black powder, 300 rawhide bags (old and new), axes, tools, and candles. In the San Cayetano were 15,000 *fanegas* of fodder, 2000 of corn, 60 mule loads of straw, and 900 cowhides for the making of water buckets. The Santa Teresa had tools, 200 miners' sacks, and some iron. In his house administrator Gregorio López stored 5000 pounds of black powder, 14,880 rawhide sacks, scrap iron, cord from Actopan, steel, paper for explosives, drawstrings for miners' sacks, cotton for wicks, tallow, and twine to tie up bundles of candles. There were bushels of chiles and beans (*habas* and *frijoles*) to nourish the Black slaves, and cloth from Querétaro to make their clothes.[16]

The refinery haciendas were solidly built and well supplied with mercury, salts, wood, sand, and pyrites, but they were not working to capacity. "Last night," a worker at San Miguel Regla told the inspectors on August 9, 1771, "no ore came in from the mines." When the day's production of the San Cayetano yielded one-half ounce of silver for 300 mule loads of ore, Pedro Romero de Terreros ordered the mine closed. The owner said his refinery San Antonio had been ruined by the labor troubles. Inspectors found the refinery Hacienda de Ixtula in Huazca to be nothing more than a water wheel amid ruins. All the construction and all the supplying in the biggest refinery, Santa María Regla El Salto, were in commendable order, but silver ore was scarce, and the five magnificent water wheels had nothing to grind. Instead of amalgamating the silver from a thousand mounds, only 266 were being mixed with mercury. Before, the stamp mill ground out 5200 *quintales* of ore and employed 600 workers. In 1771 only 200 men and women were working in the refinery.[17]

Though flood and fire on the Veta Vizcaína were property damage attributed to God, the destruction of stanchions was always blamed on workers. Mexican mines left standing blocks of stone to hold up ceilings. Owners were sure that if there were ore in them, workers would mine them. When inspectors told owners that they must replace scaffolding, rebuild all the woodwork, and mortar the stone structures, owners retorted that workers, not neglect, had ruined their mine. As a matter of fact, only four of the twenty-seven mines inspected in 1732 had suffered damage to the columns. In one mine, officials testified that waters, not workers, had undermined the stone. In another, workers said that the mine was buried in tepetates that, when water touched them, dissolved all over everything until it was impossible to distinguish pillar or dike from rockface. The workers were believed, not prosecuted. Another mine closed from neglect, and the owner gave up because he had made some repairs but could not afford all the new woodwork and stonework inspectors required. Only in one mine did the inspector fire two suspicious workers who had left their tools around a disappearing column.[18]

In 1771 five levels of the Dolores were working, with walls in good condition, but the rest of the mine was under water. Pedro Romero de Terreros blamed the workers and their "greed for the partido" which had made them "devour the dikes" until the waters entered.[19] Alan Probert wrote as if demolishing the columns was an everyday occurrence on the Veta Vizcaína: "Workmen defied authority, pirated subterranean workings, gouged out rich pockets of ore everywhere, destroyed supporting pillars and water diversion channels, despite rigorous royal ordinances against such vandalism."[20] In the inspection of 1771 only the Dolores had suffered the consequences of this alleged malice. All the other mines were in production with columns intact.

The Conde de Regla never considered the wages and partidos of his employees to be an accountable expense, and no such figures appear on any inventory. Under stress before his workers in August 1766, he said that the payroll was never less than 3000 pesos a week.[21] In 1767 Pedro de Leoz insisted that the weekly payroll amounted to more than 4000 or 5000 pesos.[22]

Statistics of silver production and profit are at best impressionistic. The few that include partidos are problematical. Pedro Romero de Terreros paid royal duties at his refineries: the *diezmo*, the king's tithe on all silver produced by a legitimate owner and refined in his own haciendas; and a fee charged when owners bought mercury and salts on account from the crown. *Señoraje* was paid on profits made at the mint. An examination of royal duties collected by the royal treasury in Pachuca, then, may help estimate what Pedro Romero de Terreros spent and kept. The chronology of all accounts varies, but it follows the same general time line: it begins in 1738, when José Alejandro de Bustamante first came to the Veta Vizcaína, or in 1739, when his claim was officially recognized, or in 1741, when Pedro Romero de Terreros became a partner, or in 1755, when he became sole owner; 1762 marked the official investigation of the new adit and its effects on mining; and 1781 was the year the Conde de Regla died.

In 1820 Josef Rodrigo de Castelar maintained that between 1738 and 1762 owners took out seven million pesos of silver and paid one million pesos to workers for partidos. From 1762 to 1781, Castelar said, Romero de Terreros took out eleven million pesos and paid 1.5 million in partidos.[23]

Pedro Romero de Terreros submitted his own accounting to the treasury in September 1755. He stated he had paid duties on 232,000 pesos of amalgamated silver and 46,305 on smelted silver. He owed the crown 164,962 pesos for mercury imported from Castile and from Peru. This was the same year he presented an account of expenses for the adits and mines amounting to 1.4 million pesos. The total silver produced by the Veta Vizcaína (1741–55) can be estimated at 2.2 million pesos.[24]

Total silver production in the Veta Vizcaína has been estimated at some 5 million pesos for the period 1761–68, which means that the strike in Real del Monte took place in an economic upswing. The effects of the strike cannot be seen in the figures for 1766 or 1767. However, the amount of silver paid in duties in 1768 was an all-time low. That is, Pedro Romero de Terreros did not at all feel the effects of the strike in production; but the results of the great *tumulto* of 1767 and its aftermath were disastrous. In 1768 he paid duties on only 16,798 *marcos* for amalgamated silver and 479 *marcos* for smelted silver. (See Table 3.)

TABLE 3: ROYAL DUTIES PAID ON SILVER PRODUCTION
BY PEDRO ROMERO DE TERREROS, 1761–68, 1776–81

Year	Amalgamated Silver[1]	Smelted Silver	Total	Percentage[2]
1761	53,731	3,924	57,655	42%
1762	56,194	6,810	63,004	57%
1763	71,680	8,397	80,077	66%
1764	76,847	12,097	88,944	61%
1765	75,906	8,828	84,734	58%
1766	62,287	21,385	83,672	65%
1767	62,148	24,359	86,057	59%
1768	16,798	479	17,277	26%
(account breaks here)				
1776	44,066	11,133	55,199	52%
1777	75,861	11,369	87,230	64%
1778	32,890	7,300	40,190	40%
1779	31,651	4,280	35,931	35%
1780	29,253	3,410	32,663	38%
1781	18,478	3,932	22,410	45%

Source: Amounts certified by royal notary Francisco de Zevallos Palacio, Libro de Contaduría de Pachuca. Published in Francisco Canterla and Martín de Tovar, *Vida y obra del primer Conde de Regla*, p. 41.

1. Quantities in *marcos:* 1 marco equals 8 ounces.

2. Percentage of total paid to royal treasury of Pachuca.

In 1770 inspector Pedro de Leoz calculated that the Veta Vizcaína had produced 1.2 million marcos of silver, worth about 11 million pesos, during the period 1740 to 1770. In that time Pedro Romero de Terreros had spent 1.8 million pesos for royal duties and mercury purchases from the crown and 5 million pesos to construct, fortify, drain, and provision his mines. [25]

Royal duties for the period 1776–81 were paid on quantities varying from a high of 87,230 marcos in 1777 to a low of 22,350 marcos in 1781. Total silver production for these last years of the owner's life may be estimated at 2 million pesos. [26]

Not disguised at all but most unusual in such inspections was an unrelieved disparagement of labor, expressed either by ignoring the contributions of working people or by accusing them of criminal activity because of how they worked, how they gained their wages, or how they assembled. When adits were lengthened and deepened, mineshafts excavated, and silver ore brought out to bolster a fortune, the entrepreneur was celebrated. Only by attributing the ills of the Veta Vizcaína to lack of workers, only by blaming workers for not going below, only by making invidious comparisons between those who worked after 1767 and those who worked before, only by the longing for Black slaves and village Indians did those in authority give grudging, indirect appreciation for the role of labor in the economic development of Real del Monte.

!¡

Some Theoretical Considerations

What happened in Real del Monte seems to go beyond the usual, predictable forms of causality in history. If no one led those workers, if no ideological prods existed to move them, if no one in their world had ever heard of a strike, how did they ever organize and maintain one? B. F. Skinner provides a psychological answer; Karl Marx, a theoretical one; and E. P. Thompson, an account of how workers developed class ways and formed the working class in England.

The best explanation is that the men of Real del Monte *learned* how to act and think like strikers. They taught themselves from an "instructional social environment," the specific situation or context in which change occurs and from which the solutions to problems are acquired. According to Skinner's studies of behavior modification, changes in this environment bring about new conditions, which allow for experiments in behavior. When one (or some) of the new behaviors is encouraged (in behavioral terms, "positively reinforced"), the behavior, strengthened, is more likely to happen again. The new actions have consequences, dependent on the stimulus, its intensity and frequency, and the response; and they are followed by the reward of reinforcement. It is these "contingencies of reinforcement" that shape complex repertoires of behavior. Feelings, attitudes, values, states of mind are collateral products.[1]

In this historical study the "instructional social environment" refers to the work of the mines and the changes that occurred in the social relations of production. Their work earned miners rewards of wages and *partidos*. The "irregular practices" of management (for example, the ones spelled out in detail by the workers themselves in the two official grievances) changed the contingencies of reinforcement on the job. The new activities are reminiscent of class struggle because workers again and again pitted themselves against management interests. As they worked out their strategies and succeeded in executing them, their behavior as strikers was strongly reinforced. What appears to be their "class consciousness" developed along with their strike activities.

Skinner, uniquely, has tried the sequences and tested the specifics of such changes. What is involved in a "science of behavior" are the subtle and complex relations among (1) the instructional social environment in which change and behavior occurs, (2) the behavior itself, (3) its consequences, and (4) the frequency of reinforcements that analogous situations provided in the past.[2]

Skinner has deep reservations about history and about Marxist interpretations. He grants that history can be entertaining but points out that its descriptive narrative of an event "can never be more than plausible."[3]

He argues that Marx has oversimplified conditioning: the environment does *not* act directly upon consciousness. Rather, it acts directly on behavior. The behavior is followed by its consequences (positive or negative reinforcements). Those consequences in turn shape the behavior. Behavior modification depends, precisely, change by change, on the reinforcement process. Values or other important aspects of consciousness emerge as part of the process. Skinner laments that Marxist history does not focus on what specifics configured the instructional social environment or what exactly accounted for the changes. He complains of Marxist interpretations as he sighs over the ineffectuality of history: "How much more we should know if the prevailing contingencies had been described rather than the feelings and 'isms' generated by them."[4]

In spite of the reservations and the differences, Skinner, Marx, and Thompson have ideas, dreams, and assumptions in common. All are, in varying degrees, determinists. The Marxist concept of "social existence" or "social being" accounts for something larger in scope and less precisely defined than Skinner's scientifically determined "social environment," but the dynamic is there, and the primacy. All share the conviction of the Perfectionists: "If human nature is determined by environment and environment can be changed, human nature can be changed."[5] All observe that the world in which people live has initiating control over their actions, but all affirm that human beings can gain the experience to attempt countercontrol. Within the complex, changing environment, "Men act upon the world, change it, and are changed in their turn by the consequences of their action."[6]

Marx argued that the mode and relations of production and the ways that they changed were the primary determinants of conditioning changes in the behavior of human beings. He, too, allowed for human initiative, under limitations: "Men make their own history, but they do not make it just as they please."[7]

E. P. Thompson, allowing for the determining influence of the environment and understanding the confusion and bafflement of men and women in struggle and the severe limitations on their opportunities to choose and act, commits himself to the proposition that people remain agents, as the English did when they "made" their working class out of thousands of situations of confrontation and struggle in the changing social environments of the Industrial Revolution.[8]

So what? What have all these theories and analogies to do with Mexican labor in the eighteenth century? To begin with, they provide descriptions, experiences, strategies, and sequences to help explain what happened and how the elements of this historical puzzle might be clarified. Is it possible? Could workers in Mexico in 1766 stage a strike without a labor union, an ideology, a charismatic leader, or exemplary models to guide them? The work of Marx, Thompson, and Skinner suggests that they could. It is possible that this happened, and it is possible that it happened this way. The documentary data of this study have built, independently, to the same conclusion. The silver miners of Real del Monte worked, protested, undertook their struggle, "made" their strike out of their own experience, confronted management and royal authority, and succeeded. But some of their success was owed to the "instructive social environment" of royal arbitration, which had been shaped by Spain's long struggle to provide justice for Indian workers.

Notes

Chapter 1. Introduction

1. William B. Taylor, *Drinking, Homicide, and Rebellion in Colonial Mexican Villages* (Stanford: Stanford University Press, 1979), p. 8.
2. Charles Tilly, Louise Tilly, and Richard Tilly, *The Rebellious Century, 1830–1930* (Cambridge, Mass.: Harvard University Press, 1975).
3. George Rudé, *The Crowd in History, 1730–1848* (New York: John Wiley and Sons, 1964), pp. 4, 5, 60, 68–70, 237–54.
4. Rudé, p. 256.
5. Rudé, p. 8. In this perspective, "the masses have no worthwhile aspirations of their own and, being naturally venal, can be prodded into activity only by the promise of a reward by outside agents or 'conspirators'" (Rudé, p. 214).
6. George Rudé, *The Crowd in the French Revolution* (London: Oxford University Press, 1967), p. 239.
7. Rudé, *The Crowd in History*, p. 234.
8. Rudé, *The Crowd in History*, p. 10; pp. 4, 7–16, 33–35; and his *The Crowd in the French Revolution*, p. 239.
9. Rudé, *The Crowd in History*, pp. 10–14.
10. Taylor, p. 128; pp. 114–17, 145.
11. John A. Fitch, "Strikes and Lockouts," *Encyclopedia of the Social Sciences* (New York: MacMillan, 1934), 14:419–25.
12. E. P. Thompson, *The Poverty of Theory* (New York: Monthly Review Press, 1978), p. 30.
13. Karl Marx and Frederick Engels, "The Contrast between the Materialist and the Idealist Conception," in *A Handbook of Marxism,* ed. Emile Burns (New York: International Publishers, n.d.), p. 211.

14. Carl Degler, *At Odds* (New York: Oxford University Press, 1981), pp. viii–ix. Degler understands the value of enabling the people of the past to speak "in their own voices," too.

15. Rodolfo Benavides, *El Doble Nueve* (Mexico City: Editores Mexicanos Unidos, 1967) and his *La vertiente* (Mexico City: Editores Mexicanos Unidos, 1979).

16. Eliot Lord, *Comstock Mining and Miners,* 1883 (reprinted, Berkeley: Howell-North, 1959); Grant H. Smith, *The History of the Comstock Lode, 1850–1920* (University of Nevada *Bulletin* 37, no. 3, July 1, 1943). Smith, who grew up in Virginia City and worked in the mines of the Comstock Lode, was a mining lawyer. He used fifty-six WPA histories of individual mines to write this study.

17. Karl Marx, "Introduction to a Critique of Political Economy," in *The German Ideology,* by Marx and Frederick Engels, ed. C. J. Arthur (New York: International Publishers, 1981), p. 146.

18. The best labor bibliography is, *El trabajo y los trabajadores en la historia de México,* by Elsa Cecilia Frost, Michael C. Meyer, Josefina Zoraida Vázquez, and Lilia Díaz (Mexico City and Tucson: El Colegio de México and University of Arizona, 1979), pp. 756–97. Pioneer studies of the working class in colonial Mexico are to be found in *La clase obrera en la historia de México* (Mexico City: Universidad Nacional Autónoma de México, Instituto de Investigaciones Sociales, Siglo Veintiúno, 1980–81), by Enrique Florescano, Isabel González Sánchez, Jorge González Angulo, Roberto Sandoval Zarauz, Cuauhtémoc Velasco A., and Alejandra Moreno Toscano.

19. Luis Chávez Orozco's great documentary collections on colonial labor include: *Los salarios y el trabajo en México durante el siglo XVIII* (Mexico City: Secretaría de Economía Nacional, 1934); *Los repartimientos de indios en la Nueva España durante el siglo XVIII* (Mexico City: Secretaría de la Economía Nacional, 1935); and *La situación del minero asalariado en la Nueva España a fines del siglo XVIII* (Mexico City: Centro de Estudios Históricos del Movimiento Obrero Mexicano, 1978).

20. Primary sources for this work are published in *Conflicto de trabajo con los mineros de Real del Monte, año de 1766,* comp. Luis Chávez Orozco (Mexico City: Instituto Nacional de Estudios Históricos de la Revolución Mexicana, 1960), hereinafter abbreviated as CO.

21. Mining studies have developed since the 1920s: 1927: J. Lloyd Mecham, "The *Real de Minas* as a Political Institution," *Hispanic American Historical Review* 7, no. 1 (February 1927): 45–83. 1949: Robert C. West, *The Mining Community in Northern New Spain: The Parral Mining District* (Berkeley: *Ibero-Americana* 30, 1949); and Walter Howe, *The Mining Guild of New Spain and Its Tribunal General, 1770–1821* (Cambridge, Mass.: Harvard University Press, 1949). 1950:

Clement G. Motten, *Mexican Silver and the Enlightenment* (Philadelphia: University of Pennsylvania Press, 1950). 1969–72: David A. Brading, "La minería de la plata en el siglo XVIII: El caso de Bolaños," *Historia mexicana* 18 (1969): 317–33; his "Mexican Silver-Mining in the Eighteenth Century: The Revival of Zacatecas," *Hispanic American Historical Review* 50, no. 4 (November 1970): 665–81; and his *Miners and Merchants of Bourbon Mexico, 1763–1810* (Cambridge: Cambridge University Press, 1971); David A. Brading and Harry E. Cross, "Colonial Silver Mining: Mexico and Peru," *Hispanic American Historical Review* 52, no. 4 (November 1972), 545–79. 1978–79: Roberto Moreno de los Arcos, "Las instituciones de la industria minera novohispana," in *La minería en México*, by Miguel León-Portilla et al. (Mexico City: Universidad Nacional Autónoma de México, 1978), pp. 67–164; and his "Régimen de trabajo en la minería del sigol XVIII," in *El trabajo y los trabajadores*, compiled by Elsa Cecilia Frost, Michael C. Meyer, Josefina Zoraida Vázquez, and Lilia Díaz (Mexico City and Tucson: El Colegio de México and the University of Arizona Press, 1979), pp. 242–67. 1980: Cuauhtémoc Velasco A., "Los trabajadores mineros de Nueva España, 1750–1810," in *La clase obrera en la historia de México: de la colonia al imperio*, by Enrique Florescano, Isabel González Sánchez, Jorge González Angulo, Roberto Sandoval Zarauz, Cuauhtémoc Velasco A., and Alejandra Moreno Toscano (Mexico City: Instituto de Investigaciones de la Universidad Nacional Autónoma de México, Siglo Veintiúno, 1980), pp. 239–301. For Peru the classic study is J. R. Fisher, *Silver Mines and Silver Miners in Colonial Peru: 1776–1824* (Liverpool: Centre for Latin-American Studies, University of Liverpool, 1977). King of the mountain is still Peter Bakewell's *Silver Mining and Society in Colonial Mexico: Zacatecas, 1546–1700* (Cambridge: Cambridge University Press, 1971).

22. Robert W. Randall, *Real del Monte: A British Mining Venture in Mexico* (Austin: Institute of Latin American Studies Press, University of Texas, 1972). Alan Probert, "The Pachuca Papers: The Real del Monte Partido Riots, 1766," *Journal of the West* 12 (January 1973): 85–125. Noblet Barry Danks, "Revolts of 1766 and 1767 in Mining Communities in New Spain" (Ph.D. dissertation, University of Colorado at Boulder, 1979).

23. Clark Kerr and Abraham Siegel, "The Interindustry Propensity to Strike—An International Comparison," in *Industrial Conflict*, ed. Arthur Kornhauser, Robert Dubin, and Arthur N. Ross (New York: McGraw-Hill, 1954), pp. 189–212. Quotation, p. 195.

24. John Leddy Phelan, *The People and the King: The Comunero Revolution in Columbia, 1781* (Madison: University of Wisconsin Press, 1978), p. 44.

25. Alexander von Humboldt, *Political Essay on the Kingdom of New Spain*, 2d ed., trans. John Black (London: Longman, Hurst, Rees, Orme, Brown, and H. Colburn, 1814), 1:124, 3:246–47.

Chapter 2. The Work of the Mines, the Matrix of the Strike

1. Robert Shrank as quoted by Lance Morrow, "What is the Point of Working?" *Time*, May 11, 1981, p. 94.
2. Francisco de Gamboa, *Comentarios* (Mexico City: Díaz de León y White, 1874), p. 302. Rodolfo Benavides, *El Doble Nueve* (Mexico City: Editores Mexicanos Unidos, 1967), pp. 1968–69; August 1, 1766, Grievance (see Appendix 2).
3. Pedro de Leoz, "Informe," June 11, 1770, Archivo General de la Nación, Mexico City (hereinafter AGN), AGN Minería 148, fs. 341–42; Roberto Moreno de los Arcos, "Régimen de trabajo en la minería del siglo XVIII," in *El trabajo y los trabajadores en la historia de México,* compiled by Elsa Cecilia Frost, Michael C. Meyer, Josefina Vázquez, and Lilia Díaz (Mexico City and Tucson: El Colegio de México and University of Arizona Press, 1979), pp. 242–67. Leoz and Moreno count twenty-two jobs in the mine; I add helpers, captains, and a few more tasks to arrive at thirty. The point is the organization and specialization of the work force.
4. Antonio de Ulloa, "Noticia i descripción de las misiones que medían entre la ciudad i puerto de Veracruz en el reino de Nueva España hasta los asientos de minas de Guanajuato, Pachuca, i Real del Norte de sus territorios, clima i produciones." Original, June 1777. MS copy in Nettie Lee Benson Collection, University of Texas at Austin. For the life of Black slaves at La Palma: El Conde de Regla, La decadencia de Real del Monte, September 2, 1771, fs. 2–2v, Archivo General de Indias, Audiencia de México, Seville (hereinafter AGI México).
5. AGN Minería 129. The great rout occurred May 29, 1755.
6. "Descripción," April 8, 1767, AGN Civil 241, fs. 185–89. Robert W. Randall has a map in his fine study, *Real del Monte* (Austin: Institute of Latin American Studies, University of Texas at Austin, 1972), p. 6.
7. "Informe," AGN Padrones 2, fs. 100–102, with map. Veeduría General, September 7, 1762, Archivo Histórico del Poder Judicial (hereinafter Pachuca: AHPJ Minería. Alexander von Humboldt, *Political Essay on the Kingdom of New Spain,* 2d ed., trans. John Black (London: Longman, Hurst, Rees, Orme, Brown, and H. Colburn, 1814), 3:238. Rodolfo Benavides wrote the beautiful phrase, *"el cielo estaba cuajado de estrellas,"* in *El Doble Nueve* (Mexico City: Editores Mexicanos Unidos, 1967), p. 137, and the part about the flowers, p. 9. In 1851 William Parish Robertson described Pachuca as wooded, with valleys lux-

uriant with shrubs and crops. He thought the trees of Real del Monte were larger and finer and "of a deeper green and thicker foliage" than Pachuca (*A Visit to Mexico* [London: Simpkin, Marshall, 1853], vol. 2, part 4:159–62). The "houses of water" are defined in U.S. Department of the Interior, *A Dictionary of Mining, Mineral and Related Terms,* comp. and ed. Paul W. Thrush and Staff (Washington, D.C.: Government Printing Office, 1968), p. 554. The serpentine labyrinths that Fausto D'Elhuyar called "rat hole mining" are described by Clement G. Motten, *Mexican Silver and the Enlightenment* (Philadelphia: University of Pennsylvania Press, 1950), p. 49.

8. Benavides, *El Doble Nueve,* pp. 9, 13; Gamboa, *Comentarios,* p. 323.

9. Benavides, *El Doble Nueve,* p. 23; Gamboa, *Comentarios,* pp. 323, 327. An English speaker would automatically translate *barretero* as "miner," but as we have seen, the word had confounding meanings in Mexico. I considered Motten's translation "pit man" but came to prefer "pikeman," Havelock Ellis's translation in Emile Zola's *Germinal.*

10. Humboldt 3:240; AGN Minería 148, fs. 517–28; AGN Civil 241, fs. 187–87v. *Tepetatl* meant to the Aztecs "rock mat" or, as geologists say, alkaline hardpan. It is not dirt. It is a porous white and yellow caliche and clayey material (Barbara J. Williams, "Tepetate in the Valley of Mexico," *Annals of the Association of American Geographers,* 62, no. 4 [December 1972]: 618–26). Nahuatl scholar and historian Sue Cline recalled this reference for me.

11. In *Conflicto de trabajo,* compiled by Luis Chávez Orozco (Mexico City: Instituto Nacional de Estudios Históricos de la Revolución Mexicana, 1960), hereinafter CO. CO, pp. 65, 109. Alan Probert estimates the sack size at 200 pounds ("The Pachuca Papers," *Journal of the West* 12 [January 1973]: 85. Humboldt estimates it at 225–350 pounds (1:125).

12. Benavides, *El Doble Nueve,* p. 19.

13. Ibid., pp. 19, 214; Rodolfo Benavides, *La vertiente* (Mexico City: Editores Mexicanos Unidos, 1979), pp. 409, 346–47; Gamboa, *Comentarios,* pp. 323–24; and the voices of the peons at Real del Monte, CO, p. 75. Motten, p. 19; Probert, "The Pachuca Papers," p. 85; Humboldt 3:238–39); AGN Minería 148, f. 398.

14. Benavides, *El Doble Nueve,* p. 25.

15. Ibid., p. 26; Benavides, *La vertiente,* p. 269.

16. *Atecas, achichinques, achichadores de agua* (all bailers) reported to Gamboa in CO, p. 110. Gamboa, *Comentarios,* pp. 321–22. Humboldt considered this part of mining operations in New Spain "barbarous." He said the leather casks wore out in a week (Humboldt 3:241–42).

17. Humboldt 3:235; Benavides, *La vertiente,* pp. 48–50, 346–47; Ademadores (timbermen) to Gamboa in CO, pp. 89–93, 110; Gamboa, *Comentarios,* p. 321; AGN Minería 148, f. 398. Robert C. West, *The Mining Community in Northern New Spain* (Berkeley: *Ibero-Americana* 30, 1949), p. 22.

18. Humboldt 3:238; *faeneros* (manual laborers) to Gamboa in CO, 109; Gamboa, *Comentarios,* p. 235.

19. Humboldt 3:218, 233–34; AGN Civil 241, fs. 185v–189; AGN Minería 148, f. 398; Benavides, *La vertiente,* p. 40; Motten, p. 19; West, pp. 21, 24; Gamboa, *Comentarios,* p. 326.

20. AGN Minería 148, f. 398.

21. Humboldt 3:211; Gamboa, *Comentarios,* p. 328; U.S. Department of the Interior, *A Dictionary of Mining,* p. 1014. Historians' accounts of what was smelted and what was amalgamated are hopelessly contradictory: Motten, p. 22; David A. Brading, *Miners and Merchants of Bourbon Mexico* (Cambridge: Cambridge University Press, 1971), pp. 137–38; West, pp. 17, 25; Bakewell, pp. 130–33. John M. Gomes, U.S. Department of the Interior, Bureau of Mines, Reno Research Center, wrote me that the question is very difficult to determine unless the ore is right there before you. It may never be straightened out because the form of refining also depended on the grade or quality of the ore, not just the kind of ore. Alvaro Alonso Barba, *Arte de los metales,* translated by R. E. Douglass and E. P. Mathewson from the Madrid 1640 edition, was most interesting but did not solve this problem.

    For ore sorters (*pepenadores*), see Benavides, *La vertiente,* p. 195.

22. Gamboa, *Comentarios,* pp. 220, 326.

23. Benavides, *La vertiente,* p. 68; Motten, p. 18; Gamboa, *Comentarios,* pp. 323, 324, 327.

24. Probert, "The Pachuca Papers," p. 86.

25. Gamboa, *Comentarios,* p. 321; *ademadores* (timbermen) to Gamboa in CO, p. 110.

26. July 28, 1766, grievance. Wages, *faeneros* (manual laborers) to Gamboa in CO, p. 95. Prices, from Pachuca: AHPJ Alcaldía Mayor 1759 and Protocolos 1751, 1770. The slave's self-purchase, Pachuca: AHPJ Protocolos, January 7, 1761.

27. José Alejandro de Bustamante, "Representación," January 18, 1748, in "José Alejandro de Bustamante, minero de Pachuca," by María del Carmen Velázquez, *Historia Mexicana* 25, no. 3 (January–March 1976): 335–62.

28. Humboldt 3:247–48.

29. Gamboa in CO, pp. 73–74.

30. Bustamante in Velázquez; Gamboa in CO, pp. 72–74.

31. Pedro José de Leoz, April 8, 1767, AGN Civil 241, fs. 186, 187v. This roster does not include dispatchers, bailers, ore sorters, or whim operators.
32. July 28, 1766, grievance.
33. The pastimes from AGN Historia 133:1; Pachuca: AHPJ Alcaldía Mayor; and AGN Criminal 303:1.
34. John Leddy Phelan, *The People and the King* (Madison: University of Wisconsin Press, 1978), p. 52.
35. Benavides, *La vertiente,* p. 59. For drinking, celebrating, and profiting from pulque from Aztec times to Independence see William B. Taylor, *Drinking, Homicide, and Rebellion in Colonial Mexican Villages* (Stanford: Stanford University Press, 1979), pp. 28—72. For the jolly activities of pulquerías, Pachuca: AHPJ Alcaldía Mayor 1775.
36. Pachuca: AHPJ Criminal 1767. In 1760 the miners of La Palma took on the workers of San Vicente and fought with stones over possession of an auger the boss had given them. Authorities threatened all involved with arrest and imprisonment (Ibid., Alcaldía Mayor, 1760).
37. Pachuca: AHPJ Bandos; Emile Zola, *Germinal* original 1885, trans. Havelock Ellis (New York: E. P. Dutton, 1952), pp. 530, 536—37; Arthur Koestler, *Darkness at Noon,* trans. Daphne Hardy (New York: MacMillan, 1941). An old silver miner in Pachua sat on a stone near a marketplace and gave me a demonstration. The miners passing by whistled back, waved, and smiled.

Chapter 3. "Bitter Wages"

1. Joseph A. Page and Mary-Win O'Brien, *Bitter Wages: Ralph Nader's Study Group Report on Disease and Injury on the Job* (New York: Grossman, 1973).
2. Karl Marx, *Enquête Ouvrière,* 1880, the passage translated in *Aspects of History and Class Consciousness,* ed. István Mészáros (London: Routledge and Kegan Paul, 1971), p. 53.
3. July 28 grievance, Appendix 1 herein. The case of Felipe Estrada is in AGN Criminal 303:1, f. 47v.
4. August 1 grievance, Appendix 2 herein.
5. Quoted by Francisco Xavier de Gamboa in *Comentarios a las Ordenanzas de Minas* (Original, 1761; reprinted, Mexico City: Díaz de León y White, 1874), pp. 302—3. This is the Richard Heathfield translation, quoted by Eliot Lord in *Comstock Mining and Miners* (original, 1883; reprinted, Berkeley: Howell-North, 1959), p. 211.
6. Alexander von Humbolt, *Political Essay on the Kingdom of New Spain,* 2d ed.,

trans. John Black (London: Longman, Hurst, Rees, Orme, Brown, and H. Colburn, 1814), 1:126, 126*n*; Grant Smith, *The History of the Comstock Lode* (University of Nevada *Bulletin* 37, no. 3, July 1, 1943), p. 243.

7. Rodolfo Benavides, *El Doble Nueve* (Mexico City: Editores Mexicanos Unidos, 1967), pp. 168–69. See also the summary in Robert C. West, *The Mining Community in Northern New Spain* (Berkeley: *Ibero-Americana* 30, 1949), pp. 54–55; and Lord, pp. 301–2.

8. Rodolfo Benavides, *La vertiente* (Mexico City: Editores Mexicanos Unidos, 1979), pp. 50, 346–47, 409; Humboldt 1:126*n*, 3:219.

9. Emile Zola, *Germinal* (original, 1885), trans. Havelock Ellis (New York: E. P. Dutton, 1952), p. 9. Landslides are described by Lord, pp. 217–20, 403, and by Benavides, *La vertiente,* pp. 50–52. On the Veta Vizcaína the San Cayetano mineshaft had been destroyed by flooding; it was rehabilitiated by Pedro Romero de Terreros and his workmen by 1762 (Pachuca: AHPJ, Alcaldías Mayores, Veeduría September 9, 1762).

10. Lord, p. 276. The terrible fire at El Encino, Real del Monte, in 1794, was described by Humboldt 3:157, 212, and by Alan Probert, "Ladders of No Return," *Journal of the West* 14, no. 2 (April 1975): 79–92. See also West, p. 22. Effects of the fires of the Santa Agueda and La Palma on the Veta Vizcaína in the 1760s are described in AGN Civil 241, fs. 185–89. Trinidad García described the devastating fire at the Quebradilla in Zacatecas in 1871 in *Los mineros mexicanos* (Mexico City: Secretaría de Fomento, 1895), pp. 64–69. For the Comstock Fires in 1869 at the Kentuck, Crown, and Yellow Jack, see Lord, chapter 14 and Smith, p. 245. No description surpasses that of Benavides, *El Doble Nueve,* pp. 197–216. Donald Hunter traces the effects of smoke inhalation in *The Diseases of Occupations,* 5th ed. (London: The English Universities Press, 1975), pp. 618–23.

11. Lord, p. 271.

12. Benavides, *La vertiente,* pp. 347–48; Bernardini Ramazzini, *De Morbis Artificum, Diseases of Workers,* the Latin text of 1713 translated by Wilmer Cave Wright (Chicago: University of Chicago Press, 1940), p. 25. (Ed Beechert kindly lent me this fascinating book.)

13. Hunter, pp. 763–67, 817–23; George Rosen, *The History of Miners' Diseases* (New York: Schuman's, 1943), p. 119. Alice M. Hamilton and Harriet L. Hardy, *Industrial Toxicology,* 3d ed. (Acton, Mass.: Publishing Sciences Group, 1974), pp. 171–72; Larry P. Gough, Hansford T. Schackletta, and Arthur A. Case, *Element Concentrations Toxic to Plants, Animals, and Man,* U.S. Geographical Survey Bulletin 1466 (Washington, D.C.: Government Printing Office,

1979); Ivan C. Smith and Bonnie L. Carson, *Trace Metals in the Environment,* vol. 2: *Silver* (Ann Arbor: Ann Arbor Science Publishers, 1977), pp. 44–46. Fans of Monty Python might be edified to read that silver is toxic to lupines.

14. Zola, p. 194; Lord, pp. 389–90.
15. Georgius Agricola [George Bauer], *De Re Metallica,* trans. from the Latin ed. of 1556 by Herbert Hoover and Lou Henry Hoover (New York: Dover, 1950), p. 215; Ramazzini, p. 21.
16. Gamboa, *Comentarios,* pp. 233–34.
17. Humboldt 3:221; Gough, et al., pp. 46–48; Hunter, pp. 631–35.
18. Gough, et al., pp. 7–8; Hunter, pp. 238–43.
19. Humboldt 1:123. Humboldt measured a temperature of 93°F down 513 meters in La Valenciana and 39–41°F at the surface (ibid., p. 125). West found a December temperature at Real del Monte of 23°F (West, pp. 7, 47).
20. "Harlan County, U.S.A.," the best feature film of 1976, directed by Barbara Kopple.
21. Lord, pp. 374, 401. R. R. Sayers and D. Harrington, *A Preliminary Study of the Physiological Effects of High Temperatures and High Humidities in Metal Mines,* U.S. Public Health Service Report 639 (Washington, D.C.: Government Printing Office, 1921); Hunter, pp. 814–15.
22. Hunter, p. 957; Rosen, p. 99; R. R. Sayers, *Silicosis among Miners,* U.S. Department of Commerce, Bureau of Mines (Washington, D.C.: Government Printing Office, 1925), p. 1; Page and O'Brien, *Bitter Wages,* p. 14.
23. Humboldt 3:258.
24. Agricola, p. 214.
25. Pachuca:AHPJ Minería, Veeduría del socabón del Real del Monte, September 6, 1762. Pro-Hidalgo miners in work clothes are portrayed in an Independence painting in the Museo Histórico, Chapultepec.
26. William Keith, C. Morgan, Anthony Seaton, et. al., *Occupational Lung Diseases* (Philadelphia: W. B. Sanders, 1975), p. 24.
27. Ibid., pp. 20–24; Page and O'Brien, *Bitter Wages,* p. 14.
28. Sayers and Harrington, p. 16; Sayers, pp. 11–12; Rosen, pp. 126–27; Page and O'Brien, p. 14; Hazel O'Hara, *Dust in the Lungs* (Washington, D.C.: Institute of Inter-American Affairs, 1952), pp. 1–3.
29. Sayers, p. 4; Lord, p. 411; International Labour Office, Studies and Reports, Series F (Industrial Hygiene), no. 13: *Silicosis: Records of the International Conference Held at Johannesburg, 13–27 August 1930* (Geneva: League of Nations, 1930): 183; Rosen, pp. 99–100, 107, 118, 127.
30. Peter Bakewell, *Silver Mining and Society in Colonial Mexico* (Cambridge: Cam-

bridge University Press, 1971), pp. 144–47; David A. Brading, *Miners and Merchants of Bourbon Mexico* (Cambridge: Cambridge University Press, 1971), p. 49.

31. Letter, November 26, 1859, quoted in Smith, pp. 16, 34n.

32. Pachuca: AHPJ Alcaldía Mayor, November 6, 1764.

33. Hunter, pp. 631–35; Gough, et al., pp. 28–31; Bakewell, p. 147.

34. Gough et al., p. 28–31; Hamilton and Hardy, pp. 85–121; Page and O'Brien, p. 31; Hunter, pp. 238–90.

35. Humboldt 3:250, 258, 268.

36. Clement G. Motten, *Mexican Silver and the Enlightenment* (Philadelphia: University of Pennsylvania Press, 1950), pp. 22–23. J. R. Fisher, *Silver Mines and Silver Miners in Colonial Peru* (Liverpool: University of Liverpool, 1977), p. 54; Humboldt 3:256–57.

37. Gamboa, *Comentarios,* ord. 66, sec. 8, p. 302.

38. Humboldt 1:127, 3:263; Fisher, p. 54.

39. Humboldt 3:265; Motten, p. 23.

40. Hamilton and Hardy, pp. 131–49; Hunter, pp. 294–315; Page and O'Brien, p. 29.

41. Benavides, *La vertiente*, p. 223.

42. Ralph Nader, Introduction to Page and O'Brien, p. xiii.

Chapter 4. Forced Labor

1. Luis Chávez Orozco, in his collection *Los repartimientos de indios en la Nueva España durante el siglo XVIII* (Mexico City: Secretaría de la Economía Nacional, 1935), includes a document describing forced labor of Indians in the mines of Guanajuato in 1779. Another treatise from the parish of San Miguel Tlalixtac argues eloquently that Indians should be forced to labor because God had created them to serve (ibid., pp. 2–24, 35–63).

2. Alexander von Humboldt, *Political Essay on the Kingdom of New Spain,* 2d ed., trans. John Black (London: Longman, Hurst, Rees, Orme, Brown, and H. Colburn, 1814), 3:246–47.

3. Denuncio de José Antonio de Bustamante, AGN Minería 29, fs. 330–330v, no. 6; *Fuentes para la historia del trabajo en Nueva España,* ed. Silvio Zavala and María Casteló (Mexico City: Fondo de Cultura Económica, 1939–45), 8:281.

4. Viceroy Marqués de las Amarillas to Pedro Romero de Terreros, February 20, 1756, AGN Minería 148, fs. 465–70; *Recopilación de Leyes de los Reynos de las Indias,* 1791 (reprinted, Madrid: Consejo de la Hispanidad, 1943), libro 6, título 12, ley 22, 2:291.

5. Pachuca: AHPJ, Protocolos de Francisco de Zevallos Palacio, mandate by Juan Antonio, archbishop-viceroy, July 1, 1739.
6. AGN Minería 149, fs. 190–95; María del Carmen Velázquez, "José Alejandro de Bustamante, minero de Pachuca," *Historia Mexicana* 25, no. 3 (January–March 1976): 360.
7. Real Cédula, San Ildefonso, September 29, 1764, AGN Minería 29, fs. 256–58. The Council of the Indies understood that the adit was completed August 29, 1759; the inspection by the royal officials of Pachuca took place on September 7, 1762; Pachuca: AHPJ Minería; AGN Minería 148, fs. 564–64v.
8. AGN Minería 148, fs. 491–91v, 483; AGN Minería 45.
9. AGN Minería 148, fs. 559–59v, September 3, 1757.
10. Cempoala: AGN Minería 148, f. 564–64v; Tulancingo: AGN Minería 148, fs. 557–58v, 572–74v.
11. August 13, 1757, AGN Minería 148, f. 557.
12. AGN Minería 45; AGN Minería 148, fs. 570–71, 575–76, 588.
13. *Recopilación,* Libro 6, título 15, ley 1, 2:308; AGN Minería 148, fs. 493, 566–67.
14. Tulancingo: September 12–13, 1757, AGN Minería 148, fs. 578–80v.
15. September 10, 1757, AGN Minería 148, fs. 566–67.
16. AGN Minería 148, fs. 582–84v.
17. AGN Minería 148, fs. 487–88v, 575–84v.
18. AGN Minería 148, fs. 474–75, 572–74. Quotation, f. 574.
19. AGN Minería 148, f. 572.
20. AGN Civil 241, fs. 85v–88v, 28v, 30, 32–32v, 154v, 16v–17, 21–26v, 36v. The defense attorney did not recall that the work Indians were complaining of in drainage was expressly forbidden by the Laws of the Indies. The viceroy's jurist, Domingo Trespalacios y Escandón, did (*Recopilación,* Libro 6, título 15, ley 12, 2:311–12).
21. AGN Civil 241, fs. 16v–17. Mexico City used it to sum up.
22. AGN Civil 241, f. 21v.
23. AGN Civil 241, fs. 17v, 19v–20, 25, 26v, 73–74.
24. AGN Civil 241, fs. 16v, 18, 21–25, 34v–35v.
25. Real Contaduría de Tributos, February 4, 1757, AGN Minería, fs. 485, 498–501, 542.
26. AGN Minería 148, fs. 488, 493–93v, 531–31v, 542; Pedro Romero de Terreros, AGN Minería 148, 487–87v, 489–89v.
27. AGN Civil 241, fs. 31, 32v, 42.
28. AGN Civil 241, fs. 18–23v, 25–27, 30, 32v. The district magistrate was out of town. The priest's notary and an Indian cacique were eyewitnesses to the kill-

ing. Bullets wounded the Indian's jaw and skull. Authorities buried him the next day without knowing who he was. The Indian cacique, who saw him die, later identified him as Eusebio Gaspar (AGN Civil 241, fs. 19, 26, 27, 30, 118v).

29. AGN Civil 241, fs. 19v, 21, 26–26v, 114–15, 117v–23v.

30. AGN Civil 241, f. 121

31. AGN Civil 241, fs. 17v, 19v, 24, 121–23, 153v–55, 157–58.

32. AGN Civil 241, fs. 121v, 153–55.

33. AGN Civil 241, 87v.

34. AGN Civil 241, fs. 43, 97, 100.

35. Antonio de la Cruz, "El Tuerto," 35, used the services of an Otomí interpreter. He was married and had five children. He languished in prison for one and a half years in Mexico City before he was finally sentenced to an *obraje*. He completed his sentence March 7, 1759 (AGN Civil 241, fs. 35v–36, 43v, 52, 53, 87v, 100–100v, 103v, 105–105v, 126–26v).

   Cristóbal Asipres, also in his thirties, was married. In Actopan everyone called him a *lobo*, the term genteelly changed to "mestizo" in Mexico City. Rumor and his reputation as a troublemaker ten years previously on a Jesuit hacienda convicted him. There is no evidence that either defendant actually organized anyone or anything. No one ever asked them if they had gone to Real del Monte (AGN Civil 241, fs. 18, 25, 41–41v, 49v, 85v, 95v, 99).

   Incredibly, the *fiscal* with the least seniority judged these two men guilty and awarded them the *death penalty* because of the deaths [sic] they had caused and the injuries at Actopan and for resisting the viceroy's order to go to the mines. The sentences were commuted higher up. Then, consulted about Cruz's long stay in jail, the same official spared him the flogging but directed prison authorities to carry out the six-*year* sentence. The errors were rectified, but this magistrate seems a marvel of incompetence and prejudice (AGN Civil 241, fs. 95v, 100, 105–105v).

36. AGN Civil 241, fs. 100, 112; AGN Minería 148, f. 543. The *oidor* also felt weary because he had not been reimbursed for the clerical expenses he incurred in Actopan while dealing with this case.

37. *Recopilación:* the sense of proportion: Libro 6, título 12, ley 19, 2:290; treatment of rebellious villages: Libro 3, título 4, ley 8, 1:565; welfare and industrial accident provisions: Libro 6, título 15, ley 1, 2:308.

38. Domingo Trespalacios, Actopan, May 30, 1757, AGN Minería 148, fs. 541–44v. *Recopilación:* Indians forbidden to work in drainage: Libro 6, título 15, ley 12, 2:311–12; penalties for abusing Indian workers: Libro 6, título 12, ley 31,

2:293; pay: Libro 6, título 15, ley 19, 2:311; travel pay: Libro 6, título 15, ley 1, 2:312.

39. AGN Minería 148, fs. 547—50.

40. AGN Minería 148, fs. 502—502v, 514—16v.

41. Pedro Romero de Terreros, Pachuca, October 22, 1764, AGN Minería 148, fs. 590—91.

42. October 27, 1764, AGN Minería 148, fs. 461—64.

43. AGN Minería 148, f. 602.

44. AGN Minería 149, fs. 153—153v; Pachuca: AHPJ Alcaldía Mayor.

45. Pedro Romero de Terreros, April 18, 1765, AGN Minería 148, fs. 605—8.

46. For an introduction: AGN Minería 45, 99, 148, 149; AGN Tributos 7, 15, 37.

47. Recogedores were defined as *lazadores* in the glossary to Gamboa's *Comentarios,* chapter 27, p. 326: "People who round up people for the work of the mines because of the scarcity of workers; named for their dexterity with the lasso." The one hundred victims a day is boasted of in AGN Minería 56. There is very little on recogedores in the primary sources, much less in the industry studies. This discussion is based on AGN Minería 56 and Pachuca: AHPJ Alcaldías Mayores and AGN Criminal 115:7, fs. 181—252v.

48. AGN Criminal 115:7.

49. Gamboa, *Comentarios,* ordenanza 37:71, capítulo 17, 25, p. 220.

Chapter 5. The Strike

1. José de Bustamante's official claim in AGN Minería 29 and AGI Mexico 2251. The official inspection of September 7, 1762, in Pachuca: AHPJ Protocolos de Francisco Zevallos Palacio. Areche's summary in AGN Minería 148, fs. 365—65v, 444—44v, 447. Pachuca: Minería, Pedro Romero de Terreros, November 11, 1755. Alan Probert, "Pedro Romero de Terreros—the Genius of the Viz-caína Vein," *Journal of the West* 14, no. 2 (April 1975), 51—78.

Antonio de Ulloa described José Alejandro de Bustamante's accident: "One day, going from San Miguel down to the adit by way of about three-quarters of a league of steep and rugged downhill terrain, his horse slipped and he fell on his knee. At first, thinking it was not a bad injury, he ignored it. But the bone had been injured, and in a few days he got worse until finally even he recognized that it was mortal. Bustamante died August 17, 1750 (Ulloa, "Noticia y descrip-ción," June 1777, ms., Nettie Lee Benson Latin American Collection, The University of Texas at Austin).

2. Francisco Canterla and Martín de Tovar, *Vida y obra del primer Conde de Regla*

(Seville: Escuela de Estudios Hispano-Americanos, 1975), p. 41. Josef Rodrigo de Castelazo, *Manifiesto de la riqueza de la negociación de minas conocida por la Veta Vizcaína . . . Real del Monte* (Mexico City: Ontiveros, 1820), in Bancroft Collection, University of California, Berkeley; Probert, "Pedro Romero de Terreros," 67–71.

3. Manuel Romero de Terreros (Marqués de San Francisco), *El Conde de Regla, Creso de la Nueva España* (Mexico City: Xóchitl, 1943). The important papers of the late marqués are now locked up by his son, who maintains that it would be lacking in filial piety to let outsiders see them. Edith Boorstin Couturier read in this archive before the noble old man died.

4. José Alejandro de Bustamante, "Representación," January 14, 1748, in María del Carmen Velázquez, "José Alejandro de Bustamante, minero de Pachuca," *Historia Mexicana* 25, no. 3 (January–March 1976): 344.

5. Francisco de Gamboa's explanations to Viceroy Marqués de la Croix, September, 1766, are published in *Conflicto de trabajo,* comp. Luis Chávez Orozco (Mexico City: Instituto Nacional de Estudios Históricos de la Revolución Mexicana) (hereinafter abbreviated as CO). CO, pp. 212, 215, 232.

6. July 28 and August 1 grievances are translated herein as Appendices 1 and 2. Gamboa's investigation and conclusion that the sacks were unequal but not overly large is published in CO, pp. 64–66, 80–81, 228, 236.

7. August 1 grievance, AGN Criminal 297:3, fs. 221v, 328v, 352.

8. July 28 grievance.

9. July 28 and August 1 grievances; AGN Criminal 297:3, f. 334v; CO, pp. 67, 76.

10. AGN Minería 148, f. 398; see procedure in the mines of the Santa Teresa and the San Cayetano, published in CO, pp. 64–65, 78–79.

11. Eyewitness accounts, CO, 64, 65, 67.

12. Names of the strike organizers were revealed by their co-worker, Juan Yedra, AGN Historia 133:1, fs. 157v–59v, 170v–71, 180, 281, 325–26. Nicolás de Zavala signed the July 28 grievance first.

13. AGN Historia 133:1, fs. 156–59v, 281, 325v.

14. Testimony of Juan González, AGN Historia 133:1, fs. 12v, 291–91v, 320.

15. Antonio Núñez de Lovera's account, September 13, 1766, AGN Historia 133:1, fs. 154–57; officials' reactions, fs. 158–69, 281; Gamboa's judgment, fs. 160–61. Lovera was about forty-nine years old, a Creole born in Mexico City. He had been in the treasury office some seven years. He admitted to the priest that he had drafted the July 28 grievance, but, fearing he would lose his job, he begged the priest not to tell his employers. The priest straightaway sent the letter to Pedro Romero de Terreros. Gamboa censured the priest for betraying the scribe, then absolved them both from suspicion of conspiring with the

strikers. Lovera forgave Dr. Díaz. In 1770 he said under oath that he was still a good friend of the priest.

16. AGN Criminal 303:1, fs. 32–33v; AGN Historia 133:1, f. 165v.

17. July 28 grievance and AGN Criminal 297:3, f. 328v.

18. AGN Criminal 303:1, fs. 33v–34v.

19. Testimonies of royal treasury officials, July 29, 1766, and of the notary Francisco de Zevallos Palacio, in CO, pp. 30, 31.

20. CO, p. 32.

21. Testimony of the notary Zevallos, in CO, pp. 33–34.

22. CO, pp. 25, 34–41; July 28 and August 1 grievances.

23. CO, p. 37; August 1 grievance.

24. All the envoys except Juan Barrón had affirmed the July 28 grievance (AGN Criminal 297:3, fs. 340v, 341); Viceroy Cruillas, CO, pp. 49–50; González himself confessed to the trip (AGN Historia 133:1, f. 171). Antonio Lovera's statement as the original scribe, f. 291. On August 23 Gamboa implied that the viceroy's original promise to investigate the grievances one by one had been suppressed by the royal officials (CO, pp. 59–60).

25. CO, p. 50; AGN Historia 133:1, fs. 325v–26, 341.

26. Pedro Romero de Terreros to the royal officials, July 30, August 1, 2, 1766, in CO, p.45; royal officials' warrant, August 8, in CO, pp. 50–51; AGN Historia 133:1, f. 45.

27. Royal officials, Pachuca, August 8, 1766, in CO, pp. 50, 187.

28. AGN Criminal 297:3, fs. 345–45v; CO, pp. 45, 54.

29. AGN Criminal 303:1, f. 35v; CO, p. 51. Spokesmen at the Dolores: Juan Diego de León, Diego Xarillo, Miguel Santos, José Sabino; at the Santa Teresa, Juan José Orizaba, Dionisio Antonio Castañeda, José Antonio Alfaro, Nicolás Luna, Paulino Bustos, Domingo Arteaga, Cayetano Antonio Rodríguez.

30. This scene and the following were described and the quotations written down by notary Francisco de Zevallos Palacio, in CO, pp. 51–58.

31. CO, p. 54.

32. CO, pp. 53–58.

33. CO, p. 58.

34. The exchange was witnessed by the royal officials and notarized August 14, 1766, in CO, pp. 53, 55. Gamboa defines recogedores as lazadores in his *Comentarios,* p. 326.

35. CO, p. 55.

36. AGN Historia 133:1, fs. 14–15.

37. AGN Criminal 303:1, f. 36; AGN Criminal 297:3, fs. 351–53v.

38. AGN Criminal 303:1, fs. 35v–36; AGN Criminal 297:3, f. 346.

39. AGN Historia 133:1, fs. 190v, 188v–189, 217v–218, 235v, 165–66v, 193, 204, 220v, 222–22v; Dr. Díaz to Gamboa, August 30, 1766, AGN Criminal 297:3, fs. 333–34v.

40. CO, pp. 70, 233; AGN Historia 133:1, fs. 193, 197v, 204v, 237, 297.

41. AGN Criminal 297:3, fs. 327, 346–47, 353–53v, 331, 351, 357v, 270–71; AGN Historia 133:1, f. 189v; CO, pp. 183, 189.

42. CO, p. 189.

43. AGN Historia 133:1, fs. 107–7v, 164–95v, 204v–48v, 326v. The priest's own account, AGN Criminal 297:3, fs. 333–38.

44. CO, pp. 183, 190, 191; AGN Criminal 297:3, fs. 327v, 331, 337, 352; AGN Historia 133:1, f. 326v; AGN Tributos 46, fs. 12, 179.

45. CO, pp. 191–94; AGN Criminal 297:3, fs. 268–68v, 328, 352.

46. AGN Historia 133:1, fs. 196–234v, 326; AGN Criminal 297:3, fs. 328–42; CO, pp. 184–88, 144, 58–59.

47. CO, pp. 59, 113–17, 200, 204–5; AGN Criminal 297:3, fs. 328, 341–41v, 357. Militiamen were paid two reales a day in AGN Criminal 298:1, f. 2.

48. AGN Historia 133:1, fs. 151–51v, 218v, 221; CO, pp. 199, 204. Testimony of an eyewitness priest, Father Juan Gutiérrez, published by Luis Sierra Nava in *El Cardenal Lorenzana y la Ilustración* (Madrid: Fundación Universitaria Española, Cisneros, 1975), p. 262.

49. Gamboa to viceroy, August 17, 1766, CO, pp. 197, 200, 241–42.

50. Royal officials of Pachuca, August 17, 1766, AGN Historia 133:1, fs. 151–51v.

51. CO, pp. 117–18, 199, 200, 225–26; AGN Historia 133:1, f. 151v. Both militiamen and regular army were paid two reales a day by Pedro Romero de Terreros (Marqués de Croix's report to the king, October 26, 1766, AGN Virreyes 2d series, 11, no. 62, fs. 109–9v).

52. CO, pp. 205–7, 57; AGN Criminal 298:1, fs. 8–10, 16–21v.

53. *Bando,* August 18, 1766, CO, pp. 200–203; AGN Criminal 298:1, fs. 5v–6, 11.

54. Gamboa to Viceroy Marqués de Croix, August 19, 1766, CO, pp. 206–7, 213.

55. CO, p. 209; AGN Criminal 298:1, f. 13.

56. CO, p. 212.

57. CO, pp. 233, 236. In 1776 Marcelo González was administrator for the mines of Manuel de Moya (Pachuca: AHPJ Minería 1776).

58. Gamboa to Viceroy Marqués de Croix, September 17, 1766, datelined Mexico City, in CO, p. 226; Roberto Moreno, "Régimen de trabajo en la minería del siglo XVIII" in *El trabajo y los trabajadores en la historia de México,* comp. Elsa Cecilia Frost, Michael C. Meyer, Josefina Zoraida Vázquez, and Lilia Díaz

(Mexico City and Tucson: El Colegio de México and University of Arizona Press, 1979), p. 248.

59. CO, p. 210.

60. CO, pp. 62, 230. The day's record is in CO, pp. 60–63.

61. CO, p. 74. The day's record was signed by ex-administrator Marcelo González, new administrator Bernadino Díaz, ex-timekeeper Francisco Lira. Pikemen who signed: Miguel Santos, Diego Xarillo, Juan Antonio Velasco, and Juan Espejel.

62. CO, p. 78, pp. 76–78. Workers also seemed "pleased" on August 29 (pp. 64–68).

63. CO, pp. 65–66, 80–81.

64. CO, pp. 72–73, 80–81. Signing and affirming the day's record for September 2, 1766, were Díaz, Marcelo González, Francisco Lira. For the peons: Manuel de Rivera, Pedro Posada, Pedro Sanz Cardela, Manuel López, and Francisco García. Pikeman signing: Pedro de Avila; and mine owner Manuel Xarillo.

65. CO, pp. 74–75, 79–80, 212–29, 232.

66. CO, p. 90.

67. CO, pp. 89–94, 230.

68. Gamboa to Viceroy Marqués de Croix, September 17, 1766, in CO, p. 228.

69. CO, pp. 200, 215, 231.

70. CO, pp. 73, 68. Workers thanked Gamboa as they left and promised to obey him as a father. Gamboa's Ordinances for Real del Monte are published in AGN Minería 148, f. 398, and CO, pp. 104–10.

71. CO, p. 237.

72. CO, pp. 200, 226.

73. CO, pp. 207, 208.

74. CO, pp. 212–13. Suspects are listed in AGN Criminal 297:3, fs. 348–51, 270–71v; for their disposition in 1771 and 1772, see "Lista de reos," AGI México 2251. On the basis of their support (signed or affirmed) of the grievances, these men were considered by authorities to be strikeleaders: Lucas Angulo, Juan Barrón, José Galarza, Juan Diego de León, Juan Luna, Nicolás Luna, José Oviedo, Vicente Oviedo, Cayetano Antonio Rodríguez, Miguel Rosales, José Sabino, Miguel Santos, and Nicolás de Zavala. The thirty-four others presumably had little to do with the strike and may or may not have had anything to do with the riot. That is, they were probably the "usual suspects."

75. Gamboa to Viceroy Marqués de Croix, September 8, 1766, in CO, pp. 216–17.

76. Marqués de Croix to Gamboa, September 10, 1766, CO, p. 215.

77. CO, p. 218.

78. CO, pp. 238, 244, 266.

79. Gamboa to Viceroy Marqués de Croix, October 6, 1766, and the viceroy's directive, October 7, 1766, CO, pp. 277–79.

Chapter 6. Direct Action: October 1766–February 1767

1. Pedro de Leoz, CO, p. 178.
2. Ordinance no. 3, October 6, 1766 (published), AGN Minería 148, f. 398.
3. Gamboa to Viceroy Croix, September 17, 1766, CO, p. 229.
4. The *causa* of October 14, 1766, is published in its entirety in CO, pp. 123–76. It is summarized by fiscal Areche in AGN Minería 148, fs. 291–96. This is one of the best criminal cases I have ever read: the issues are clear, all the parties are articulate, and the prisoners are ably defended by Joseph Clemente de Villaseñor, who played the part of public defender in Real del Monte.
5. Joseph Patricio Nolasco, age 25, a mestizo, was the leader. October 24, 1766, CO, p. 136.
6. Timekeeper Marcos Jaramillo, CO, p. 128; administrator Bernadino Díaz, p. 170.
7. Writ, October 17, 1766, CO, p. 124.
8. Francisco de Gamboa, Ordinances, AGN Minería 148, f. 398.
9. CO, p. 162.
10. Testimony of Simon Vicente García, Creole, age 52, CO, pp. 162–63.
11. CO, pp. 140–43.
12. CO, p. 170.
13. AGN Minería 148, 518, no. 103.
14. CO, p. 172.
15. Bernadino Díaz to the royal officials of Pachuca, December 31, 1766, CO, pp. 170–74.
16. Gamboa to viceroy, January 30, 1767, CO, p. 176.
17. CO, pp. 136, 137, 139, 142, 145, 152.
18. AGN Minería 148, f. 292.
19. There is nothing in the literature to explain the meteoric career of don Manuel José de Moya. In 1767 he proposed to rehabilitate all his mines by whim because the shafts were so deep that an adit would not serve. He seems to have received more privileges than Pedro Romero de Terreros: the right to use Indian labor; lowered taxes; and mercury supplied at cost. The privileges did not pay off. On July 20, 1773 the king put Moya's mines into receivership until his principal backer, Antonio Rodríguez de Pedroso, recovered the 100,000 pesos he had invested (AGN Reales Cédulas Originales 103:26–26v; AGN Minería 224; AGN

Minería 38, fs. 1−153v, 155−212; and Pachuca: AHPJ, Minería: Posesiones and Denuncios y Protocolos de Francisco de Zevallos Palacio).

20. AGN Criminal 303:1, f. 64.

21. Fiscal José Antonio Areche, AGN Minería 148, f. 292v.

22. AGN Minería 148, fs. 292v−293v.

23. AGN Criminal 303:1, fs. 12, 17, 34, 35v.

24. AGN Criminal 303:1, f. 11.

25. AGN Criminal 303:1, f. 28.

26. AGN Criminal 303:1, f. 151.

27. AGN Criminal 303:1, f. 6v.

28. This is the recogedores' version, AGN Criminal 303:1, fs. 2, 4, 6, 8v, 11v, 12, 15, 17, 22, 25.

29. During the arbitration Gamboa told the timbermen that ore would be taken away from them if it came from a place other than where they were assigned to work (CO, p. 110; quote from AGN Criminal 303:1, f. 62).

30. AGN Criminal 303:1, f. 62.

31. AGN Criminal 303:1, f. 88.

32. AGN Criminal 303:1, fs. 138v, 140.

33. AGN Criminal 303:1, f. 88.

34. AGN Criminal 303:1, fs. 31−31v.

35. AGN Criminal 303:1, f. 4v.

36. AGN Criminal 303:1, fs. 2−3, 4v, 10, 28v, 30.

37. AGN Criminal 303:1, f. 2.

38. AGN Criminal fs. 11v, 12, 17, 22, 30, 24, 25v, 28v.

39. AGN Criminal 303:1, f. 93v.

40. AGN Criminal 303:1, fs. 24v, 35v, 93−94.

41. I deeply regret never being able to accompany Pedro de Leoz on one of his little investigations. I would like to see them count the marks of stones on the wall. Leoz's investigation, February 25, 1767, AGN Criminal 303:1, fs. 91v, 71, 25v.

42. Ibid. Investigation, March 1767, f. 91v.

43. Fiscal José Antonio Areche, AGN Minería 148, f. 294.

44. AGN Criminal 303:1, f. 112v.

45. AGN Criminal 303:1, f. 16.

46. AGN Criminal 303:1, f. 5v.

47. AGN Criminal 303:1, f. 47v.

48. AGN Criminal 303:1, f. 46.

49. AGN Criminal 303:1, f. 144.

50. AGN Criminal 303:1, fs. 124–25.
51. AGN Criminal 303:1, fs. 96, 98.
52. AGN Criminal 303:1, f. 60v.
53. AGN Criminal 303:1, fs. 115v–16v, 45.
54. AGN Criminal 303:1, f. 168v.
55. AGN Criminal 303:1 passim.
56. AGN Criminal 303:1, fs. 36, 36v, 54, 81, 151, 166, 177v.
57. AGN Criminal 303:1, f. 126.
58. AGN Criminal 303:1, fs. 62, 63v, 75v, 126–27, 64, 177v, 169v.
59. AGN Criminal 303:1, f. 191. "Exile" in all these cases meant staying away from the district twenty leagues roundabout Pachuca.
60. AGN Criminal 303:1, fs. 50, 97, 97v, 131v, 178.
61. AGN Criminal 303:1, fs. 177, 155, 189, 171, 143.
62. AGN Criminal 303:1, fs. 37v, 38v, 76v, 66v, 128, 54, 121v–122, 58v, 138–138v, 147, 147v, 172.
63. AGN Criminal 303:1, fs. 41–151 passim.
64. AGN Criminal 303:1, fs. 49, 89, 133v, 177v.
65. José de Gálvez, visitor general, executed almost a hundred people for protesting the expulsion of the Jesuits. Authorities interpreted the protest as "a contagion of rebellion" (Hubert Howe Bancroft, *History of Mexico,* vol. 3: *1600–1813* [San Francisco: A. L. Bancroft, 1883], chapter 23; Herbert Ingram Priestley, *José de Gálvez, Visitor-General of New Spain (1765–1771)* [Berkeley: University of California Press, 1916]).

    Priestley wrote that José de Gálvez corralled thousands of Indians suspected of defending the Jesuits. He tortured and hanged 90, then ordered them drawn and quartered and their heads exposed on pikes. Some 125 were flogged, 34 were given life imprisonment, 192 were exiled, and 674 were remanded to prison (pp. 213–28). In Sonora 20 Charay Indians were beheaded and 17 given two hundred lashes *after* they surrendered to his promise of amnesty (p. 276). On October 14, 1769, in Sonora, Gálvez came undone. He told the leader of the expedition that St. Francis had told him all the mutinous officers were incompetent. He himself would solve the problem by importing six hundred apes from Guatemala. The officers and the leader confined him for forty days because he was irrational and violent. He raved that he was the king of Prussia, king of Sweden, protector of the House of Bourbon, sent by God . . . and the Eternal Father himself. Officers, when they returned to Mexico City, were seized and imprisoned when they swore he was insane (pp. 278–81). Gálvez got better. Spain made him a member of the Council of the Indies. Gálvez maintained that he had always acted with clemency toward those Indians who had defended the

Jesuits. Priestley concluded that his sentences were "heartlessly cruel" (p. 228).
66. AGN Criminal 303:1, f. 173.
67. AGN Criminal 303:1, fs. 173–75.
68. AGN Criminal 303:1, f. 169.
69. John C. Super, "Querétaro *Obrajes:* Industry and Society in Provincial Mexico, 1600–1810," *Hispanic American Historical Review* 56, no. 2 (May 1976): 197–216; Manuel Carrera Estampa, "El obraje novohispano," *Memorias de la Academia Mexicana de la Historia* 20 (April–June 1961): 148–71; Richard E. Greenleaf, "The *obraje* in the Late Mexican Colony," *The Americas* 23: no. 3 (January 1967), 227–50. Military preparedness at minimum cost was effected by employing convict labor at Havana and Veracruz (Ruth Pike, *Penal Servitude in Early Modern Spain* [Madison: The University of Wisconsin Press, 1983], chapter 8).
70. AGN Criminal 303:1, fs. 166v–67.
71. Mohandas K. Gandhi, *An Autobiography: The Story of My Experiments with the Truth,* trans. from the Gujarti by Mahadev Desai (Boston: Beacon Press, 1957), p. 471.
72. July 28 grievance, Appendix 1; CO, p. 29.
73. Pedro José de Leoz, Real del Monte: Descripción de las minas, April 8, 1767, AGN Civil 241, f. 186.
74. Veeduría de don José de Rojas, March 14, 1732, AGN Minería 149, fs. 208–345v; Informe de Pedro de Leoz, February 12, 1770, AGN Minería 148, fs. 300v, 301, 332–34.
75. Silver production figures are given for the entire Real del Monte–Pachuca region:

1744	69,159 *marcos* of silver
1766	129,607
1768	67,210

Libros de Contaduría de Pachuca, 1735–81, in AGI México 2133, 2134, 2136; AGI Contaduría 937. Francisco Canterla and Martín de Tovar, *Vida y obra del primer Conde de Regla* (Seville: Escuela de Estudios Hispano–Americanos, 1975), pp. 39–41. A marco measures eight ounces of silver.

Chapter 7. Pedro Romero de Terreros

1. CO, pp. 13, 18.
2. Alan Probert, "Pedro Romero de Terreros—The Genius of the Vizcaína Vein," *Journal of the West* 14, no. 2 (April 1975): 73.
3. The man being described as lucky is Adolph Sutro, a kindred spirit of Pedro

Romero de Terreros. Sutro drained the Comstock Lode in Virginia City, Nevada (Eliot Lord, *Comstock Mining and Miners,* original, 1883 [reprinted, Berkeley: Howell-North, 1959], pp. 264–65).

4. Doris M. Ladd, *The Mexican Nobility at Independence* (Austin: Institute of Latin American Studies, University of Texas at Austin, 1976), chapter 3; AGN Media Annata 43.

5. Ladd, chapter 3.

6. Ibid., chapter 4. Exactly how it was possible for an individual to entail mines belonging to the king is not clear. Royal decrees of May 18, 1775, and December 22, 1777, obliged the Conde de Regla and his heirs to work the mines of the Veta Vizcaína according to royal ordinances. If the rules were not complied with, the mines would escheat to the crown. In 1824 British mining interests feared the claims of primogeniture, and the new Mexican nation promised to abrogate them. A contract between the British company and the third Conde de Regla was signed in 1824. Entail was abolished in Mexico in 1826 (Robert W. Randall, *Real del Monte* [Austin: University of Texas Press, 1972], p. 226).

7. Antonio de Ulloa, "Noticia i descripción," June 1777, ms., Nettie Lee Benson Latin American Collection, University of Texas at Austin. The Archbishop of Mexico officially praised Romero de Terreros as a modest, charitable man, "father of orphans" (Archbishop Manuel Joseph to the king, September 26, 1755, AGI México, fs. 263–66v).

8. AGN Vínculos 142; AGN Tierras 2033:1; Charles Gibson, *The Aztecs under Spanish Rule* (Stanford: Stanford University, 1964), pp. 290, 548n; Antonio Maria Bucareli, *La administración* . . . (Mexico City: Publications 29, 30, Archivo General de la Nación, 1936) 29:4–33; Miguel Domínguez, *Manifiesto del derecho que asiste el Conde de Regla* (Mexico City, 1795); Manuel Romero de Terreros (Marqués de San Francisco), *El Conde de Regla, Creso de la Nueva España* (Mexico City: Xóchitl, 1943).

9. AGN Virreyes 1ª, 41, fs. 51–53; 120, f. 47. Romero de Terreros, pp. 136–39. The will of the first Conde de Regla is published in Francisco Canterla and Martín de Tovar, *Vida y obra del primer Conde de Regla* (Seville: Escuela de Estudios Hispano-Americanos, 1975), pp. xix, 3.

10. The incident at El Salto is described in AGN Minería 148, fs. 289–91; CO, pp. 177–79; AGN Criminal 298:2; and AGN Criminal 303:1, fs. 166v, 179.

11. Alan Probert's version is distinctly antilabor: the worker is caught red-handed stealing silver, the lashing was his just deserts, the mob was organized by "a group of labor agitators from Pachuquilla" who had "coached" the local people in their revolting roles, the woman who yelled was crazy and was committed to

an "insane asylum" (Probert, "The Pachuca Papers: The Real del Monte Partido Riots, 1766," *Journal of the West* 12 [January 1973], 114–15).

12. Two "leaders" were condemned to six years' exile and hard labor at Vera Cruz; fourteen were exiled (AGN Criminal 303:1, f. 179).

13. AGN Minería 148, f. 298.

14. Conde de Regla to the king, printed in Canterla y Tovar, pp. 94–95, 99.

15. AGN Minería 148, fs. 354–55.

16. Pedro de Leoz, Informe, June 11, 1770, AGN Minería 148, fs. 340–60v.

17. AGN Minería 148, fs. 352–53.

18. AGN Minería 148, f. 359v.

19. AGN Minería 148, fs. 341v–42.

20. AGN Minería 148, f. 342.

21. AGN Minería 148, f. 350.

22. AGN Minería 148, fs. 350–50v.

23. AGN Minería 148, fs. 376–76v.

24. AGN Minería 148, fs. 294v, 299.

25. AGN Minería 148, f. 302v.

26. AGN Minería 148, f. 304.

27. AGN Minería 148, fs. 303, 305.

28. José Antonio Areche to the viceroy, Estado de la Veta, February 12, 1770, AGN Minería 148, fs. 289–308v; El Fiscal Dice, 1770, fs. 363–86v; Puntos: Las Nuevas Ordenanzas, September 14, 1770, fs. 387–96v; Resolution, April 20, 1771, fs. 449v–52v.

29. AGN Minería 148, f. 384v.

30. José de Gálvez, Arancel de salarios, Real de Alamos, June 2, 1769, published in Luis Chávez Orozco, *Los salarios y el trabajo en México durante el siglo XVIII* (Mexico City: Secretaría de Economía Nacional, 1934), p. 67.

31. AGN Minería 148, fs. 407v–8v.

32. José de Gálvez, Ynstrucción particular para el restablecimiento y govierno de las minas del Real del Monte, AGN Minería 148, fs. 401–18v; Gálvez to Viceroy Marqués de Croix, February 18, 1771, fs. 419–39; Gálvez to Viceroy Bucareli, November 23, 1771, fs. 458–59.

33. Viceroy Marqués de Croix, February 26, 1771, AGN Minería 148, fs. 440–40v; Viceroy Bucareli to the king, December 24, 1771, AGN Virreyes 1ª, 6, no. 12.

34. Conde de Regla to the king, September 1, 1771, AGI México 2251, published in Canterla y Tovar, doc. 4, pp. 90–97; Conde de Regla to Viceroy Bucareli, November 27, 1771, Ibid., doc. 6, pp. 99–101; Conde de Regla to Viceroy Bucareli, December 15, 1771, Ibid., doc. 7, pp. 102–6.

35. Viceroy Bucareli to Conde de Regla, December 20, 1771, in Canterla y Tovar, p. 98; Viceroy Bucareli to the king, December 24, 1771, AGN Virreyes 1ª, 6, no. 12; same to same, AGN Virreyes 1ª, 19, no. 130, fs. 345−47v; Bucareli, *La administración* 30, pp. 376−77n; Viceroy Bucareli to Conde de Regla in Canterla y Tovar, p. 78.

36. Lista de reos, oficiales reales de Pachuca, December 1771; fiscal José Antonio Areche to José de Allés, January 16, 1772, AGI México 2251. Four on the list were women. The original 1766 list is in AGN Criminal 297:6, fs. 348−59, 270−71v.

37. Fiscal Areche, January 7, 1772; royal officials, Pachuca, January 18, 1772; fiscal Areche, January 20, 1772, AGI México 2251.

38. *Bando,* January 26, 1772; report by royal officials of Pachuca, February 22, 1772; royal officials to the viceroy, March 1, 1772; fiscal Areche to the viceroy, March 15, 1772, AGI Mexico 2251.

39. Pachuca to Mexico City, January 18, 25, February 8, 22, March 8, 1772; Mexico City to Pachuca, February 12, 26, March 3, 1772, AGI México 2251.

40. Mexico City to don Agustín Callis, February 24, 1772 (copy to Pachuca, March 3, 1772), AGI México 2251. Captain Callis was still collecting 700 pesos a month from the treasury in Pachuca in 1779 (Pachuca: AHPJ Alcaldías Mayores, 1779).

41. Conde de Regla to the viceroy, September 1, 1773, AGN Minería 48, fs. 491−91v.

42. Viceroy Bucareli to the king, December 24, 1771, AGN Virreyes 1ª, 6, no. 12. This important letter, which is the basis of the discussion on how partidos were preserved, is published in Spanish in Bucareli, *La administración,* 30:359−76. For another English translation see Bernard E. Bobb, *The Viceregency of Antonio María Bucareli* (Austin: University of Texas Press, 1962), pp. 177−78.

Chapter 8. The Priest

1. AGN Historia 133:1, fs. 106−7. This *expediente* provides the principal primary source for this chapter.
2. Ibid., f. 213v.
3. Bachiller Joaquín Doistue, ibid., fs. 90, 106.
4. AGN Historia 133:1, fs. 175, 190, 194, 282.
5. Ibid., fs. 136v, 166v−68, 170−71, 179.
6. Ibid., fs. 164v−75, 189v, 194, 200v.
7. Ibid., f. 19.
8. Ibid., f. 261v.

9. Ibid., 12–18, 320v–321.

10. Informe, January 16, 1770, AGI México 2252, published in Francisco Canterla and Martín de Tovar, *Vida y obra del primer Conde de Regla* (Seville: Escuela de Estudios Hispano-Americanos, 1975), p. 46.

11. AGN Historia 133:1, fs. 26–27, 30–36v, 53–55. Though the archbishop had not forbidden Dr. Díaz from coming to Mexico City, the viceroy told the archbishop on September 10, 1770, that the authorities would not allow him to remain there (ibid., fs. 30, 36–36v).

12. Ibid., fs. 181, 213, 250v, 265.

13. Published by Luis Sierra Nava in *El Cardenal Lorenzana y la Ilustración* (Madrid: Fundación Universitaria Española, Cisneros, 1975), pp. 267–68.

14. AGN Historia 133:1, f. 125v.

15. Ibid., f. 302v.

16. Ibid., f. 160.

17. Ibid., fs. 29v, 95, 185.

18. Ibid., fs. 291–91v, 320.

19. Ibid., fs. 170, 172.

20. Ibid., fs. 191v, 291v.

21. Ibid., fs. 26, 53–55.

22. Ibid., fs. 4v–5, 10, 99v, 321–21v.

23. Ibid., f. 94.

24. Ibid.

25. Ibid., f. 113v.

26. Ibid., f. 185v.

27. Ibid., 282v, 284v–85, 286v.

28. Ibid., f. 113v.

29. Ibid., fs. 126–26v.

30. Ibid., fs. 88, 104, 137, 170–71, 279v, 282.

31. Ibid., fs. 104, 279v.

32. Ibid., fs. 16v–17, 87v, 95v.

33. Father Andrew M. Greeley, University of Arizona, "The Thorn Birds," *TV Guide* (March 26, 1983), 5–6.

34. AGN Historia 133:1, fs. 95v–96.

35. Ibid., fs. 87–134, 268v–89v, 306v–10v.

36. Ibid., fs. 99–135, 272v–90.

37. Ibid., f. 164.

38. Ibid., fs. 90–91. Shelters for women are described by Josefina Muriel in *Los recogimientos de mujeres* (Mexico City: Universidad Nacional Autónoma de México, Instituto de Investigaciones Históricas, 1974).

39. AGN Historia 133:1, fs. 87–91, 135v–36, 290, 306.

40. Ibid., fs. 17, 98.

41. Ibid., fs. 17v, 266–76, 290.

42. Ibid., fs. 99–313v passim.

43. Ibid., fs. 93–121, 131–31v, 293–95.

44. Ibid., fs. 290–91; quotation, f. 313.

45. Ibid., f. 134.

46. Ibid., f. 137.

47. Ibid., f. 147v.

48. Ibid., f. 138.

49. Ibid., f. 255v.

50. Ibid., fs. 30, 142.

51. Ibid., f. 146.

52. Ibid., f. 145.

53. Ibid., f. 144v.

54. Ibid., f. 148–48v.

55. Ibid., fs. 332–42v.

Chapter 9. An Interpreting

1. Karl Marx, *The Poverty of Philosophy*. (Original, 1847; reprinted, Peking: Foreign Languages Press, 1978), p. 167; Rosa Luxemburg, *The Mass Strike*, original, 1906, trans. Patrick Lavin (New York: Harper and Row, 1971), p. 44.

2. E. P. Thompson, "A Special Case," in *Writing By Candlelight* (London: The Merlin Press, 1980), p. 71.

3. B. F. Skinner, *About Behaviorism*, New York: Vintage, 1976), p. 144. See Appendix 4 herein, "Some Theoretical Considerations."

4. E. P. Thompson, *The Making of the English Working Class* (London: Penguin, 1968), pp. 485, 586; Skinner, *About Behaviorism*, pp. 51–55, 81–82, 170, 226; and Skinner, *Beyond Freedom and Dignity* (New York: Knopf, 1971), pp. 8–9, 211. Karl Marx, *A Contribution to the Critique of Political Economy*, trans. S. W. Ryazanskaya, ed. Maurice Dobb (New York: International Publishers, 1972), pp. 20–21; Marx, "Theses on Feuerbach," in *The German Ideology*, by Karl Marx and Frederick Engels, ed. C. J. Arthur (New York: International Publishers, 1981), pp. 42–65, 79n; and Karl Marx, *The Eighteenth Brumaire of Louis Bonaparte* (New York: International Publishers, 1963), p. 15.

5. Norman McCord, *Strikes* (New York: St. Martin's Press, 1980), pp. 117–18.

6. Thompson, *The Making of the English Working Class*, pp. 40, 64; Skinner, *About Behaviorism*, pp., 144–45, 170, 184; Skinner, *Beyond Freedom and Dignity*,

p. 18; Skinner, *Verbal Behavior* (New York: Appleton, Century, Crofts, 1957), p. 21; Marx, "Theses on Feuerbach," in *The German Ideology,* by Marx and Engels, pp. 121–23; Marx, *Contribution to the Critique of Political Economy,* p. 21.

7. McCord, p. 12.

8. August 1 grievance.

9. John Womack, Jr., *Zapata and the Mexican Revolution* (New York: Random House, 1968), p. 79. Zapata used the word *cariño* to explain why the villagers of Morelos followed him.

10. AGN Historia 133:1, f. 144v.

11. McCord, p. 117. The question of satisfactions from Thompson, *Making of the English Working Class,* pp. 267–68, 329.

12. ". . . nothing more favours irregular and lawless habits of life among the inferior class . . . than scattered and sequestered habitations" (an 18th-century commissioner of forests, quoted by E. P. Thompson, *Whigs and Hunters* [New York: Random House/Pantheon, 1975], p. 240).

13. E. P. Thompson, *The Poverty of Theory* (New York: Monthly Review Press, 1978), p. 171.

14. Marx, "Theses on Feuerbach," *The German Ideology,* by Marx and Engels, p. 51; quoted by Skinner, *About Behaviorism,* p. 242 (with discussion, pp. 162–69); Thompson, *The Making of the English Working Class,* p. 485; Thompson, *The Poverty of Theory,* pp. 114, 171.

15. Thompson, *The Making of the English Working Class,* p. 485; Skinner, *Beyond Freedom and Dignity,* p. 125.

16. Thompson, *The Making of the English Working Class,* p. 485; Thompson, *Whigs and Hunters,* p. 239; Skinner, *Beyond Freedom and Dignity,* pp. 104, 125; Skinner, *About Behaviorism,* pp. 75, 142, 216–17.

17. August 1 grievance.

18. August 1 grievance. It is datelined Pachuca, but authorities believed that Zavala had consulted the lawyer Manuel Cordero in Mexico City.

19. Thompson, *The Making of the English Working Class,* p. 603. Stressing violence, Malcolm I. Thomis interprets the same events as social anarchy: "striking a few blows," "collective bargaining by riot," in *The Luddites: Machine-Breaking in Regency England* (New York: Schocken, 1972).

20. Thompson, *The Making of the English Working Class,* p. 604

21. William B. Taylor, *Drinking, Homicide, and Rebellion in Colonial Mexican Villages* (Stanford: Stanford University Press, 1979), p. 151.

22. Thompson, *The Poverty of Theory,* p. 106

23. Thompson, *The Making of the English Working Class,* pp. 9–10, 40; Skinner, *About Behaviorism,* p. 213.

24. Thompson, *The Poverty of Theory,* pp. 106—7; Thompson, *The Making of the English Working Class,* pp. 9—10.

25. Karl Marx, *The Eighteenth Brumaire of Louis Napoleon,* p. 15.

26. AGN Minería 148, f. 602. Las Casas's story in Lewis Hanke, *The Spanish Struggle for Justice in the Conquest of America* (Boston: Little, Brown, 1965; *The Laws of Burgos 1512—1513,* trans. Lesley Byrd Simpson (San Francisco: John Howell, 1960), pp. 11—47.

27. August 1 grievance.

28. August 1 grievance.

29. John Leddy Phelan spent his whole career illuminating the mediating functions of the Spanish imperial state and emphasizing that its power was limited by an unwritten constitution which involved consultation, negotiation, and compromise, *The People and the King* (Madison: University of Wisconsin Press, 1978); *The Kingdom of Quito in the Seventeenth Century* (Madison: University of Wisconsin Press, 1967); "Authority and Flexibility in the Spanish Imperial Bureaucracy," *Administrative Science Quarterly* 5, no. 1 (June 1960); 47—65; *The Hispanization of the Philippines: Spanish Aims and Filipino Responses, 1565—1700* (Madison: University of Wisconsin, 1959); *The Millennial Kingdom of the Franciscans in the New World* (Berkeley: University of California Press, 1956). The idea of the Spanish imperial government as patrimonial: Richard Morse, "The Heritage of Latin America," in *The Founding of New Societies,* ed. Louis Hartz (New York: Harcourt, Brace and World, 1964); Charles Gibson, *Spain in America* (New York: Harper and Row, 1966).

30. Lyle N. McAlister, "Social Structure and Social Change in New Spain," *Hispanic American Historical Review* 43; no. 3 (August 1963): 349—70. Quotation, p. 364.

31. Pachuca: AHPJ, Alcaldías Mayores, February 22, 1769.

32. Martín Luis Guzmán, *The Eagle and the Serpent,* trans. Harriet de Onís (Garden City, N.Y.: Doubleday/Dolphin, 1960). pp. 163—74.

33. AGN Virreyes 1ª, 59, 86. *Representación que a nombre de la minería de esta Nueva España . . .* (Mexico City: Zúñiga y Ontiveros, 1774); Walter Howe, *The Mining Guild of New Spain and Its Tribunal General, 1770—1821* (Cambridge, Mass: Harvard University Press, 1949).

34. Real Tribunal de Minería de la Nueva España, Ordenanzas, May 21, 1778, AGN Minería 38, fs. 214—96v.

35. *Reales Ordenanzas de Minería,* Aranjuez, May 22, 1783, promulgated in Mexico City, January 15, 1784, by Viceroy Matías de Gálvez, published by Silvio Zavala and María Casteló in *Fuentes para la historia del trabajo en Nueva España* (Mexico City: Fondo de Cultura Económica, 1939—45), 8:301—7.

36. Pragmática sanción, April 17, 1774, AGN Bandos 8, fs. 485—90.
37. Robert Randall, *Real del Monte: A British Mining Venture in Mexico* (Austin: Institute of Latin American Studies, University of Texas at Austin, 1972), pp. 141—52, 152n. Randall describes Cornish tutwork as a system of gang labor with incentives. Workers furnished all their own equipment and worked a full day for a wage of four reales. Each week the work gangs would bid on which stopes they would work. The British idea of the proper proportion of quota to partido had been seven quota sacks to one partido sack (Randall, pp. 141, 227—28).
38. Ricardo Palma, "Friar Juan the Unafraid," in *The Knights of the Cape,* trans. Harriet de Onís (New York: A. A. Knopf, 1945), p. 119.
39. Viceroy Marqués de Croix to Francisco de Gamboa, September 18, 1766, in CO, pp. 215—18.

Appendix 3. Developing the Mines of the Veta Vizcaína

1. Veeduría 1732, AGN Minería 149, fs. 208—354; Condición de la Veta Vizcaína 1755, AGI México 2251, fs. 152—52v, 30, 79—79v. Depth of six meters by ordinance, Juan Antonio, Arzobispo-virrey de la Nueva España, June 1, 1739, confirming the claim of José Alejandro de Bustamante (AGI México 2251, f. 30. José Galindo, *El distrito minero Pachuca-Real del Monte* (Mexico City: Compañía de Real del Monte y Pachuca, n.d.).
2. AGN Minería 29; Condición de la Veta Vizcaína 1755, AGI México 2251, fs. 120—239; Gamboa, *Comentarios,* pp. 313, 317. The adit is described as bounded by La Palma to the east and Acontecillo to the west and "Azoyautla" to the south (Pachuca: AHPJ, Protocolos of Francisco Zevallos Palacio, December 9, 1740). The will of Juan de Barandiarán in Ibid., December 29, 1753.
3. Condición de la Veta Vizcaína 1755, AGI México 2251, fs. 83—245.
4. Condición de la Veta Vizcaína 1755, AGI México 2251, fs. 80v—109; Diligencias de Veeduría 1771, AGI México 2252.
5. Condición de la Veta Vizcaína, AGI México 2251, fs. 50v, 52—52v, 116, 154—56v, 244—45; Veeduría General 1762, Pachuca: AHPJ Minería.
6. Condición de la Veta Vizcaína 1755, AGI México 2251, fs. 83—84v, 94—95; Diligencias de Veeduría 1771, AGI México 2252, f. 7v.
7. Condición de la Veta Vizcaína 1755, AGI México 2251, fs. 102v, 105, 107, 122—25v, 151v, 252v.
    On August 8, 1771, the same kind of hail and rain storm caught the inspecting team in an adit at 2:30 P.M. The summer deluge and the underground waters rushing in from ravines inundated San Cayetano. Waters lifted the scaffolding from a ventilation shaft, and some 34 meters of walls and paths were

damaged. The main shaft was unharmed, this time; reconstruction work was soon accomplished; and San Cayetano was restored to operation without any lasting ill effects (Diligencias de Veeduría 1771, AGI México 2252, fs. 20–27).

8. Condición de la Veta Vizcaína 1755, AGI México 2251, fs. 252–55v, 85, 80v–83, 55v, 70–72v, 209, 215v–25v.

9. Veeduría General, September 9, 1762, Pachuca: AHPJ Minería.

10. Pedro de Leoz, Descripción de las Minas, April 8, 1767, AGN Civil 241, fs. 185v–189.

11. Diligencias de Veeduría 1771, AGI México 2252, f. 30v.

12. Diligencias de Veeduría 1771, AGI México 2252, fs. 30v–31.

13. Diligencias de Veeduría 1771, AGI México 2252, f. 31. Emphasis mine.

14. Diligencias de Veeduría 1771, AGI México 2252, fs. 1–9.

15. Diligencias de Veeduría 1771, AGI México 2252, fs. 8v–9.

16. Diligencias de Veeduría 1771, AGI México 2252, fs. 3–5.

17. Diligencias de Veeduría 1771, AGI México 2252, fs. 11–15.

18. Veeduría 1732, AGN Minería 149, fs. 220v–52v, 275–78, 363v.

19. Diligencias de Veeduría 1771, AGI México 2252, fs. 3–3v, 7v.

20. Alan Probert, "Pedro Romero de Terreros—The Genius of the Vizcaína Vein," *Journal of the West* 14, no. 2 (April 1975): 72–73.

21. co, p. 54. He said, "three *talegas*," and a talega is a bag of one thousand silver pesos.

22. Descripción de las Minas 1767, AGN Civil 241, f. 187.

23. Josef Rodrigo de Castelazo, *Manifiesto de la riqueza de la negociación de minas, conocida por la Veta Vizcaína ubicada en el Real del Monte* . . . Mexico City: Ontiveros, 1820), in the Bancroft Collection, University of California, Berkeley. The patron was the second Conde de Regla, and his purpose, finally fulfilled, was to provide supporting documents and incentives to persuade the British to contract to run the mines of Real del Monte. Peter Bakewell has the clearest explanation of *diezmos* and *quintos* and the problem of understanding accounts in his *Silver Mining and Society in Colonial Mexico: Zacatecas, 1546–1700* (Cambridge: Cambridge University Press, 1971), pp. 181–95.

24. Pedro Romero de Terreros, September 19, 1755, AGI México 2251, fs. 257–63, for the accounting and fs. 55v–59, 98–99v, for the expenses of the adits. Alan Probert, "Pedro Romero de Terreros—The Genius," p. 67.

25. Pedro de Leoz, Informe, June 11, 1770, AGN Minería 148, fs. 356–58.

26. Francisco Canterla and Martín de Tovar, *Vida y obra del primer Conde de Regla* (Seville: Escuela de Estudios Hispano-Américanos, 1975), p. 41.

Appendix 4. Some Theoretical Considerations

1. The term "instructional social environment" is from B. F. Skinner, *About Behaviorism* (New York: Vintage, 1976), p. 144; "contingencies of reinforcement" from Skinner, "An Operant Analysis of Problem-Solving," paper, April 16, 1985; feelings as collateral, from *About Behaviorism,* p. 75. In his *Beyond Freedom and Dignity* (New York: Knopf, 1971), p. 104, Skinner explains, "The value is to be found in the social contingencies."

2. Skinner, *About Behaviorism,* pp. 77, 162.

3. Ibid., pp. 67, 150.

4. Ibid., p. 162; discussed on pp. 72, 213, 255, 259; Skinner, *Beyond Freedom and Dignity,* p. 142.

5. B. F. Skinner, *Reflections on Behaviorism and Society* (Englewood Cliffs, N.J.: Prentice-Hall, 1978), p. 330.

6. B. F. Skinner, *Verbal Behavior* (New York: Appleton, Century, Crofts, 1957), p. 1.

7. Karl Marx, *The Eighteenth Brumaire of Louis Bonaparte* (New York: International Publishers, 1963), p. 15.

8. E. P. Thompson, *The Poverty of Theory* (New York: Monthly Review Press, 1978), pp. 106–7; E. P. Thompson, *The Making of the English Working Class* (London: Penguin, 1968).

!¡

Glossary

a ingenio: a mine worked "by contrivance," not according to royal ordinances. Such mines paid *partidos* but no wages.

ademes, ademadores: timbermen in charge of the wooden supports and structures of a mine.

adit: drainage earthworks which divert groundwater from mines into controlled runoffs.

alcalde mayor: district magistrate, governing areas of local administration and jurisdiction. Pachuca and Tulancingo were district magistracies.

amo: boss, employer, owner.

arastradero: stamp mill, crushing ore inside a refinery.

arroba: measure of weight, equivalent to 25 pounds.

atecas, achichadores, achichinques: bailers, manual laborers who worked to keep the mines free of water. The work of scooping up the water and carrying it in heavy leather buckets to the whim or crane was so fatiguing that Indians were forbidden to do it.

barra: share in a business enterprise (to the investors); work gang (to the workers).

barragana: priest's woman.

barretero: pikeman skilled in the work of taking out ore and setting explosives.

"blacks": silver ore colored by a high content of lead sulfide.

bray: to pound, to grind into a powder.

cañón: drift, underground passage, horizontal gallery. Mexican drifts were neither straight nor parallel. Because they followed the vein, they were labyrinths; hence the term "rat hole mining."

castizo: person of Spanish and or Creole and mestizo heritage.

cofradía: laymen's church group.

costal: rawhide ore sack.

crowd: group of people, sometimes with deep convictions and seeking political solutions for their own grievances through mass action that may or may not end in violence. (Rudé).

cuera y gorra: miners' work clothes, a leather or cotton tunic and a soft cap.

cura: rector, a secular priest assigned the living of a parish.

dry diggings: mining operations in terrain without ore.

en borrasca: describes mines in ruins, played out.

español: Mexican Creole or peninsular Spaniard.

estado: measure of the depth of a mine or shaft. One estado equals 1.967 meters.

faeneros: manual laborers.

fandango: dance, party.

fiscal: attorney general.

gachupín: derogatory Mexican term for peninsular Spaniard.

gente decente: townsfolk who consider themselves "nice people."

hacienda de beneficio: silver refinery.

league: a measure of distance; one Spanish league equals 3.5 miles.

lumbrera: ventilation shaft in an adit.

marco: mesures eight ounces of silver.

medio: half a pottery jar; the vessel in which pulque was served.

mestizo: person of Spanish and/or Creole and Indian heritage.

minero: owner, investor; mine foreman.

mob: from the perspective of authorities, a group of people stirred up by "outside agitators," a "disorderly rabble," often bent on violence. (Rudé).

muriate: chloride.

partido: share, a customary wage in the form of a portion of ore.

peons: in mines they are miners' helpers.

pepenador: rock crusher and sorter of ores.

plan: level or tier.

pueble: workers in a shift, the work force of a mine during the day or night.

pulquería: small tavern, licensed or illicit, serving fermented maguey sap and snacks.

quota (tequio): the task of ore sacks set for the work of the shift, the size adjusted for its difficulty; a proportional share of silver ore designated for management.

ratio: a fixed relation between two things; here between quota and partido.

rayador: timekeeper, registrar, paymaster of mines.

real: one-eighth of a silver peso or piece of eight.

Real: a mining community where production was governed by royal ordinances. Such places today are called "Mineral," as in Mineral del Monte.

recogedores: "press gangs" used to round up forced labor for the dry diggings.

"reds" (colorados): silver ore colored from a high content of iron oxide.

smith (herrero): man who repaired iron tools on a charcoal forge and doled out water for the workers below.

stopes: excavations within a mine in which miners cut ore; the workplaces inside a mine, where ore is pried out.

surco: a "water inch." A measure of water (as at the mouth of an adit), amounting to 198.8 liters of water per minute.

taco: paper packet for black powder and fuse.

tepetates: alkaline rubble.

tiro: shaft in a mine.

tumulto: riot.

vara: a measure of distance equalling .838 meters.

veeduría: official inspection of mines and adits.

velador: watchman, inspector.

veta: lode. The Veta Vizcaína is the Biscayan Lode at Real del Monte.

vicario: curate.

whims (malacates): horse-driven capstans used to control pulleys that raised ore, rubble, or water.

!¡

Bibliography

Archival and Manuscript Sources

Bancroft Collection, University of California, Berkeley.
AGI. Archivo General de Indias, Seville:
   Audiencia de México 2251, 2252.
AGN. Archivo General de la Nación, Mexico City:
   Bandos
   Civil
   Clero Regular y Secular
   Criminal
   Historia
   Minería
   Padrones
   Reales Cédulas Duplicadas
   Reales Cédulas Originales
   Tierras
   Tributos
   Vínculos
   Virreyes, primera serie de correspondencia
   Virreyes, segunda serie de correspondencia
Pachuca: AHPJ. Archivo Histórico del Poder Judicial,
   Pachuca, Hidalgo.
Texas. Nettie Lee Benson Latin American Collection,
   The University of Texas at Austin.

Published Documents

Bucareli, Antonio María. *La administración.* . . . Mexico City, Publications 29, 30, Archivo General de la Nación, 1936. 2 vols.

Chávez Orozco, Luis, compiler. *La minería en la Nueva España a postrimerías del siglo XVIII.* Mexico City: Secretaría de la Economía Nacional, 1938.

―――. *Los repartimientos de indios en la Nueva España durante el siglo XVIII.* Mexico City: Secretaría de la Economía Nacional, 1935.

―――. *Los salarios y el trabajo en México durante el siglo XVIII.* Mexico City: Secretaría de Economía Nacional, 1934.

―――. *La situación del minero asalariado en la Nueva España a fines del siglo XVIII.* Compiled in 1935. Mexico City: Centro de Estuidos Históricos del Movimiento Obrero Mexicano, 1978.

CO. Chávez Orozco, Luis, compiler. *Conflicto de trabajo con los mineros de Real del Monte, año de 1766.* Mexico City: Instituto Nacional de Estudios Históricos de la Revolución Mexicana, 1960.

Gamboa, Francisco Xavier de. *Comentarios a las Ordenanzas de Minas.* Original, 1761. Reprinted, Mexico City: Díaz de León y White, 1874.

The Laws of Burgos of 1512–1513. Royal Ordinances for the Good Government and Treatment of the Indians. Translated by Lesley Byrd Simpson. San Francisco: John Howell, 1960.

Recopilación de Leyes de los Reynos de las Indias. 3 vols. Original, 1791. Reprinted, Madrid: Consejo de la Hispanidad, 1943.

Zavala, Silvio, and María Casteló, eds. *Fuentes para la historia del trabajo en Nueva España.* 8 vols. Mexico City: Fondo de Cultura Económica, 1939–45.

Books, Articles, Dissertations

Agricola, Georgius [George Bauer]. *De Re Metallica.* Original, 1556. Translated from the Latin by Herbert C. Hoover and Lou Henry Hoover. New York: Dover, 1950.

Bakewell, Peter. *Silver Mining and Society in Colonial Mexico: Zacatecas, 1546–1700.* Cambridge: Cambridge University Press, 1971.

Bancroft, Hubert Howe. *History of Mexico, vol. 3: 1600–1803.* San Francisco: A. L. Bancroft, 1883.

Barba, Alvaro Alonso. *Arte de los metales.* Original, 1640. Translated by Ross. E. Douglass and E. P. Mathewson. New York: J. Wiley, 1923.

Bargalló, Modesto. *La minería y la metalurgia en la América Española durante la época colonial.* Mexico City: Fondo de Cultura Económica, 1955.

Benavides, Rodolfo. *El Doble Nueve*. Mexico City: Editores Mexicanos Unidos, 1967.

————. *La vertiente*. Mexico City: Editores Mexicanos Unidos, 1979.

Bobb, Bernard E. *The Viceregency of Antonio María Bucareli in New Spain, 1771 – 1779*. Austin: University of Texas Press, 1962.

Brading, David A. "Mexican Silver-Mining in the Eighteenth Century: The Revival of Zacatecas." *Hispanic American Historical Review* 50, no. 4 (November 1970): 665 – 81.

————. "La minería de la plata en el siglo XVIII: El caso de Bolaños." *Historia Mexicana* 18 (1969): 317 – 33.

————. *Miners and Merchants of Bourbon Mexico, 1763 – 1810*. Cambridge: Cambridge University Press, 1971.

Brading, David A., and Harry E. Cross. "Colonial Silver Mining: Mexico and Peru." *Hispanic American Historical Review* 52, no. 4 (November 1972): 545 – 79.

Cam, Helen Maude. *Liberties and Communities in Medieval England: Collected Studies in Local Administration and Topography*. Original, 1944. Reprinted, New York: Barnes and Noble, 1963.

Canterla, Francisco, and Martín de Tovar. *Vida y obra del primer Conde de Regla*. Seville: Escuela de Estudios Hispano-Americanos, 1975.

Carrera Estampa, Manuel. "El obraje novohispano." *Memorias de la Academia Mexicana de la Historia* 20 (April – June 1961): 148 – 71.

Castelazo, Josef Rodrigo de. *Manifiesto de la riqueza de la negociación de minas conocida por la Veta Vizcaína . . . Real del Monte*. Mexico City: Ontiveros, 1820. (In Bancroft Collection, University of California, Berkeley.)

Centro Hidalgüense de Investigaciones Históricas. "Ciudad de Pachuca." Sobretiro de la *Encyclopedia de México*. Mexico City, 1975.

————. *Historiografía hidalgüense*. Vol 2. Pachuca, 1979.

Cutler, Antony, et al. *Marx's "Capital" and Capitalism Today*. Translated by S. W. Ryazanskaya. 2 vols. Edited by Maurice Dobb. London: Henley; Boston: Routledge and Kegan Paul, 1977 – 78.

Danks, Noblet Barry. "Revolts of 1766 and 1767 in Mining Communities in New Spain." Ph.D. Dissertation, Department of History, University of Colorado at Boulder, 1979.

Davis, Natalie Zemon. *Society and Culture in Early Modern France*. Stanford: Stanford University Press, 1975.

Dawley, Alan. "E. P. Thompson and the Peculiarities of the Americans." *Radical Historical Review* 19 (Winter 1978 – 1979): 33 – 59.

Degler, Carl. *At Odds*. New York: Oxford University Press, 1980.

Domínguez, Miguel. *Manifiesto del derecho que asiste el Conde de Regla.* Mexico City, 1795.

Esquivel Obregón, Tc_:bio. *Biografía de don Francisco Javier Gamboa.* Mexico City: Talleres Gráfico Laguna, 1941.

Fisher, J. R. *Silver Mines and Silver Miners in Colonial Peru: 1776–1824.* Liverpool: Centre for Latin-American Studies, University of Liverpool, 1977.

Fisher, John. "Soldiers, Society, and Politics in Spanish America, 1750–1821." *Latin American Research Review* 17, no. 1 (1982): 217–22.

Fitch, John A. "Strikes and Lockouts." *Encyclopedia of the Social Sciences,* 14:419–25. New York: MacMillan, 1934.

Florescano, Enrique, Isabel González Sánchez, Jorge Gónzález Angulo, Roberto Sandoval Zarauz, Cuauhtémoc Velasco A., and Alejandra Moreno Toscano. *La clase obrera en la historia de México.* Mexico City: Universidad Nacional Autónoma de México, Instituto de Investigaciones Sociales. Siglo Veintiúno Editores, 1980–81.

Frost, Elsa Cecilia, Michael C. Meyer, Josefina Zoraida Vázquez, and Lilia Díaz. *El trabajo y los trabajadores en la historia de México.* Mexico City and Tucson: El Colegio de México and University of Arizona, 1979.

Galindo, José J. *El distrito minero Pachuca–Real del Monte.* Pachuca: Compañía de Real del Monte y Pachuca, n.d.

Gandhi, Mohandas K. *An Autobiography: The Story of My Experiments with the Truth.* Translated from the Gujarati by Mahadev Desai. Boston: Beacon Press, 1957.

García, Trinidad. *Los mineros mexicanos.* Mexico City: Secretaría de Fomento, 1895.

Gerhard, Peter. *A Guide to the Historical Geography of New Spain.* Cambridge: Cambridge University Press, 1972.

Gibson, Charles. *The Aztecs under Spanish Rule.* Stanford: Stanford University Press, 1964.

———. *Spain in America.* New York: Harper and Row, 1966.

Gough, Larry P., Hansford T. Schackletta, and Arthur A. Case. *Element Concentrations Toxic to Plants, Animals, and Man.* U.S. Geographical Survey Bulletin 1466. Washington, D.C.: Government Printing Office, 1979.

Greenleaf, Richard E. "The *obraje* in the Late Mexican Colony," *The Americas* 23, no. 3 (January 1967), 227–50.

Guzmán, Martin Luís. *The Eagle and the Serpent.* Translated by Harriet de Onís. Garden City, New York: Doubleday-Dolphin, 1960.

Hadley, Phillip Lance. "Mining and Society in the Santa Eulalia Mining Complex, Chihuahua, Mexico, 1790–1950." Ph.D. dissertation, Department of History, University of Texas at Austin, 1975.

Hamilton, Alice, and Harriet L. Hardy, *Industrial Toxicology.* 3d edition. Acton,

Mass.: Publishing Sciences Group, 1974.

Hanke, Lewis. *The Spanish Struggle for Justice in the Conquest of America*. Boston: Little, Brown, 1965.

Harrison, Royden, ed. *Independent Collier: The Coal Miner as Archetypal Proletarian Reconsidered*. New York: St. Martin's Press, 1978.

Howe, Walter. *The Mining Guild of New Spain and Its Tribunal General, 1770–1821*. Cambridge, Mass.: Harvard University Press, 1949.

Humboldt, Alexander von. *Political Essay on the Kingdom of New Spain*. 4 vols. 2d. ed. Translated by John Black. London: Longman, Hurst, Rees, Orme, Brown and H. Colburn, 1814.

Hunter, Donald. *The Diseases of Occupations*. 5th ed. London: The English Universities Press, 1975.

International Labour Office. Studies and Reports, Series F (Industrial Hygiene), no. 13: *Silicosis: Records of the International Conference Held at Johannesburg, 13–27 August, 1930*. Geneva: League of Nations, 1930.

Keith, William, C. Morgan, Anthony Seaton, et. al. *Occupational Lung Diseases*. Philadelphia: W. B. Sanders, 1975.

Kerr, Clark, and Abraham Siegel. "The Interindustry Propensity to Strike—An International Comparison." In *Industrial Conflict*, ed. Arthur Kornhauser, Robert Dubin and Arthur M. Ross, pp. 189–212. New York: McGraw-Hill, 1954.

Koestler, Arthur. *Darkness at Noon*. Translated by Daphne Hardy. New York: Mac-Millan, 1941.

Ladd, Doris M. *The Mexican Nobility at Independence: 1780–1826*. Austin: Institute of Latin American Studies, University of Texas at Austin, 1976.

León Portilla, Miguel, Jorge Gurría Lacroix, Roberto Moreno de los Arcos, Enrique Madero Bracho. *La minería en México*. Mexico City: Universidad Nacional Autónoma de México, Instituto de Investigaciones Históricas, 1978.

López Cancelada, Juan. "Vocabulario." In *Minas de oro y plata en España*, pp. 182–97. Madrid, 1834.

López Miramontes, Alvaro. *Las minas en Nueva España en 1753*. Mexico City: Instituto Nacional de Antropología e Historia, Departamento de Investigaciones Históricas, 1975.

Lord, Eliot. *Comstock Mining and Miners*. Original, 1883. Reprinted, Berkeley: Howell-North, 1959.

Lugo, Theodomiro. *The Characteristic Minerals of the Lodes in the Mining Districts of Pachuca and Mineral del* [Atotonilco el] *Chico*. Pachuca: Daniel Quiroz, 1901.

Lukács, Georg. *History and Class Consciousness: Studies in Marxist Dialectics*. Translated by Rodney Livingstone. Cambridge, Mass.: M.I.T. Press, 1971.

Luxemburg, Rosa. *The Mass Strike*. Original, 1916. Translated by Patrick Lavin.

New York: Harper and Row, 1971.

Marcus Aurelius. *Meditations*. Translated by Maxwell Staniforth. Baltimore: Penguin, 1964.

Marx, Karl. *The Class Struggles in France, 1848–1850*. Moscow: Progress, 1972.

———. *A Contribution to the Critique of Political Economy*. Translated by S. W. Ryazanskaya. Edited by Maurice Dobb. New York: International Publishers, 1972.

———. *The Eighteenth Brumaire of Louis Bonaparte*. New York: International Publishers, 1963.

———. *The Poverty of Philosophy*. Original, 1847. Reprinted, Peking: Foreign Languages Press, 1978.

———. *Wage-Labor and Capital*. Introduction for workingmen by Frederick Engels. Original, 1849. Reprinted, Chicago: Charles H. Kerr, 1948.

Marx, Karl, and Frederick Engels. *Basic Writings in Politics and Philosophy*. Edited by Lewis S. Feuer. Garden City, N.Y.: Doubleday/Anchor, 1959.

———. *The German Ideology*. Edited by C. J. Arthur. New York: International Publishers, 1981.

———. *A Handbook of Marxism*. Edited by Emile Burns. New York: International Publishers, n.d.

McAlister, Lyle N. "Social Structure and Social Change in New Spain." *Hispanic American Historical Review* 43, no. 3 (August 1963): 349–70.

McCord, Norman. *Strikes*. New York: St. Martin's Press, 1980.

McFarlane, Anthony. "Riot and Rebellion in Colonial Spanish America." *Latin American Research Review* 17, no. 2 (1982): 212–21.

Mecham, J. Lloyd. "The *Real de Minas* as a Political Institution." *Hispanic American Historical Review* 7, no. 1 (February 1927): 45–83.

Mendizábal, Miguel O. de, "Los minerales de Pachuca y Real del Monte en la época colonial." *El trimestre económico* 8, no. 2 (July–September 1941): 253–309.

Mesa-Lago, Luis. *El Cardenal Lorenzana y la Ilustración*. Madrid: Fundación Universitaria Española, Seminario Cisneros, 1975.

Meseguer Pardo, José. *Vocabulario minero hispano-americano*. Madrid: C. Bermejo, 1959.

Mészáros, István, ed. *Aspects of History and Class Consciousness*. London: Routledge and Kegan Paul, 1971.

Moreno de los Arcos, Roberto. "Las instituciones de la industria minera novohispana," in *La minería en Mexico* by Miguel León Portilla, et al., pp. 67–164.

———. "Régimen de trabajo en la minería del siglo XVIII." In *El trabajo y los trabajadores en la historia de México,* by Elsa Cecelia Frost, Michael C. Meyer, Josefina Zoraida Vázquez, and Lilia Díaz, pp. 242–67. Mexico City and Tucson: El Colegio de México and University of Arizona, 1979.

————. "Salario, tequio y partido en las ordenanzas para la minera novohispana del siglo XVIII." *Revista de la Facultad de Derecho,* Universidad Nacional Autónoma de México 26: no. 101 (January–June 1976): 465–83.

Morse, Richard. "The Heritage of Latin America." In *The Founding of New Societies,* ed. Louis Hartz, pp. 123–77. New York: Harcourt, Brace, and World, 1964.

Motten, Clement G. *Mexican Silver and the Enlightenment.* Philadelphia: University of Pennsylvania Press, 1950.

Muriel, Josefina. *Los recogimientos de mujeres.* Mexico City: Universidad Nacional Autónoma de México, Instituto de Investigaciones Históricas, 1974.

O'Hara, Hazel. *Dust in the Lungs.* Building a Better Hemisphere Series, no. 9. Washington, D.C.: Institute of Inter-American Affairs, 1952.

Page, Joseph A., and Mary-Win O'Brien. *Bitter Wages: Ralph Nader's Study Group Report on Disease and Injury on the Job.* New York: Grossman, 1973.

Palacio Atard, Vicente. *Areche y Gurior: Observaciones sobre el fracaso de una visita al Perú.* Seville: Escuela de Estudios Hispano-Americanos, 1946.

Palma, Ricardo. *The Knights of the Cape.* Translated from *Tradiciones peruanas* by Harriet de Onís. New York: A. A. Knopf, 1945.

Phelan, John Leddy. "Authority and Flexibility in the Spanish Imperial Bureaucracy." *Administrative Science Quarterly* 5, no. 1 (June 1960): 47–65.

————. *The Hispanization of the Philippines: Spanish Aims and Filipino Responses, 1565–1700.* Madison: University of Wisconsin Press, 1959.

————. *The Kingdom of Quito in the Seventeenth Century: Bureaucratic Politics in the Spanish Empire.* Madison: University of Wisconsin Press, 1967.

————. *The Millennial Kingdom of the Franciscans in the New World: A Study of the Writings of Gerónimo de Mendieta (1525–1604).* Berkeley: University of California Press, 1956.

————. *The People and the King: The Comunero Revolution in Colombia, 1781.* Madison: University of Wisconsin Press, 1978.

Pike, Ruth. *Penal Servitude in Early Modern Spain.* Madison: University of Wisconsin Press, 1983.

Priestley, Herbert Ingram. *José de Gálvez, Visitor-General of New Spain (1765–1771).* Berkeley: University of California Press, 1916.

Probert, Alan. "A Lost Art Rediscovered: Primitive Smelting in Central America." *Journal of the West* 2, no. 1 (January 1971): 116–28.

————. "Ladders of No Return." *Journal of the West* 14, no. 2 (April 1975): 79–92.

————. "The Pachuca Papers: The Real de Monte Partido Riots, 1766." *Journal of the West* 12, no. 1 (January 1973): 85–125.

————. "Pedro Romero de Terreros—the Genius of the Vizcaína Vein." *Journal of the West* 14, no. 2 (April 1975), 51–78.

————. "Reseña histórica del distrito minero de Pachuca–Real del Monte hasta

1906." In A. R. Geyne, et al., *Geología y yacimientos minerales del Distrito de Pachuca—Real del Monte."* Consejo de Recursos Minerales, Publication 5E, pp. 93–104. Mexico City: Helio-México, 1963.

Ramazzini, Bernardini. *De Morbis Artificum, Diseases of Workers.* Original Latin text, 1713. Translated and revised by Wilmer Cave Wright. Chicago: University of Chicago Press, 1940.

Ramírez, Santiago. *Noticia histórica de riqueza minera de México.* Mexico City: Secretaría de Fomento, 1884.

Randall, Robert W. *Real del Monte: A British Mining Venture in Mexico.* Austin: Institute of Latin American Studies, University of Texas at Austin, 1972.

Robertson, William Parish. *A Visit to Mexico.* 2 vols. London: Simpkin, Marshall, 1853.

Romero de Terreros, Manuel (Marqués de San Francisco). *El Conde de Regla, Creso de la Nueva España.* Mexico City: Xóchitl, 1943.

Rosen, George. *The History of Miners' Diseases: A Medical and Social Interpretation.* New York: Schuman's, 1943.

Rudé, George. *The Crowd in History: A Study of Popular Disturbances in France and England, 1730–1848.* New York: John Wiley and Sons, 1964.

————. *The Crowd in the French Revolution.* London: Oxford University Press, 1967.

Sayer, R. R. *Silicosis among Miners.* U.S. Department of Commerce, Bureau of Mines. Washington, D.C.: Government Printing Office, 1925.

Sayers, R. R., and D. Harrington. *A Preliminary Study of the Physiological Effects of High Temperatures and High Humidities in Metal Mines.* U.S. Public Health Service Report 639. Washington, D.C.: Government Printing Office, 1921.

Sayers, R. R., F. V. Meriwether, A. J. Lanza, and W.W. Adams. *Silicosis and Tuberculosis among Miners of the Tri-State District of Oklahoma, Kansas and Missouri.* Vol. 1 for the year ended June 30, 1928. U.S. Department of Commerce, Bureau of Mines. Washington, D.C.: Government Printing Office, 1933.

Sierra Nava, Luis. *El Cardenal Lorenzana y la Ilustración.* Madrid: Fundación Universitaria Española, Cisneros, 1975.

Skinner, B. F. *About Behaviorism.* New York: Vintage, 1976.

————. *Beyond Freedom and Dignity.* New York: Knopf, 1971.

————. "An Operant Analysis of Problem-solving." Paper presented at Carnegie Institute of Technology, Pittsburgh, April 16, 1965.

————. *Reflections on Behaviorism and Society.* Englewood Cliffs, N.J.: Prentice-Hall, 1978.

————. *Science and Human Behavior.* New York: The Free Press, 1965.

————. *Verbal Behavior.* New York: Appleton, Century, Crofts, 1957.

Smith, Grant H. *The History of the Comstock Lode, 1850–1920.* University of Nevada

Bulletin 37, no. 3 (July 1, 1943).

Smith, Ivan C., and Bonnie L. Carson. *Trace Metals in the Environment,* vol. 2: *Silver.* Ann Arbor: Ann Arbor Science Publishers, 1977.

Super, John C. "Querétaro Obrajes: Industry and Society in Provincial Mexico, 1600–1810." *Hispanic American Historical Review* 56, no. 2 (May 1976): 197–216.

Taylor, William B. *Drinking, Homicide, and Rebellion in Colonial Mexican Villages.* Stanford: Stanford University Press, 1979.

Thomis, Malcolm I. *The Luddites: Machine-Breaking in Regency England.* New York: Schocken, 1972.

Thompson, E. P. *The Making of the English Working Class.* London: Penguin, 1968.

———. "The Moral Economy of the English Crowd in the Eighteenth Century." *Past and Present* 50 (February 1971): 76–136.

———. "Patrician Society, Plebeian Culture." *Journal of Social History* 7, no. 4 (Summer 1974), 382–405.

———. *The Poverty of Theory.* New York: Monthly Review Press, 1978.

———. *Whigs and Hunters.* New York: Random House / Pantheon, 1975.

———. *Writing by Candlelight.* London: The Merlin Press, 1980.

Thompson, E. P. et al. *Visions of History: Interviews by the Mid-Atlantic Radical Historians' Organization.* New York: Pantheon, 1984. Pp. 3–25.

Tilly, Charles, Louise Tilly, and Richard Tilly. *The Rebellious Century, 1830–1930.* Cambridge, Mass.: Harvard University Press, 1975.

Ulloa, Antonio de. "Noticia i descripción de los países que medían entre la ciudad i puerto de Vera Cruz en el reino de Nueva España hasta los asientos de minas de Guanajuato, Pachuca, i Real del Monte de sus territorios, clima i producción." Original, June 1777. MS copy in Nettie Lee Benson Latin American Collection, The University of Texas at Austin.

U.S. Department of the Interior. Bureau of Mines. *A Dictionary of Mining, Mineral and Related Terms.* Compiled and edited by Paul W. Thrush and Staff. Washington, D.C.: Government Printing Office, 1968.

———. *Mineral Facts and Problems.* Bicentennial Edition. Washington, D.C.: Government Printing Office, 1975.

Velasco A., Cuauhtémoc. "Los trabajadores mineros de Nueva España, 1750–1810." In *La clase obrera en la historia de Mexico: de la colonia al imperio.* By Enrique Florescano, Isabel González Sánchez, Jorge González Angulo, Roberto Sandoval Zarauz, Cuauhtémoc Velasco A., and Alejandra Moreno Toscano. Mexico City: Instituto de Investigaciones de la Universidad Nacional Autónoma de México, Siglo Veintiúno, 1980.

Velázquez, María del Carmen. "José Alejandro de Bustamante, minero de Pachuca."

Historia Mexicana 25, no. 3 (January–March 1976): 335–62.

West, Robert C. *The Mining Community in Northern New Spain: The Parral Mining District*. Berkeley: *Ibero-Americana* 30 (1949).

Williams, Barbara J. "Tepetates in the Valley of Mexico." *Annals of the Association of American Geographers* 62, no. 4 (December 1972): 618–26.

Womack, John, Jr. "The Historiography of Mexican Labor." In *El trabajo y los trabajadores en la historia de México*. By Elsa Cecelia Frost, Michael C. Meyer, Josefina Zoraida Vázquez, and Lilia Díaz. Mexico City and Tucson: El Colegio de Mexico and the University of Arizona Press, 1979.

———. *Zapata and the Mexican Revolution*. New York: Random House, 1968.

Zola, Emile Edouard Charles Antoine. *Germinal*. Original, 1885. Translated by Havelock Ellis. New York: E. P. Dutton, 1952.

Index